"Henry's commitment to both s⌐   of Christians to engage the world. This book will deepen your understanding of how Carl Henry sought to place all aspects of life under the banner of the gospel."

    Richard Stearns, President, World Vision US; author, *Unfinished* and *The Hole in Our Gospel*

"It has been a marked blessing of God in my life to have known Carl and Helga Henry personally. I do what I do and live where I have lived now for over twenty years in no small because of Carl Henry. Carefully reading each of these essays has left me feeling like I've just spent time with him again. Careful research, clear writing, and shared concerns mark the chapters in this book. The authors are to be commended."

    Mark Dever, Pastor, Capitol Hill Baptist Church, Washington, DC; President, 9Marks

"It would be hard to overstate the importance and ongoing relevance of the writings of Carl Henry, one of the fathers of modern evangelicalism. Henry was a close friend of my organization's founder, Chuck Colson. His impact continues to be felt on our board of directors, in the Christian worldview ministry he helped to inspire, and in the hundreds of thousands of men and women behind bars who have also been impacted through his teaching. This book belongs on the must-buy list of today's evangelical readers."

    Jim Liske, President and CEO, Prison Fellowship Ministries

"Too many evangelical churches today are enamored with a therapeutic gospel and pander after yet another spiritual experience. What we need is a good dose of the theological depth and intellectual rigor of the likes of Carl Henry. You don't have to agree with everything he wrote, but you will be wise for having wrestled with his great mind."

    Mark Galli, Editor, *Christianity Today*

"Carl F. H. Henry is a writing mentor to me. Like Francis Schaeffer, I fear losing him to a generation that desperately needs to hear both their voices. This book will help contemporary evangelicals understand why they need to know this man and delve into his writings. It will stretch them intellectually. It will guide them spiritually. And it will greatly aid them in not repeating mistakes from the past—mistakes already uncovered and handled by this princely theologian."

    Daniel L. Akin, President, Southeastern Baptist Theological Seminary

"The brilliant essays found in *Essential Evangelicalism* provide readers with a masterful and comprehensive look at the life and work of Carl F. H. Henry. So much more than a historical reflection, this timely and extraordinary volume not only presents Henry's massive thought to a new generation of readers, but carefully explores the identity and theology of the evangelical movement with remarkable insight. With great enthusiasm, it is a privilege to recommend this outstanding publication."

David S. Dockery, President, Trinity International University

"Carl Henry was a giant on whose shoulders all contemporary evangelicals stand—whether or not they know that. This volume represents another significant contribution to celebrating, assessing, and reclaiming Henry's massive influence. One need not agree with every aspect of Henry's thought (or this volume's claims about Henry) to rejoice in this multivoiced wrestling with Henry's huge role in shaping contemporary evangelicalism."

Ronald J. Sider, Senior Distinguished Professor of Theology,
Holistic Ministry, and Public Policy, Palmer Theological Seminary,
King of Prussia, Pennsylvania

Essential Evangelicalism

ESSENTIAL EVANGELICALISM

The Enduring Influence of Carl F. H. Henry

MATTHEW J. HALL AND
OWEN STRACHAN, EDITORS

Foreword by Timothy George

WHEATON, ILLINOIS

Essential Evangelicalism: The Enduring Influence of Carl F. H. Henry

Copyright © 2015 by Matthew J. Hall and Owen Strachan

Published by Crossway
   1300 Crescent Street
   Wheaton, Illinois 60187

Cover design: Josh Dennis

Cover image: Richard Solomon Artists, Gary Kelley

First printing 2015

Printed in the United States of America

Trade paperback ISBN: 978-1-4335-4726-3
ePub ISBN: 978-1-4335-4729-4
PDF ISBN: 978-1-4335-4727-0
Mobipocket ISBN: 978-1-4335-4728-7

Library of Congress Cataloging-in-Publication Data
Essential evangelicalism : the enduring influence of Carl
F. H. Henry / Matthew J. Hall and Owen Strachan,
editors ; foreword by Timothy George.
  pages cm
 Includes bibliographical references and index.
 ISBN 978-1-4335-4726-3 (tp)
 1. Henry, Carl F. H. (Carl Ferdinand Howard),
1913–2003. 2. Theologians—United States.
3. Evangelicalism—United States—History—20th
century. 4. Theology—United States—History—
20th century. I. Hall, Matthew, 1980– editor.
BX4827.H38E87   2015
230'.044092—dc23   2015008948

Crossway is a publishing ministry of Good News Publishers.

VP   25 24 23 22 21 20 19 18 17 16 15
15 14 13 12 11 10 9 8 7 6 5 4 3 2 1

Contents

Foreword

American evangelicals and *serious theology* are terms that do not just naturally snuggle up to each other with easy equipoise. That, despite the fact that Jonathan Edwards, the greatest theologian America has produced, stands at the headwaters of the evangelical tradition. The diminution of the evangelical mind since Edwards—and not only in theology—has been often rehearsed. The lure of pragmatism, individualism, revivalism (not to be confused with revival, about which Edwards knew a thing or two), expressivism, and fissiparous fundamentalism have all taken their toll when it comes to the nurturing of a theological tradition that is wise and deep. But in recent history, there is one evangelical theologian who stands above others in depth of insight and clarity of vision: Carl Ferdinand Howard Henry.

Born in New York City in 1913, Henry came of age at a time when the modernist-fundamentalist battles were going strong. But he heard no talk of these struggles, or of anything else religious, at the family dinner table. His father, a master baker from Germany, was a nominal Lutheran; his mother, a nominal Catholic.

Skilled in typing, Henry landed a job as a sportswriter. He eventually became a reporter and then an editor of the small newspaper on Long Island while also writing stories as a stringer for the *New York Times*. By all accounts, he was a hard-nosed journalist given to pagan pleasures, with no knowledge or use for God, much less the church.

His conversion to Jesus Christ was dramatic, unexpected, and unforgettable. Sitting alone in his car in 1933, he was startled by a violent thunderstorm—shades of Luther. He later described this event in this way:

A fiery bolt of lightning, like a giant flaming arrow, seemed to pin me to the driver's seat, and a mighty roll of thunder unnerved me. When the fire fell, I knew instinctively the Great Archer had nailed me to my own footsteps. Looking back, it was as if the transcendent *Tetragrammaton* wished me to know that I could not save myself and that heaven's intervention was my only hope.[1]

Henry the convert became Henry the evangelist and Henry the student. He went on to earn two degrees from Wheaton College (where one of his classmates was the young Billy Graham) and eventually the PhD from Boston University under Edgar S. Brightman.

Soon after the National Association of Evangelicals was formed in 1942, the *Christian Century* announced in a headline, "Sectarianism Receives New Lease on Life." But sectarian retrenchment was the last thing Boston pastor Harold John Ockenga, the ringleader of the so-called New Evangelicalism, or the far-thinking Carl Henry had in mind. In 1947, thirty-four-year-old Henry published *The Uneasy Conscience of Modern Fundamentalism*, a seventy-five-page booklet that sold for one dollar per copy. Henry called on his fellow evangelicals to leave behind the legalism, obscurantism, and judgmentalism that had left a blight on conservative Christianity in the twentieth century. Sectarian isolation, Henry said, must give way to evangelical engagement. The new movement had its manifesto.

In 1956 Henry was invited to become the first editor of a new publication, *Christianity Today*. CT was to be "a magazine of evangelical conviction," a thoughtful conservative alternative to the more liberal *Christian Century*. In his first editorial, Henry told his readers that he could see the lawn of the White House from his office. He was saying, in effect, that evangelicals would no longer be confined to the gospel ghettos of the culture. The mission of the evangelical church was both personal and public. The aim was to capture minds as well as to save souls, to struggle for a just social structure, and to preach the gospel to the ends of the earth.

To accomplish these goals, Henry not only wrote editorials, but he also published serious theology. He wrote more than forty books in his

---

[1] Carl F. H. Henry, *Confessions of a Theologian* (Waco, TX: Word, 1986), 45–46.

lifetime, dealing with a range of issues from theological ethics to higher education and human rights. One of his most interesting essays was called "Christian Fund-raising Heresies." But his magnum opus was a massive six-volume study, *God, Revelation, and Authority*, published from 1976 to 1983. It contains more than three thousand pages, and none of them is meant for light bedtime reading. *God, Revelation, and Authority* is not a systematic theology proper but rather a sustained theological epistemology offering a comprehensive overview of revelation in biblical terms—the living God who speaks and shows, who stands and stays, who stoops and saves.

God, Revelation, and Authority is an extended discourse built on fifteen principal theses. Luther had ninety-five; Henry had fifteen. The first of Henry's fifteen theses is the most important, the basis for all the others: "Revelation is a divinely initiated activity, God's free communication by which he alone turns his personal privacy into a deliberate disclosure of his reality."[2] He argues that all merely human affirmations about God that are based on something other than his divinely initiated, freely communicated, and deliberately disclosed reality will inevitably curl into a question mark.

The awesome disclosure of God precipitates human surprise. Perhaps thinking about his own encounter in the thunderstorm, Henry declares that divine revelation is "like a fiery bolt of lightning that unexpectedly zooms towards us and scores a direct hit." Or, it is like an earthquake that suddenly shakes and engulfs us. Or, it is like "some piercing air-raid siren" which sends us "scurrying from life's preoccupations and warns us that no escape remains if we neglect the only sure sanctuary."[3]

During the latter years of his life, Henry became *theologus non gratus* within large sectors of the evangelical academy. In far less nuanced fashion than the postliberal criticism he had received from Yale theologians Hans Frei and Brevard Childs, postconservative, postevangelical, and semi-post-Christian critics blasted Henry for what they called his pure propositionalism and conformity to the canons of Enlightenment rationalism. But Kevin J. Vanhoozer, an evangelical theologian whose own work is marked by

---

[2] Carl F. H. Henry, *God, Revelation, and Authority*, vol. 2, *God, Who Speaks and Shows: Fifteen Theses, Part 1* (Waco, TX: Word, 1976), 8.
[3] Ibid., 17.

acuity and insight, has been much more balanced. Using speech-act theory as an aid to understanding biblical discourse, Vanhoozer criticizes Henry for his lack of interest in genre along with some of his hermeneutical pre-suppositions. But Vanhoozer is a friendly critic and openly admits, "Carl Henry said the right thing at the right time."[4]

In a tribute I wrote on Henry at the time of his death in 2003, I predicted that despite his eclipse at the time, a new generation of evangelicals would arise to rediscover "Uncle Carl" and once again find his work vibrant, provocative, and relevant to the issues of the day. Now, more than twelve years after his death, my prediction is coming true. The essays in this volume are among the firstfruits of a harvest of renewed engagement with the most significant American evangelical theologian since World War II.

There is a sense that postmodernism with its stops, gaps, and radical breaks with all traditions of received wisdom is suffocating in its own exhaust fumes. This is a good time to affirm something truly awesome: that the God of eternity, the creator and Lord of time, has come among us as one of us in the person of his Son, Jesus Christ, and that this God still speaks to troubled and confused human beings using "comprehensible ideas and meaningful words."

I applaud and welcome the Henrician renaissance now under way, with this one caveat: what we need is not a repristination of Henry, nor a new defense of his methods and views in every respect, but rather a renewed commitment to doing theology in the service of the church, and to doing it with a Henry-like passion for truth and with love for the God who is both the source and object of truth.

In the closing paragraph of *God, Revelation, and Authority*, Henry describes the wonder and joy that is the true calling of every theologian and of theology itself. He points us to the contemplation of the living God of creation and redemption, the God who stands and stoops and speaks and stays:

He it is who preserves and governs and consummates his cosmic purpose. But the awesome wonder of the biblical revelation is not

---

[4] http://www.biblicalfoundations.org/vanhoozer-responds-to-my-review/ (May 8, 2007).

his creation and preservation of our vastly immense and complex universe. Its wonder, rather, is that he came as God-man to planet Earth in the form of the Babe of Bethlehem; he thus reminds us that no point in the universe is too remote for his presence and no speck too small for his care and love. He came as God-man to announce to a rebellious race the offer of a costly mercy grounded in the death and resurrection of his only Son and to assure his people that he who stays will remain with him forever and they with him. He is come in Christ incarnate to exhibit ideal human nature and will return in Christ glorified to fully implement the Omega-realities of the dawning future.[5]

Beyond all of his accomplishments, two things about Carl Henry stand out in my mind. On his last visit to Beeson Divinity School, he spoke in chapel about his conversion to Christ. He never got over the sheer wonder and joy of having been chosen and rescued by God's surprising grace. He knew what it meant to be born again. The other thing that stands out was his extraordinary humility and kindness toward others. His commitment to the orthodox Christian faith was solid as a rock, but I never heard him speak in a bitter or disparaging way about anybody, not even those with whom he disagreed.

I shall never forget my last visit with Carl. Dr. Greg Waybright, then president of Trinity International University, and I made a pilgrimage to his bedside at the little Moravian nursing home where Henry and his dear wife, Helga, lived. He could not walk and could barely talk, but his mind was abuzz with ideas and plans and new ventures for the advance of God's kingdom. We prayed and read the Scriptures together. Even though he was in pain, his eyes still sparkled with the joy of Christ. Carl loved to quote Vance Havner's prayer: "Lord, get me safely home before dark." Although Carl Henry has been home for some years now, his legacy lives on and still illumines the path we tread toward that Light, which can never be extinguished.

Timothy George

---

[5] Carl F. H. Henry, *God, Revelation, and Authority*, vol. 6, *God Who Stands and Stays* (Waco, TX: Word, 1983), 513.

Editors' Preface

We begin a book about a Long Island–born theologian with a quote from a Swiss scholar reflecting on a French churchman. In 1922, writing to his friend Eduard Thurneysen, Karl Barth said the following about John Calvin:

> Calvin is a cataract, a primeval forest, a demonic power, something directly down from Himalaya, absolutely Chinese, strange, mythological; I lack completely the means, the suction cups, even to assimilate this phenomenon, not to speak of presenting it adequately.
>
> What I receive is only a thin little stream and what I can then give out again is only a yet thinner extract of this little stream.
>
> I could gladly and profitably set myself down and spend all the rest of my life just with Calvin.[1]

Barth's words are memorable on their own terms. It is not every day that a magisterial theologian is described by another master scholar as "something directly down from Himalaya," after all.

Descriptive gymnastics aside, our real interest in Barth's description is his effort to take the measure of a man whose varied life and voluminous work defy easy summation. So it is with Carl Ferdinand Howard Henry, a man so eminent he bore two middle names. Carl Henry is a distant reality for many modern Christians. Perhaps we should amend that: to a good many folks, he is unknown. He is recognized primarily among scholars, seminarians, and some pastors. Those who are aware

---

[1] Eberhard Busch, *Karl Barth: His Life from Letters and Autobiographical Texts*, trans. John Bowden (Grand Rapids, MI: Eerdmans, 1994), 57.

of Henry know him to be a formidable theologian, a sometimes impenetrable writer, and an evangelical-at-large of the postwar twentieth century.

These senses are correct. Henry was all these things. But he was more: a tireless evangelist, an incurable optimist, a gifted administrator, a loving father, a devoted husband, a fierce opponent, an eternal journalist, an unstoppable-hatcher-of-grand-schemes, a Sunday school teacher, and a primeval forest. The last of these does not in truth apply; it is true, though, that one could profitably set down with Henry and spend a very long time following his trail of thought.

As two young evangelical scholars, we ourselves are committed to some form of this program. Like many of our peers, we have found ourselves drawn, even mythologically, to Henry. Our lives overlapped to a relatively significant degree with his; he died on December 7, 2003, when both of us were recent college graduates. While we shared an understanding of the massive loss his death represented to evangelicalism, neither of us had a full appreciation of the extent of this man's singular contribution to the shaping of much of the world we inhabited. We had seminary professors, pastors, and mentors who spoke of their own firsthand dependence on Dr. Henry's influence and guidance. We heard the stories and legends of his influence in the genesis of Fuller Theological Seminary and in the launch of *Christianity Today* and of his place in the galvanization of postwar neo-evangelicalism.

Owen was a church member at Capitol Hill Baptist Church in Washington, DC, while Henry was a "watchcare member" of the same congregation, living in Watertown, Wisconsin. That secondhand connection aside, we never actually knew the man. We never met him, much as we wish we had. But we are convinced that there are few better or more urgently vital models for young evangelicals interested in theological engagement of an unsteady church and a secular age. As historians, we believe that we are best positioned to thrive when we face the future with the wisdom and training of the past, not when we engage in create-your-own-evangelical-polity-and-theology. We are young, but we actually *like* the past. We like, furthermore, faithful leaders who would train us in thinking and living unto God. We're eager to learn from their successes and failures, their strengths and weaknesses.

This book represents our best effort to collect reflections and essays from some of those who knew Henry or who have dedicated significant time and effort to assessing his influence and place in the story of American evangelicalism. To be even more pointed, we count ourselves among the tribe of evangelicals who routinely survey the landscape of American religion and lament the absence of Henry in our own day. Yes, in case you're wondering, we'd love to hear the answer to, "Dr. Henry, what do you make of Joel Osteen?" though we would have his heart medication close at hand in posing the query.

We'll assume for a moment that you're not that different from us. You know you're *supposed* to respect, admire, and appreciate the legacy of someone like Carl Henry. But, if pressed, you'd have a hard time explaining why. And you might not even have a clear sense of where to begin if you did want to learn more about this titan of American evangelicalism. Before you launch into this book and are introduced to Henry from several individuals who did have the privilege of knowing him and working alongside him, allow us to lay out a few reasons we find Henry to be as urgently relevant for evangelicals in the twenty-first century.

FIVE REASONS TO ENGAGE CARL HENRY TODAY

First, Henry provides a model of orthodox theological engagement with an unorthodox world. Henry grounded his entire program in divine authority mediated through divine revelation. If you know nothing about Carl Henry, mark this. Henry's six-volume trilogy, *God, Revelation, and Authority* (or GRA), is a masterwork, the most serious contribution to a synthesis of evangelical hermeneutics and first theology of the twentieth century. No other work by one of Henry's fellow evangelicals even tried for this title. In GRA, and in numerous other works less well known, Henry set out to define, delimit, and defend divine truth. In the 1970s and 1980s, at the end of his career, he saw that humanity had entered into a "crisis of word and truth," as he put it.[2] He believed that it was his call to address the crisis and to do so by reattaching that

---

[2] Carl F. H. Henry, *God, Revelation, and Authority*, vol. 1, *God Who Speaks and Shows, Preliminary Considerations* (Waco, TX: Word, 1976), 21.

which modernity had sundered. The Word was the Truth; the Truth derived from the Word.

GRA sets out this vision in six volumes that total nearly three thousand pages. Let us be clear: GRA is to the Christian academy what Tolstoy is to the literary guild. His books may in past days have served more as doorstops in the office than as doorways into another realm. It has become somewhat fashionable to drop into conversation at an evangelical seminary that one has acquired GRA, but to read him is another matter altogether. We are happy to commend GRA to those whose interest in Henry is whetted by this volume. It is true that the prose can at times grow thick. It is correct that he never lost his quick-fire journalistic instincts and that this can lead to digressive sections. Yet it is also the case that Henry was a brilliant mind. He was, as all the best theologians are, in regular conversation with the guild. He argued with the living and the dead and engaged them, sometimes multiple scholars in one paragraph, in his masterwork. What is more, he accomplished something in GRA: he showed that the Christian faith is rationally defensible yet spiritually vital. In Henry, one sees that word and truth, heart and mind, authority and piety are one, joined as they must ultimately be not in an abstract concept but in a flesh-and-blood person: Jesus Christ.

Second, Henry's philosophical engagement can provide young evangelicals with the framework for navigating the perils of encroaching secularism. Somehow, we suspect Henry would be neither surprised nor intimidated by the so-called new atheism, deconstructionist theories, or challenges to ideas of revealed truth. In fact, his own work seemed to have a nearly prophetic ability to foresee some of the most vexing intellectual challenges to the Christian worldview. Are you wrestling with understanding the Christian tradition of moral ethics? Henry wrote on that. Troubled with understanding ideas of epistemology and philosophy? He wrote on that too. And if you cannot quite seem to wrap your mind around concepts of biblical revelation, truth, and inspiration— well, as mentioned, we have a six-volume magnum opus just waiting for you.

This is a promise that has real weight and depth. One of our colleagues and contributors to this book was helped enormously by Henry's work. Gregory Thornbury was a budding intellectual at a Northeastern college whose Christian piety crashed into the wall of higher criticism in one survey class. Thornbury, now the president of a resurgent The King's College in Manhattan, read Marcus Borg's *Jesus: A New Vision* and "reeled" at the materials.[3] He was trained in faithful Christian living, but Greg was knocked off his game by a "well-studied and per-suasive scholar with an Oxford DPhil." who brought him "within a whisker" of losing trust in the Bible.[4] In God's kind providence, Thornbury remembered the name of Carl F. H. Henry, a scholar his father, a pastor, greatly respected. He began devouring Henry's writings and recovering his trust in God's Word. It was, he later reflected, "a turning point for me."[5]

We suspect that there are a good number of bright young thinkers out there much like the collegiate Thornbury. Their evangelical upbring-ing was warm and even rich, but in their educational years, they have encountered influential voices that threaten to overwhelm their own understanding of the faith. Where this is the case, we want to freshly commend Henry's work. It is not perfect; it will not answer every ques-tion; it is, like every body of texts ever crafted, a product of its time. But its depth of thought, its level of scholarly interaction, and its abiding zeal for Christ lift it out of the half-priced bookstore consignment bin and beckon us to take and read once more.

Third, Henry provides young evangelicals with a vision for gospel-centered social justice. Of the making of arguments about the connec-tions of the *evangelion* and the call to peace and justice, there shall be no end. But we believe that Henry provided more light than heat, offering evangelicals a vision and ethic of the kingdom of Christ that managed to affirm the centrality of the atonement and resurrection for sinners, but to also understand that the church must play a part in calling for peace, justice, righteousness, and virtue. What Henry rightly knew, and what evangelicals in our time so easily miss, is that social jus-tice and the gospel must be tethered together closely if there will be true justice and if there will be much of a gospel that really is "good news."

---

[3] Marcus Borg, *Jesus: A New Vision: Spirit, Culture, and the Life of Discipleship* (New York: HarperOne, 1991).
[4] Gregory Alan Thornbury, *Recovering Classic Evangelicalism: Applying the Wisdom and Vision of Carl F. H. Henry* (Wheaton, IL: Crossway, 2013), 14.
[5] Ibid., 15.

Henry made this case in his best-selling *The Uneasy Conscience of Modern Fundamentalism*, the most widely read of all his books. Clocking in at eighty-eight pages, the text is almost shockingly ahead of its time, anticipating both a secularizing society and the desperate need for Christians to love their neighbor in tangible ways in such a society. Henry came up in a time when to be a conservative Christian meant accepting cultural marginalization, and perhaps even taking cold comfort in it. He walked a fine line in sociological terms, for the fundamentalists of his day were ready to brand him as a gospel-softening deed-doer, while the liberals of his day were ready to denounce him as a backwater brimstone evangelist whose charitable work was only a means to an end.

Henry was far closer to the fundamentalists in his theological commitments, but he could not tolerate cultural retreat. His sense of idealism and his love for his fellow man impelled him to do everything he could to stir up the church to love and good deeds. So it is that he popped up in surprising places, including the organizing meeting of the 1973 Chicago Declaration of Evangelical Social Concern, a project championed by Ron Sider and others. Henry's interest in gospel-shaped social justice led him outside his normal circles. It is for this and other reasons that it is thoroughly unfair to label Henry. He was an unabashedly conservative theologian who offered the most forthright defense of biblical authority of any thinker of the twentieth century—and yet he was also powerfully motivated by the need to love justice and pursue righteousness. He is as inspiring as he is iconoclastic.

Fourth, Henry models a broad evangelical ecumenism that is framed by confessional identity. While seemingly paradoxical, Henry managed to reconcile a vision for a broad evangelical coalition with a commitment to necessary theological first principles of orthodoxy. We suspect Dr. Henry would be delighted by some of the broadening coalitions within some corridors of confessional evangelicalism. As cultural Christianity evaporates before our eyes in Western Europe and the United States, the necessity of cooperative efforts among evangelicals of diverse traditions and denominations becomes increasingly imperative. But, as Henry would have warned, these coalitions must be framed by and held in check by the truth of Scripture and the message of the gospel of Christ.

We recognize that some may push against this vision of Henry as a "confessional" thinker. Wasn't he the man, with Harold John Ockenga and Billy Graham, who was most responsible for minimizing traditional ecclesiological boundaries in the mid-twentieth century? There is some truth to this characterization, we admit. But we must also think carefully about Henry's identity and his role. With his peers, he made a major contribution to the Christian church in his day. He helped it to see that unity in the gospel was a more powerful unifying force than separating from one's foes. This, in truth, is what the neo-evangelical project was. It was a referendum on gospel unity, not an attack on meaningful confessionalism.

With many young friends, we are grateful for the example of Henry and his friends. We believe that their recovery of an evangel-driven identity was a contribution for the ages, akin to the pioneering work of Edwards and Whitefield in the First Great Awakening and of Luther and Calvin in the Reformation. We ourselves are happily evangelical. But none of this should distract us from the reality that Henry was a Baptist. Perhaps we see this most clearly in his churchmanship, which is, after all, vitally important to laying hold of a person's truest, deepest commitments. Henry was a faithful member at Capitol Hill Baptist Church and a longtime Sunday school teacher there. Years after his passing, he was warmly remembered by congregants. He did not carry himself like a world-class scholar but like a fellow worshiper at the feet of Jesus.

Henry would very likely have struck much deeper roots in Baptist theological territory than he did, save for one thing: not all Baptists of his era liked him. He was an outspoken evangelical. In sectors of the Southern Baptist Convention, this was not the pathway to making friends and influencing people. It was the opposite. When R. Albert Mohler Jr. first encountered Henry in the 1980s, he was shocked to find that the best-known evangelical Baptist theologian of his day was not permitted to speak in his graduate seminar at the Southern Baptist Theological Seminary. Henry, we should reiterate, was very much a Baptist. He worked out of his tradition in ways obvious and obscure. But he came unto his own, and his own received him not. It is our delight to, in a very small way, redress past wrongs in a volume of this kind. It is a particular point of pleasure that, alongside other similarly denominated academic centers, the Carl F. H. Henry Institute for Evangelical Engagement is alive and flourishing on the campus of Southern.

Fifth, Henry understood that theology and evangelism are inseparable. It is now the stuff of legend, but Henry famously once told a group of seminarians that the most important theological question of our time is, Do you know the risen Christ? Henry understood that the gospel was only good news if it got there on time. And this conviction and commitment to the truth claims of the gospel undergirded and animated his urgent commitment to global evangelization. As evangelicals become a shrinking minority in the West—and a surging group in the southern hemisphere—we could learn much from Henry's vision and hope. If the gospel really is true and the promises of God are reliable, then the church universal has good reason to be hopeful and confident in its task.

Here we see how important it is to understand Henry's theology as a body of thought. Too often we approach theologians in discrete terms, dividing up their work into nicely spliced seminars and reading groups. In reality, there is a straight line between Henry the GRA writer and Henry the evangelist. Biblical authority mattered for the man. He knew what it was to walk through life a lost soul, to have no foundation for hope, to possess no direction for the soul, no light for the mind. He was himself saved by a traveling evangelist when a young man. He never lost his sense of the serendipity of conversion. It could strike at a moment's notice, giving no warning to a lifetime of unbelief and sin. It is no accident that some of Henry's closest associates, including the prison reformer Chuck Colson, came from similarly non-Christian backgrounds. Like Colson, Henry understood the convulsive power of the gospel, a gospel that rushes over the most formidable of personal barriers to redeem the depraved in heart.

Any theologian or philosopher who lived by his or her convictions is to be granted special consideration. Henry falls in this category. Not everyone who reads this volume will come away agreeing with him. They cannot fail, however, to find in the stories and reminisces and theological reflections that he was a man who lived what he believed. To be most specific, he believed what divine revelation teaches as a unified message: that the God who speaks does so to save a people for himself.

For his teaching, writing, and living, he deserves commendation. Not only this, though—he deserves emulation, the ultimate honor.

THE BROADER CONVERSATION

We publish this book recognizing that it is part of a broader conversation. The discussion of Henry is not waning; it is growing apace. There was an earlier period of Henry-related publishing some twenty-five to thirty years ago. One thinks of works such as the following: Henry's own *Confessions of a Theologian: An Autobiography* (Waco, TX: Word, 1986); Bob Patterson's *Carl F. H. Henry*, Makers of the Modern Theological Mind (Waco, TX: Word, 1983); R. Albert Mohler Jr.'s chapter "Carl F. H. Henry," in *Baptist Theologians*, edited by Timothy George and David S. Dockery (Nashville: Broadman, 1990), 518–38; and a number of the more personal essays in Henry's *Gods of This Age or God of the Ages?*, edited by R. Albert Mohler Jr. (Nashville: Broadman, 1994).

The second wave of books interacting with Henry appeared about fifteen years ago. These included Kevin Vanhoozer's *The Drama of Doctrine: A Canonical-Linguistic Approach to Christian Theology* (Louisville, KY: Westminster, 2005); Stanley Grenz and John Franke's *Beyond Foundationalism: Shaping Theology in a Postmodern Context* (Louisville, KY: Westminster, 2001); and most sympathetically and extensively, Russell D. Moore's *The Kingdom of Christ: The New Evangelical Perspective* (Wheaton, IL: Crossway, 2004). In 2004 the *Southern Baptist Journal of Theology* devoted its entire Winter 2004 edition to evaluating and honoring Henry.[6] We may group two more recent volumes in this later school: Gregory Alan Thornbury's *Recovering Classic Evangelicalism: Applying the Wisdom and Vision of Carl F. H. Henry* (Wheaton, IL: Crossway, 2013), and G. Wright Doyle's *Carl Henry—A Theologian for All Seasons: An Introduction and Guide to Carl Henry's God, Revelation and Authority* (Eugene, OR: Pickwick, 2010).

In terms of institutional commitment, Henry's name has graced the nameplates of no less than three scholarly centers: the Carl F. H. Henry

---

[6] http://www.sbts.edu/resources/category/journal-of-theology/sbjt-84-winter-2004.

Center for Theological Understanding at Trinity Evangelical Divinity School; the Carl F. H. Henry Institute for Intellectual Discipleship at Union University; and the aforementioned Henry Institute at Southern Seminary. Capitol Hill Baptist Church of Washington, DC, has for over a decade sponsored "Henry Forums" on theology and culture in honor of its former member, Sunday school teacher, and mentor to pastor Mark Dever.

CONCLUSION

We began this preface by reference to the words of Karl Barth on John Calvin. Barth was one of Henry's most frequently referenced sparring partners. The two men labored in the same task from different theological poles. Both wished to vindicate Christianity as a system of revelation in a century that viewed the Word as outmoded. Barth, though a churchman, championed the neoorthodox position, claiming that the Bible-in-itself was not the Word of God, but contained the Word of God; Henry, though recognizing Barth's prodigious gifts—he called his writings an "epochal contribution to theology"[7]—sided with the evangelical tradition in identifying the Scripture as the revealed mind of God itself.

The two men did not cross paths on many occasions. In 1962, Barth came to America from Switzerland for a lecture tour. Henry attended his lectures at the McCormick Divinity School in Chicago and engaged him in the question-and-answer session. The exchange that followed, recounted by Henry in his *Confessions*, captured perfectly the differences between the two theologians.

> "The question, Dr. Barth, concerns the historical factuality of the resurrection of Jesus." I pointed to the press table and noted the presence of leading religion editors or reporters representing United Press, Religious News Service, Washington Post, Washington Star and other media. If these journalists had their present duties in the time of Jesus, I asked, was the resurrection of such a nature that covering some aspect of it would have fallen into their area of re-

---

[7] Carl F. H. Henry, "The Dilemma of Facing Karl Barth," *Christianity Today*, January 4, 1963, 27–28.

sponsibility? "Was it news," I asked, "in the sense that the man in the street understands news?"

Barth became angry. Pointing at me, and recalling my identification, he asked: "Did you say *Christianity Today* or *Christianity Yesterday?*" The audience—largely nonevangelical professors and clergy—roared with delight. When countered unexpectedly in this way, one often reaches for a Scripture verse. So I replied, assuredly out of biblical context, "Yesterday, today and forever."[8]

Wherever one lands, this is one of the all-time great trading of wits of the Christian church. Henry's last response—which Barth followed up with a question about whether photographers would take pictures of the virgin birth—crystallized his optimism about the future God directs. The church would suffer violence, and violent men would seek to destroy it. But they would fail. The kingdom of God might suffer violence but never defeat.

We need many things in our day, but this kind of God-centered hope is paramount. As future chapters will show, Carl Henry did not only quip about his confidence in God's promises. He made good on it. He fashioned a life by it. He produced a body of thought according to it. We young evangelicals may never have had the privilege of knowing Henry in the flesh. We can, however, encounter both his piety and his theology, profiting from the meeting, discovering in it a godly man who lived what he believed and a Christian theologian who wrote what he had seen: Jesus high and lifted up, the Word once and for all delivered to the saints.

Books like this one are by necessity collaborative efforts. We therefore owe a debt of gratitude to many who have contributed to its completion. We are especially grateful to the various institutions and organizations that collaborated in one form or another to mark the occasion of the centennial of Carl Henry's birth in 2013. Two conferences in particular, hosted at the Southern Baptist Theological Seminary and Trinity Evangelical Divinity School, provided venues for many of this book's chapters to be delivered first in address form.[9]

---

[8] Carl F. H. Henry, *Confessions of a Theologian* (Waco, TX: Word, 1986), 210–11.
[9] We were especially delighted to see the broad constellation of evangelical sponsors behind the event in Louisville, including Beeson Divinity School, *Christianity Today*, Fuller Evangelical Theological Seminary,

We also note our appreciation to the administration at Southern Seminary, including President Albert Mohler and Provost Randy Stinson. Both have provided keen institutional leadership and influence, fostering an environment that reflects the best virtues of Carl Henry's vision for theological education and scholarship. We are thankful to call that place home.

Deep thanks are especially due to the wonderful team at Crossway. We found it to be a particularly sweet providence that Lane Dennis and Justin Taylor would support this project, especially in light of the long history and partnership between Crossway and Dr. Henry. Jill Carter and Lydia Brownback provided outstanding editorial assistance along the way, and Lauren Harvey led the effort to produce the book's extraordinary cover.

We are particularly grateful to our wives, Jeannie Hall and Bethany Strachan, who always lovingly and patiently endure our academic enterprises and broadly eccentric scholarly pursuits.

American evangelicalism now faces, as it has at various points in its complex history, something of a crisis moment. In the face of stiffening cultural opposition and the evaporation of cultural Christianity, the movement is once again required to return to its first principles, those convictions and beliefs that anchor our faith and direct our mission. We remain optimistic and hopeful. The faith once for all delivered to the saints remains as true and steadfast as ever, because the God "who speaks and shows" remains unchanging, and his promises are sure. We pray you sense that hopefulness even as you read this book and are strengthened afresh for the task at hand.

Matthew J. Hall and Owen Strachan

Prison Fellowship Ministries, the Southern Baptist Theological Seminary, Trinity Evangelical Divinity School, and Union University.

1

The Indispensable Evangelical

Carl F. H. Henry and Evangelical Ambition in the Twentieth Century

R. Albert Mohler Jr.

Historians often overplay the term *indispensable*. Charles De Gaulle once quipped that cemeteries are filled with "indispensable" men. Nevertheless, it is certainly true that some men are indeed indispensable in the stories of nations, movements, and institutions. Historians of the founding era of the United States, for example, increasingly understand the indispensability of certain men whose lives proved consequential in the founding of the American nation. James Thomas Flexner, for example, wrote a Pulitzer Prize–winning biography entitled *Washington: The Indispensable Man*, a monograph that describes Washington's indispensable role in the birth of America.[1]

Carl Henry had a similar stature within the evangelical movement in the United States during the twentieth century. His role in the neo-evangelical movement was, without overstatement, indispensable. Just as the story of America's founding is impossible to tell without the indispensable George Washington and his network of colaborers, so

---

[1] James Thomas Flexner, *Washington: The Indispensable Man* (Boston: Back Bay Books, 1994).

also it is impossible to tell the story of the evangelical movement in the twentieth century without the indispensable Carl Henry and his fellow laborers Harold John Ockenga and Billy Graham.

In 1983 Word Publishing released a monograph on Carl Henry in their series Makers of the Modern Theological Mind. Bob Patterson, the general editor of the series, chose to write the volume on Carl Henry. He explained in the book's foreword, "As the editor of this series . . . I had to select an (or the) outstanding American evangelical theologian about whom to write a book. That choice was simplicity itself—Carl F. H. Henry, of course. Carl Henry is the prime interpreter of evangelical theology—one of its leading theoreticians and now in his seventies, the unofficial spokesman for the entire tradition."[2] Later he wrote, "Carl Henry has been the prime mover in helping evangelical theology in America re-assert its self-respect."[3] In 1978, *Time* magazine named Carl Henry evangelicalism's leading theologian. In his obituary in the *New York Times*, published on December 13, 2003, Laurie Goodstein described Carl Henry as the "brain of the evangelical movement"—a line that served as the headline of the obituary.[4]

The description of Henry as the "brain" of the evangelical movement was not original to Goodstein. She adopted the phrase from none other than David Neff, the then-editor of *Christianity Today*. Neff told the *New York Times*, "If we see Billy Graham as the great public face and general spirit of the evangelical movement, Carl Henry was the brains." Goodstein also said, "In more than 40 books he wrote or edited, Dr. Henry laid out an intellectual defense both for a literal understanding of Scripture and for the imperative of spreading the faith." She went on to conclude, "Dr. Henry helped start several of the institutional pillars of the evangelical movement: Fuller Theological Seminary, where he was the first acting dean, and the National Association of Evangelicals, in addition to *Christianity Today*." Greg Thornbury later added a similar assessment of Henry's role in the neo-evangelical movement: "It would be fair to say that if Billy Graham was the heart of evangelical-

---

[2] Bob Patterson, *Carl F. H. Henry*, Makers of the Modern Theological Mind (Waco, TX: Word, 1983), 9.
[3] Ibid., 10.
[4] Laurie Goodstein, "Rev. Dr. Carl F. H. Henry, 90, Brain of Evangelical Movement," *New York Times*, December 13, 2003, accessed November 1, 2014, http://www.nytimes.com/2003/12/13/us/rev-dr-carl-f-h -henry-90-brain-of-evangelical-movement.html.

ism, Carl F. H. Henry was its head. The man with a massive brain, a journalist's pen, and an Athanasian fortitude."[5] Paul House also noted, "It is historically untenable to ignore or dismiss Carl Henry's role in the shaping of twentieth century American evangelicalism. His involvement in evangelical life is well known, and has been well documented by himself and others."[6] My own assessment of Henry already published in *Baptist Theologians* is in accord with the statements above: "In an age of declining theological vigor and few theological giants, Carl F. H. Henry has emerged as one of the theological luminaries of the twentieth century. His experience as journalist, teacher, theologian, editor, and world spokesman for evangelical Christianity ranks him among the few individuals who can claim to have shaped a major movement."[7] I continue to stand by those words and the assessment made in that essay.

A PERSONAL ACCOUNT

HENRY AT SOUTHERN SEMINARY

I first encountered Dr. Henry in his theological literature. *Remaking the Modern Mind* was the first of his books I read. This work and others on the modern mind were written a generation before I read them. These books, however, described exactly what I was seeing and experiencing both in the modern world and in classrooms at the Southern Baptist Theological Seminary during the 1980s.

I met Dr. Henry personally when he visited Southern Seminary at the invitation of the Student Evangelical Fellowship (SEF) in the 1984–1985 academic year. This was a critical time for both the seminary and the Southern Baptist Convention. Just one year prior (1983), Glenn Hinson, one of the most influential professors on the campus of Southern Seminary, and James Leo Garrett of Southwestern Baptist Theological Seminary participated in a literary project that asked the question, Are Southern Baptists evangelicals? Garrett was more open to the notion

---

[5] Gregory Alan Thornbury, *Recovering Classic Evangelicalism: Applying the Wisdom and Vision of Carl F. H. Henry* (Wheaton, IL: Crossway, 2013), 22.
[6] Paul R. House, "Remaking the Modern Mind: Revisiting Carl Henry's Theological Vision," *Southern Baptist Journal of Theology* 8/4 (2004): 4. Paul House's sentence is strategically written. Winston Churchill once said, "History will be kind to me, for I intend to write it"! Dr. Henry intended to do very much the same.
[7] R. Albert Mohler Jr., "Carl F. H. Henry," in *Baptist Theologians*, ed. Timothy George and David Dockery (Nashville: Broadman Press, 1990), 518.

that Southern Baptists were evangelical of a sort. Hinson, however, was adamant that Southern Baptists were not evangelicals. Evangelicals were not only a different theological tribe but of a different species! As both he and other SBC moderates saw it, *evangelical* was an undesirable adjective and a noun they did not intend to be.

Furthermore, in 1984 Jimmy Draper, then president of the Southern Baptist Convention, published *Authority: The Critical Issue for Southern Baptists*. That the president of the SBC was writing about serious theological issues within the church was an important achievement for the convention. Draper's book is also notable because it was largely dependent on the work of Carl Henry. Further, Draper, as president of the convention, included Henry and other prominent evangelicals in many important conversations taking place in Southern Baptist circles.

When Dr. Henry arrived on campus at Southern Seminary, I was serving as the assistant to my predecessor, President Roy Honeycutt. Dr. Honeycutt called me and indicated that we were facing an institutional challenge due to Henry's presence on campus. Henry, the most distinguished evangelical theologian of our time, had come to Southern Seminary, and yet no faculty member would host him.[8] In light of this crisis, I was asked to host Henry. This was an experience that, for me, was a bit like discovering one had been asked to have breakfast with a visiting head of state!

Dr. Henry's arrival proved an intimidating experience—a massive, titanic theological presence had been delivered unto me for hosting. Having admired Henry's work and having listened to so many audio recordings of his lectures, I wondered what he was going to do with this twenty-something who had been appointed as his official host simply because the members of the faculty did not want to host him.

Dr. Henry accompanied me to my PhD theological colloquium, where I introduced him to Dr. Frank Tupper, the chairman of that colloquium and a senior faculty member at Southern. The faculty, having met prior to my arrival with Henry, had decided that Henry was certainly welcome to participate as an observer but was not allowed to

---

[8] I want to absolve Dr. Timothy George who also contributed to this volume and taught at SBTS during this time. He was unavailable during this time to offer assistance to Dr. Henry.

speak. As usual, Henry was incredibly gracious. He folded himself into a chair among the students, took out a tattered, leather briefcase with "C. H." in gold on the clasp, retrieved some notes, and listened quietly.

The student presenting in colloquium that day was Charles Scalise, who now serves as professor of church history at Fuller Theological Seminary. Scalise had written a very incisive paper on Brevard Childs's pioneering work on canonical theology. After roughly thirty minutes of cross-examination from the students, the faculty entered the conversation with a very lively debate about Hans Frei, James Barr, and Brevard Childs. Though I could almost feel the energy coming out of Dr. Henry, he exercised restraint and said nothing. At the end of the colloquium he privately made some very kind comments to Scalise about the paper.

Later that day Dr. Henry pulled three large manila envelopes out of his briefcase and handed them to me. The first was dated two weeks previous and labeled "Debate with Brevard Childs—Yale University." The next envelope was also dated very recently and labeled "Dialogue with Hans Frei." The final envelope was also recently dated and labeled "Debate with James Barr, Tyndale Fellowship, Edinburgh." Each of these conversations had taken place just within the past few weeks! The PhD colloquium and faculty had just been discussing Brevard Childs, Hans Frei, and James Barr, and here was the man who not only had written about them but had just engaged them in public conversation. Yet he was not allowed to speak in colloquium. Of course, that did not keep him from speaking thereafter.

As readers may imagine, Dr. Henry and I had a great deal of conversation thereafter, particularly during the time he delivered an address to the SEF. During this time I learned that Henry could talk and walk at equal pace. He was a torrent of conversation. He had an unusual ability to put so many places and people on a theological and intellectual map of conversation. He connected so many dots into a cohesive theological worldview. I often wish I could now replay all of those conversations.

His conversation was also challenging. During his visit, I was writing my dissertation on Karl Barth and American evangelicalism. At one point, he decided to grill me on my reading of Karl Barth. Those who have read portions of Barth's *Church Dogmatics* will know that there are sections in large print and sections in small print (the *minuscula*).

Thankfully, due to my attention to the *minuscula*, I was able to respond to each of Dr. Henry's questions to his satisfaction. Henry concluded the conversation by reminding me, "Always read the *minuscula*. That's where Barth is at his greatest and most dangerous."

He grilled me with other theological questions as well. He had a knack for positing the most challenging theological questions in casual conversation. Though he was enormously kind, he was not a man given to many pleasantries. Conversations almost always seemed to end with a discussion of epistemology. On one occasion as we drove to dinner, he turned to me in the car and asked, "Which is prior, correspondence or coherence?" At the time I was more concerned about which is better, Italian or Thai? However, after being thrust into the deep end of the epistemological pool, I had to either sink or swim. My answer: "Correspondence is prior, coherence is meaningful only after correspondence." He simply responded, "We can eat now."

As his autobiography, *Confessions of a Theologian*, makes clear, Dr. Henry had something of a "vagabond ministry" during this time. His travel schedule was quite rigorous. Thankfully, his next engagement after his trip to Southern Seminary turned out to be some time away, so he continued to stay on campus. This time was a tremendously rich experience for me. One of the most important encounters I had with Henry during that time came as we walked across the seminary lawn after lunch. I can still remember exactly where we were on the seminary lawn when Henry asked me, "What is your position on women in the pastorate?" Until then, I had happily been an egalitarian. In fact, in 1984 the Southern Baptist Convention had adopted a resolution stating that the office of pastor was limited by Scripture to qualified men. In response, I instigated a public statement and bought a full-page ad in the Louisville *Courier Journal* to write a manifesto about how wrong the Southern Baptist Convention was on that issue. I do not know if Henry was aware of that information, but my guess is that someone in the SEF had informed him. After I stated my convictions, Dr. Henry looked at me over his glasses and said "One day, you'll be embarrassed to have made that argument."

Of course, I found Dr. Henry's statement rather devastating. That night, I went to Southern Seminary's library and tried to find everything

I could on the issue of the ordination of women—which was not much. This, of course, was before publications such as *Recovering Biblical Manhood and Womanhood* and other literature upholding modern evangelical complementarianism. As a matter of fact, the only book I could find that opposed women's ordination was *Man and Woman in Christ* by Stephen Clark, a rather eccentric Roman Catholic. Both Clark's book and a fresh evaluation of Scripture's teaching on the issue forced me to realize I had the wrong position—a position that was inconsistent with other theological commitments I had made. The experience now feels something like when Apollos was taken aside and instructed more accurately. Henry had a way of doing just that. I am very grateful for these experiences.

THE YEARS THAT FOLLOWED

Dr. Henry and I remained in contact, especially as I was writing my dissertation. In 1987 he came as a visiting professor to the campus, as part of a Pew Charitable Trusts' funded project on Southern Baptists and American evangelicals. This experience allowed me to spend more time with him and witness how he worked—an experience for which I am profoundly grateful. In 1989 I was elected editor of the *Christian Index*, the oldest newspaper serving the Southern Baptist Convention and now the oldest religious periodical in America. Carl Henry was the one man whom I had as a role model for editorial work, and we corresponded regularly. Henry never offered a critical word about my editorials, though he would often suggest other issues that should have been addressed. His letters regularly included statements such as, "You could have said such and such . . . but you're always going to run out of space"—a final sentence that he would usually write in tiny script at the end of the letter because he himself had just run out of space. Henry's *Christianity Today* was the standard I hoped to accomplish at the *Christian Index*.

In 1993, I was elected president of Southern Seminary. During my inauguration, a time of volatility almost impossible to describe, one of my goals was to make a statement about the direction that Southern Seminary needed to take. I asked several people for help in that task. The first was Billy Graham, who not only came and spoke at my inauguration but also allowed us to name our graduate school of missions and evangelism after him. It remains the only graduate school that bears his name. I asked Henry to deliver the inaugural address at lunch, to which he graciously agreed.

Dr. Henry's address at the inaugural luncheon was entitled "Theology in the Balance." His address was both profound and incisive.

At this turning time in the history of Southern Seminary . . . the institution can exert enormous influences in view of its role in the denomination and the manner in which theoretical and practical studies are coordinated and in which the great heritage is perpetuated. There are always free spirits who think theologians, like magicians, need only carry a special bag of tricks or think that a pastor's main asset is his ready effervescence and his discharge of charismatic dynamism. Instead of looking to God and his self-disclosure and to the Bible and God's enduring promises, they look to self-esteem, to humanity, and its potential. . . . The time is right therefore to emphasize that truth is the highest asset the Christian religion can have. Nothing else much matters: the nature of God, the content of the Christian faith, redemption, regeneration, resurrection, and heaven and eternal bliss. If we remain only in the realm of myth, none of this matters. . . . Yet theology once again hangs insecurely in the balances . . . it is once again at a crucial stage, at a decisive juncture, at a critical turning point. We who profess to be its champions, and who welcome it for what it authentically and genuinely presents, need more aggressively to herald the direction it gives, and the truth and justice it affirms. The grace and moral energy it offers needs a larger sounding board. . . . Even an inaugural occasion like this reminds us that Baptists were among the earliest in founding Christian universities and seminaries. They've also had one of the poorest records in preserving their theological stability. We need more than two hands to count up the number of Baptist institutions that have gone down the drain doctrinally. . . . There are gratifying signs, however, of a recovery of academic heritage. . . . Even the launching of a large Christian university in the New York/New Jersey area is again being discussed, sixty years after it was first seriously probed. If a comprehensive Christian alternative to a turbulent secular outlook is to arrive, it will come from a Christian academia. The foes of Christian education can hardly be expected to respond critically to their own theories. The time has come to put things right again. Theology may no longer be king or queen of the sciences, but that is not reason for demeaning it to a bargain basement closeout.

From you for whom the Word of God has come alive, the world waits for a message that throbs with the heart of God. It is time for all of us to do theology in the dark again. It is not too late for America, if we stay true to the Savior and remain dedicated to his Word. Neither politics, nor the media, nor science, nor public education will make us truly happier or better or wiser. May the Southern Baptist Theological Seminary be a theological terrain where the Book and the Redeemer and the Returning King become the source of our theological preoccupations and moral power. It's time for revelry, and Louisville can lead the way again.[9]

Those words were marching orders. They were both bracing and challenging at the same time.

In 1994 Dr. Henry and I were invited to a think tank at Geneva College sponsored by the National Association of Evangelicals. The two of us were asked to deliver papers about how evangelicals should think about the increasingly relevant and controversial issue of homosexuality. After presenting our papers, Henry asked if we could travel home together. It was then that I realized he was not able to get himself around as he once did. On this same occasion, I lost Henry in the airport. After paging him several times, I eventually had to enlist the aid of airport security. We finally found him sitting on a bench, wearing an overcoat, with his briefcase and book open, and jotting notes. I said, "Dr. Henry, we've been looking for you." He simply responded, "I've been here reading."

In 1994 I also served as the general editor—at Dr. Henry's invitation—for one of his final books, *The Gods of This Age or God of the Ages?* On this occasion, I discovered that Henry, though no longer serv-

---

[9] Carl F. H. Henry, "Theology in the Balance," inaugural luncheon address, the Southern Baptist Theological Seminary, October 15, 1993.

ing in an editorial role, was still very much an editor. Not only did he edit his own work; he also edited my editing of his work. On one occasion, he chided me for nearly publishing a sentence that, in his estimation, inappropriately used the word *indicate* instead of *demonstrate*—even though it was Henry who had written the sentence using the word *indicate*. He wrote me a few paragraphs on the difference between what it would mean merely to *indicate* something as opposed to what it would mean to *demonstrate* something. While I was tempted to send back Henry's original draft to show that he had used the word *indicate*, I decided to simply make the change and not mention the issue again. Not so with Henry. The next time we met, he asked, "Do you really understand the distinction between 'indicates' and 'demonstrates'?" I assured him I did.

On January 22, 1999, Dr. Henry came back to Southern Seminary. That same day was also his eighty-sixth birthday. At that point, Southern Seminary named him senior professor of Christian theology. We hoped he would be able to have at least an episodic classroom ministry. Regretfully, Henry was never able to take a lectern at Southern. We were, however, able to celebrate that Henry's six-volume magnum opus, *God, Revelation, and Authority*, was republished under the cosponsorship of Southern Seminary and Crossway—an achievement I now look back on with incredible satisfaction.

AN EVANGELICAL AMBITION

My friendship with Dr. Henry is one of the kindest gifts he could have given me. His interest in me, my ministry, the ministry of Southern Seminary, and Southern Baptists was generous. Our friendship continued all the way to his death. In the conclusion to my essay on Henry in *Baptist Theologians*, I wrote: "[Dr. Henry] has been recognized by evangelicals and non-evangelicals as the premier theological representative of the evangelical movement in the last half of the twentieth century. As E. G. Homrighausen of Princeton Theological Seminary remarked, Henry 'has championed evangelical Christianity with clarity of language, comprehensiveness of scholarship, clarity of mind and vigor of spirit.' Baptists and their fellow evangelicals stand in his debt."[10]

---

[10] Mohler, "Carl F. H. Henry," 531.

Now, over one hundred years after his birth, I continue to stand by that assessment. There is also a sense in which I understand my own words even more. As we look at the twentieth century, the only conclusion we can draw is that Carl Henry is an "indispensable evangelical." Even his personal achievements reveal something of the importance of his influence: Wheaton College, Fuller Theological Seminary, *Christianity Today*, and beyond. This list is only more impressive when one thinks of his associations: Pacific Garden Mission, Moody Bible Institute, Prison Fellowship, World Vision, the World Congress on Evangelism in Berlin, and many other events, movements, and organizations he helped organize.

Part of what made Carl Henry an indispensable evangelical was his relentless ambition. The roots for this ambition are found prior to World War II in the wreckage of American fundamentalism. The neo-evangelical ambition was driven by a sense of urgency mixed with opportunity. In fact, it is difficult to understand which was greater, the opportunity or the urgency. Carl Henry's birth in the very year before World War I placed him in one of the most transformative periods of human history. It also placed him in one of the most urgent moments of the history of American Christianity.

Suggesting that fundamentalism was entirely a failed project is churlish and condescending. If nothing else, the status of "fundamentalist" was forced upon many simply by the fact that they were cast out of denominations, removed from institutional structures, and eliminated from the opportunity of influence or engagement. Yet there are good reasons for understanding fundamentalism as a failure. Those who would become the leaders of the New Evangelicalism recognized that this failure was rooted in an anti-intellectualism, cultural disengagement, doctrinal eccentricity, pugilistic infighting, and the assured marginalization of a movement that complained about being marginalized but worked hard at times, seemingly, to be marginalized.

Thus, New Evangelicals were looking in two different directions. As they looked backward, they saw the collapse of obscurantist fundamentalism. They understood it was not only a failed project, but a closed option. There was no mode of moving forward. Readers can find in the writings of these early neo-evangelicals a sense of near desperation as they struggled to find a way to perpetuate classical Christianity in a modern world without all of the shackles and the embarrassments of fundamentalism.

As the neo-evangelicals looked backward at the collapse of fundamentalism, they looked forward to the future and saw the collapse of liberal Protestantism. In reviewing their literature, I am amazed again at just how prescient the neo-evangelicals were about the collapse of liberal Protestantism. While the perpetual decline of mainline, liberal Protestant denominations is familiar to us now, the notion that these denominational crashes were coming was anything but obvious in the mid-twentieth century. Evidence of the optimism about the future of mainline denominations during this time can be found in Will Herberg's book *Protestant, Catholic, Jew*, the National Council of Churches, and conciliar Protestantism after World War II. Yet during his editorship at *Christianity Today* Henry recognized that the foundations of liberal Protestantism were beginning to crack. He argued that liberal Protestantism simply could not provide compelling answers to the questions modern society was asking. The result of the collapse of liberal Protestantism would be not only the abandonment of biblical authority and doctrinal essentials, but also a retreat from mission fields, and a perpetual mode of cultural accommodationism. In this light, a New Evangelicalism became the dream of Henry and his colleagues. Their ambition was to project a reinvigorated Christianity that was truly orthodox, biblical, and comprehensively, even boldly, engaged.

It could be argued that Carl Henry arrived at Wheaton College as a student in 1935 with at least the embryonic form of this ambition. He was driven by his Christian passion but also by his experience as a young journalist. As a journalist, he witnessed an era that saw the rise of international organizations with both deep structural integrity and far-reaching influence. If Henry arrived at Wheaton with this ambition already brewing in his mind, it may explain why he networked and made the friends and associations he did. It may explain why he shared with Billy Graham and others an institutional, organizational, and Great Commission ambition that gave fruit to so many ministries. At Wheaton, Henry met friends who, with him, would become the luminaries of the New Evangelicalism. Their shared vision was marked by an almost unbridled ambition.

Carl Henry drove, shaped, publicized, edited, advertised, criticized, rationalized, and institutionalized that ambition. The neo-evangelical ambition was an ambition to reawaken and rescue conservative Christianity, to reengage the mind of the age with the revealed truths of God's Word, to marshal the finest minds and seize the intellectual opportunity, to build a great evangelical empire, and to organize evangelicals worldwide into a massive, world-changing Great Commission movement. Together these neo-evangelicals intended to meet the theological liberals on their own ground—the ground especially of academia and elite intellectual centers.

Carl Henry went beyond that, of course. He argued in *Christianity Today* that it was not enough to change minds—you had to change policies. Repeatedly within his editorials he would make the argument that we needed to change policies and reshape institutions. It was not enough to agree on cognitive issues if it did not have a practical effect. At the same time, he always knew that cognitive issues came first. The ambition of the New Evangelicals was to meet theological liberals on their own ground and beat them at their own game, especially in the arenas of theology and philosophy. They wanted to build greater institutions than liberal Protestantism had built and, unlike the mainline Protestants, they intended to retain them for evangelical faithfulness. They wanted to do more than engage the culture. They wanted to reshape it.

Without Carl Henry, the story of evangelicalism would be a very different story. To speak of Carl Henry is to tell the story of evangelical ambition and all of its glory—the conferences, colleges, seminaries, publishing houses, evangelistic organizations, youth movements, mission agencies, and congregations. To tell his story is also to speak honestly about the failures of that evangelical ambition—its overreach, its personality conflicts, its celebrity culture, its unfulfilled dreams, and its own accommodations, both cultural and theological.

The institutional ambitions were not without tremendous effect. Glancing at the contributors to this volume and their associated places of ministry is itself evidence to the fact that those evangelical ambitions were realized, even if they were not completely fulfilled. Fuller Theological Seminary, *Christianity Today*, the National Association of

Evangelicals, and the Evangelical Theological Society all live because of the ambition of the New Evangelicals.

One dream of the New Evangelicals and of Carl Henry that never materialized was a great evangelical university in a major metropolitan area. Dr. Henry insisted that the school could be established only in one of two places: Boston or New York. Evangelicals, he argued, needed to be located in the great centers where culture was being shaped. Even as late as my inauguration as president in 1993, he was still talking about that idea and engaged in conversations about the possibility of building this university. Several years ago, one evangelical leader told me, "Most of those conversations were going on in Carl Henry's brain." The man had a dream he simply would not let die.

This dream for a university was, in historical perspective, too late. There are very few major universities, evangelical or otherwise, that have emerged de novo out of the mid-twentieth century. As a matter of fact, a recent major volume on higher education points out that it is now virtually impossible to found what would be a major research university. For example, research institutions such as Stanford University or the University of Chicago were built upon the foundations of grants given by philanthropists such as John Rockefeller and others—men who at the time individually controlled 1 percent of the gross national product or gross domestic product of the United States.[11]

While the ambition to see an evangelical university never materialized, Dr. Henry's dream lives on in the lives of scholars and scholarly organizations that produce rigorous academic work with evangelical commitments. This dream also lives on in institutional representations such as King's College and others in the New York/New Jersey area.

Many of Dr. Henry's institutional ambitions live on. Some of them would please him more than others, but, frankly, it is something of a miracle that they actually do exist. When you consider what the evangelical founders established that has lasted, it is astounding—even if all their dreams were not realized. Henry's theological ambitions were just as staggering. As I once again look at dozens of books written by

---

[11] See Alison R. Bernstein, *Funding the Future: Philanthropy's Influence on American Higher Education* (Lanham, MD: Rowman & Littlefield Education), 2013.

Carl Henry, I realize that few of his successors (if any) have written anything of that stature. The evangelical movement we know today would not be what it is had Carl Henry not written that library as a singular individual.

In all of his personal ambitions, what drove Dr. Henry ultimately can be boiled down to one word—*conversion*. He knew himself "to be completely owned by a Savior."

In 1986, in his memoir, *Confessions of an Evangelical Theologian*, he said:

> I have two main convictions about the near-term future of American Christianity. One is that American evangelicals presently face their biggest opportunity since the Protestant Reformation, if not since the apostolic age. The other is that Americans are forfeiting that opportunity stage by stage, despite the fact that evangelical outcomes in the twentieth century depend upon decisions currently in the making.[12]

Our ambitions may be somewhat different from those of the evangelical movement's founders, but they are no nobler. Chastened by the realities of a new century and its challenges, I identify without hesitation or compromise upon the theological tradition or confession that Carl Henry and his friends so capably defined, defended, and declared. We stand not only in their debt but in their shadows. In an age that will require an even greater theological clarity and theological wisdom from us, may we be worthy to pick up the mantle they have handed to us.

Shortly before his death Dr. Henry wrote:

> Our weak batteries can be recharged by a jump cable that reconnects believers to the divine current held in store for us by our supernatural Creator, Preserver, and Redeemer. We rely too much on our own finite power and world energy; we are dazzled by technology more than by theology and morality. To gain God's empowerment for mission we must first acknowledge our vulnerabilities and our

---

[12] Carl F. H. Henry, *Confessions of a Theologian: An Autobiography* (Waco, TX: Word, 1986), 381.

spiritual immaturity. Beyond our lifetime, if Christ tarries, others will run the relay and carry the torch. For us, in the rocky terrain of the present-day cultural conflict, the time is now, and the race is now.[13]

The race has been over for Carl F. H. Henry for some time now. But it is not over for us. The real question is this: Will the present generation of evangelicals run the race or run from it?

---

[13] Carl F. H. Henry, *Gods of This Age or God of the Ages?* (Nashville: Broadman, 1994), 43.

2

Toward a Full-Orbed Evangelical Ethic

The Pioneering Contribution of Carl F. H. Henry

Richard J. Mouw

My first encounter with Carl Henry occurred when the inaugural issue of *Christianity Today* arrived at our family's home in the fall of 1956. My father was a pastor, and in those early years the magazine was sent to many clergy free of charge.

I was sixteen years old when that first issue appeared, and while I can't say that I picked it up and devoured it, I did see Billy Graham's name on the cover, and since Graham was (and still is!) one of my spiritual heroes, I opened the magazine to read his article on biblical authority. And having gotten into the magazine, I also read Dr. Henry's editorial, "Why *Christianity Today*?" I was not well versed in the complexities of evangelical identity in those days, but when Henry referred to the need for evangelical scholarship, and to the reality of a network of evangelical scholars working in various academic settings around the world, I did sense, in my teenage naïveté, that this was something new in my spiritual environs.

I had not heard much about the importance of evangelical scholarship, or even many encouraging words about the need for careful thinking, during my evangelical upbringing. On the contrary, I frequently heard anti-intellectual jabs aimed at folks who took the life of the mind seriously. In my childhood, for example, I could not have given any kind of definition of the word *exegesis*, but I could have told you that whatever it was, it was something that true Christians were to avoid at all costs. I had learned that from a traveling revival preacher who had proclaimed that, in contrast to what he had learned in the few seminary courses he had taken, "you don't need exegesis, you just need Jesus!" When I opened that first issue of *Christianity Today*, then, I had the sense that Carl Henry was trying to tell us something different. And I clearly remember that "my heart was strangely warmed."

The warming increased significantly when, a few years later, as a student at Houghton College, I enrolled in a course entitled "Christian Ethics," and once again I had a significant encounter with Carl Henry. His book *Christian Personal Ethics* was not required reading for the course, but it was listed as one of the recommended readings for students who wanted to go a little deeper, and since Henry's name was to me by now a very familiar one, I checked out the book from the library's reserved reading shelf and made my way through its pages.

As my own later career as an ethicist has developed, I have often returned to the more theological chapters of *Christian Personal Ethics*, which make up the last three-fourths of the book. But I must confess that as I sat in the Houghton College library in 1959, it was the first 144 pages of Henry's discussion that grabbed me. In those pages he offered a clear and concise survey of the history of philosophical ethics. Five years later I was to begin graduate studies in philosophy, and I took seminars where we studied, for example, the pre-Socratics in considerable detail. But when I began teaching that subject matter in my own courses, I often went back to Henry's thirty-seven-page overview for insights into, for example, the varieties of Epicurean thought, making use particularly of Henry's discussion of the hedonists' understanding of *ataraxia*, the Greek word for *tranquility*—and always with a sense of gratitude that it was Carl Henry who opened up for me that exciting world of ethical ideas.

HENRY AND EVANGELICAL SOCIAL ETHICS

In 1947 Carl Henry had published his *The Uneasy Conscience of Modern Fundamentalism*. That too was a work in ethics but much less rigorous than *Christian Personal Ethics*, which he was to publish a decade later. I also read *Uneasy Conscience* as a college student, and it did open up for me issues that prepared me to take on many of the social-political questions that were so prominent on the secular campuses where I did my graduate study in the 1960s. But, again, *Uneasy Conscience* was more of jeremiad than it was a systematic study. When a group of us began to call for more social action in the evangelical community of the 1970s, I was known to complain publicly that Henry had restricted his pioneering foundational work in ethics to the personal dimensions.

While that complaint was factually accurate, it failed to take some important considerations into account. For one thing, Henry himself understood the limits of restricting ethical attention to the personal, and he had fully intended to take the next step into a scholarly treatment of the social. In his autobiography he tells us that "originally alongside *Christian Personal Ethics* I had hoped to produce a companion work on Christian Social Ethics as a follow-up to *The Uneasy Conscience of Modern Fundamentalism*."[1] The longer book was not to be written, however, because as soon as he finished writing *Christian Personal Ethics*, he took up the editorship of *Christianity Today*—a task that was to require his full attention for the next twelve years—after which he turned to other theological issues that he had come to see as requiring sustained attention, specifically matters of epistemology, authority, and revelation. He did, however, take a stab at laying out some basic issues in the social sphere, in his 1963 Payton Lectures at Fuller Seminary, which were published in 1964 as *Aspects of Christian Social Ethics*. The focus of those lectures was largely topical, however—he discussed work and leisure, the role of legislation, church-state relations, and the like—without the sustained historical-systematic character of *Christian Personal Ethics*.

In *Aspects of Christian Social Ethics*, though, Henry did touch upon the issues that he would have explored with greater depth if he had been able to follow through on his original intention to write a second major

---

[1] Carl F. H. Henry, *Confessions of a Theologian: An Autobiography* (Waco, TX: Word, 1986), 151.

volume. In the book's introduction, Henry points to the final chapter as being "of fundamental import for the structure of social ethics."[2] In that chapter, titled "The Nature of God and Social Ideals," he zeroes in on the ways in which social thought must be grounded on a proper understanding of God and the divine attributes. Because "Christian doctrine is a harmonious unity whose main axis is the nature of God," he argues, much hangs on our clarity concerning the divine attributes.[3] This topic is so fundamental, he says, that "even the least adjustment of the divine perfections has consequences for theology and ethics."[4] More specifically, he insists that "righteousness and benevolence are equally ultimate in the unity of the divine nature," which means that we must worry when one is emphasized at the expense of the other. "Even the smallest deviation from the biblical view of divine justice and divine benevolence eventually implies far-reaching consequences for the entire realm of Christian truth and life."[5]

Here, then, is another good reason not to complain that Henry simply left us guessing about what a systematic treatment of social ethics would look like. To be sure, we would have been greatly helped had he written that more comprehensive volume. But we can be assured that it would have emphasized precisely the same foundational concerns that characterized his treatment of personal ethics—that all ethical thought that deserves to be called "Christian," whether focusing on the personal or the social, has to be grounded in a proper, biblically faithful theology of the nature of God. And this is precisely what Henry was getting at when, at the beginning of *Christian Personal Ethics*, he called for evangelicals to formulate a "comprehensive revealed ethic, full-orbed as Christian theology."[6]

FULL-ORBED THEOLOGY AND
GENERIC EVANGELICALISM

As we look back to Henry's pioneering work in evangelical ethics, it is important to linger a bit over the significance of his call for ethics to be

---

[2] Carl F. H. Henry, *Aspects of Christian Social Ethics* (Grand Rapids, MI: Eerdmans, 1964), 14.
[3] Ibid., 146.
[4] Ibid., 147.
[5] Ibid., 146.
[6] Carl F. H. Henry, *Christian Personal Ethics* (Grand Rapids, MI: Eerdmans, 1957), 16.

"full-orbed as Christian theology." For a long time, I was content in my own thought to settle for less than this—not, I must quickly add, because I was against a theology that is full-orbed, but because I did not think that we could ever find something worthy of that label that would be serviceable to the evangelical movement as a whole.

My argument went along these lines.[7] Given the coalition character of the evangelical movement, we cannot insist on an all-encompassing, tightly defined system of thought. Our evangelical coalition embraces a diverse mix of theological traditions—Reformed, Wesleyan, Pentecostal, Anglican, Free Church, dispensationalist, and so on. The most we can hope for is that we can agree to rally around a common set of *corrective* emphases in theology and spiritual practice—the kinds of things associated, for example, with what has come to be known as "the Bebbington quadrilateral," referring to the British historian David Bebbington's account of evangelicalism as essentially characterized by these four features: an emphasis on the need for conversion, a fidelity to biblical authority, a central emphasis of the atoning work of Christ on the cross of Calvary, and the insistence on a life of active discipleship.[8]

And what is true of evangelical theology in general, I argued, applies to ethics in particular. The most we can hope for as evangelicals is a shared set of corrective emphases in ethics rather than a detailed moral theology. Some of these ethical correctives have to do with matters that would have been almost universally taken for granted in the Christian past but are widely ignored today in much ethical discussion, such as the insistence that there is a God who has issued clear directives for the moral life; that these directives are presented to us in an authoritative Scripture; and that we sinners, if we are left to our own devices, will inevitably be led astray by a human heart that "is deceitful above all things, and desperately sick" (Jer. 17:9).

Let me explain that I do not think that this argument of mine, which I have endorsed in the past, is completely wrongheaded. We do need an evangelical movement that can unite around common commitments,

---

[7] See, e.g., my essay in *Where Should My Wond'ring Soul Begin? The Landscape of Evangelical Piety and Thought*, ed. Mark Noll and Ronald Thiemann (Grand Rapids, MI: Eerdmans, 2000).
[8] David Bebbington, *Evangelicalism in Modern Britain: A History from the 1730s to the 1980s* (Grand Rapids, MI: Baker, 1989), 2–3.

especially those that can serve as crucial correctives to much that is missing in present-day theology and ethics. But I do not think it is adequate simply to take those corrective emphases for granted and proceed from there to a common evangelical witness.

Here is a bit of history to unpack my concerns on this topic. It is now over four decades since the issuing of the Chicago Declaration of Evangelical Social Concern, a document drawn up in November of 1973 by a group of us gathered in Chicago's downtown YMCA, to affirm our shared commitment to working as evangelicals for issues of social justice. Carl Henry was a participant, and he gave his blessing as a signer of the Declaration, even though many of us had the clear impression that he was not altogether happy with everything the document affirmed—a fact confirmed by Henry's reflections on the Declaration in his autobiographical *Confessions of a Theologian*, published in 1986.

Henry was not alone in his concerns. The Mennonite theologian John Howard Yoder refused to sign, and a number of others expressed their disappointment that this or that item in the declaration was not dealt with adequately.

In retrospect it is clear that this occasion was really the last time that many of us who were present could agree on a document of that sort. We would soon be engaging in serious debates among ourselves about matters of theology—not the sorts of consensus commitments typified by Bebbington's four-point list but about more basic "framing" theological questions that had long been disputed in historic evangelicalism. For those of us who then represented the younger generation, our social consciences had been stirred up, as students in the 1960s, by the opposition to the Vietnam War and the civil rights struggles—all happening during a time when many evangelicals were still immersed in the "other-worldly" mentality that Henry had associated with "the uneasy conscience" in his 1947 book. For us, in 1973, it was encouraging simply to join with other evangelicals—including such venerable evangelical leaders as Carl Henry, Paul Rees, and Vernon Grounds—in letting it be known that from here on at least some evangelicals were going to be addressing structural-systemic societal issues.

It soon became clear to many of us, however, that being activist was not enough. We needed the kind of ethical discernment that could come only from a more substantive theological grounding. And this is where we began to move in separate directions after that Chicago gathering. Some—influenced by Yoder's seminal 1972 book, *The Politics of Jesus*—looked to the Anabaptist tradition. Others worked at recovering relevant themes from the Wesleyan past. The witness of Dietrich Bonhoeffer held promise for some looking to Lutheran resources. Others of us found our inspiration in Calvinism, particularly as it was developed by the great nineteenth-century theologian-statesman Abraham Kuyper.

It will surprise no one familiar with my own work that I have embraced the Kuyperian option. And for me this has meant that one of the most important intra-evangelical engagements to pursue with great diligence has been a dialogue with representatives of the Anabaptist perspective, particularly with John Howard Yoder. The issues that Yoder and I debated, both in print and in a number of public settings, went deeper than our obvious disagreement about pacifism and just-war theory. Yoder once declared at a conference at Calvin College—organized, incidentally, by my dear friend and colleague of blessed memory Paul Henry, son of Carl and Helga—that when Jesus rejected Satan's offer of the nations of the earth in exchange for Jesus bowing before him, the Savior was, said Yoder, resisting the temptation to be a Calvinist!

That assessment was Yoder's—admittedly, not very nice—way of pointing to important differences between the Reformed and Anabaptist traditions regarding the permissibility of Christian participation in civil government as such. Yoder was calling for a Christian activism that stood over against the political-social-economic status quo. And the fact that he grounded this kind of active engagement in a strong "following Jesus" ethical emphasis was (and still is!) attractive to many evangelicals who were looking for a pattern of radical discipleship that is centered on a strong commitment to the person of Jesus Christ.

The passion that characterized these post–Chicago Declaration intra-evangelical debates demonstrated for many of us that it is not enough simply to pledge to work together as evangelical activists who focus primarily on a set of consensus convictions about issues in moral theology. Yes, there is much in liberal Protestantism and Roman Catholicism that desperately needs correctives grounded in our shared evangelical convictions. And, yes, there is much in the "uneasy conscience" of our collective evangelical past that we can also work together to correct. But the more we look to the diverse theological-confessional traditions for much-needed wisdom for present societal challenges and opportunities, the more we will find ourselves arguing with each other about matters that have always loomed large in theological discussion. In an important sense, for evangelicals our talk about our shared commitment to the historic Christian faith masks the realities of what is more accurately thought of as the historic Christian *faiths*.

Again, I am not opposed to the idea of a diverse evangelical movement that is bonded together by a shared commitment to the supreme authority of God's Word, a passion for evangelism, and a firm desire to honor the Lord Jesus as the heaven-sent Savior who alone can save. Indeed, I love that kind of theological consensus, having happily presided for the past twenty years in a seminary community that has counted over a hundred denominations represented in its student body and faculty. Henry himself promoted that broad-movement spirit in his leadership at *Christianity Today*.

My problem is not with a transconfessional, transdenominational evangelical-theological consensus. It is with a movement in which the only operative theology is of a generic evangelical variety. Here is an example of what I mean by this: evangelicals are often accused of having a weak ecclesiology, which is certainly a legitimate observation if we focus primarily on what we evangelicals do or do not say when describing what we hold in common. Billy Graham has said little about the nature of the church in his wonderful ministry. The National Association of Evangelicals does not require its members to subscribe to a detailed ecclesiology. Nor has *Christianity Today* focused much on what we Reformed types label "the marks of the true church." Among influential evangelical scholars, F. F. Bruce and James Houston were formed by the Plymouth Brethren movement, while James Packer and John Stott have ministered as Anglicans. The ecclesiological spectrum evident in those examples is a broad one.

None of that should mean, however, that "thick" ecclesiology is not important for the evangelical movement. Indeed, my own conviction is that the impression we often give about a lack of robust ecclesiological understandings is in fact based on a genuine weakness in evangelical-ism. To be sure, as a matter of mere social history Alister McGrath was right when he responded to the charge that evangelicals have an "under-developed ecclesiology" by suggesting that maybe "it is others who have over-developed ecclesiologies."[9] We evangelicals have long worried about ecclesiological perspectives that are so highly detailed and all-consuming that they crowd out other important theological concerns. So we respond by emphasizing some things, such as the need for a personal relationship with Jesus Christ and the need for evange-lizing the lost, that are often neglected by people who take delight in detailed ecclesiologies.

Fair enough. But without careful attention to ecclesiology we can get into serious theological trouble. There is plenty of evidence today that when we start with a theology that features only the emphases in the Bebbington quadrilateral and then begin to water down one or more of those items, we are left with a movement that can easily be blown about by every wind of doctrine. A generic evangelical theology is a weak basis for sustaining biblical orthodoxy. Much to be preferred is an evangelicalism that, sharing some fundamental convictions that are ignored and even explicitly denied in the larger Christian community, eagerly enters into a free-wheeling discussion of what we can best draw upon from the "thick" confessional traditions of the past in addressing urgent questions today about the church's life and mission.

Gregory Thornbury put it well in his recent fine study of what he labels Carl Henry's "classic evangelicalism." It is important, writes Thornbury, that "we get over our addiction to novelty and the misper-ceived pursuit of freedom from tradition, which leaves us lifeless to the legacy of those who went before us."[10]

CARL HENRY'S ECCLESIOLOGY AND ETHICS

Carl Henry was not simply a generic evangelical. To repeat his call in the opening pages of *Christian Personal Ethics*, evangelicals need, in

---

[9] Alister McGrath, "Evangelical Anglicanism: A Contradiction in Terms?," in *Evangelical Anglicans: Their Role and Influence in the Church Today*, ed. R. T. France and A. E. McGrath (London: Society for Promoting Christian Knowledge, 1993), 14.
[10] Gregory Alan Thornbury, *Recovering Classic Evangelicalism: Applying the Wisdom and Vision of Carl F. H. Henry* (Wheaton, IL: Crossway, 2013), 208.

his words, a "comprehensive revealed ethic, full-orbed as Christian theology." I do agree with several Southern Baptist scholars—Russell Moore, Albert Mohler, Timothy George, and others—who have pointed out that Henry did not pay much attention to the doctrine of the church in most of his major publications. There is virtually nothing on that subject, for example, in his six-volume magisterial *God, Revelation, and Authority*.[11] But I do find some excellent attention to the church as a crucial community for spiritual-moral formation in his *Christian Personal Ethics*, as in his insistence that Christian ethics must be *the ethics of the believing church*. It is the moral inheritance of a fellowship of men and women "separated unto God." The church is a spiritual, ethical, and vital creation that is divinely called into being with Christ as its head. It is the household of God, whose mission is to hold before the world the realities of a redemptive morality.[12]

My own reading of Henry's theological intentions is that he did in fact have a "thick" ecclesiology but that he chose not to push ecclesiological questions to the fore in his writings because he had deep concerns about other theological issues, and that on those other issues he was also operating with a "thick" theology that was clearly shaped by an awareness of traditional theological resources. The issues that he did address, specifically the doctrine of God and the nature of revelation, were ones on which Henry was willing—as he was not, in the case of the theology of the church—to go to the wall to defend as what he saw as nonnegotiable for a full-orbed evangelical theology. Furthermore, on those nonnegotiables Henry was grounded in a classic Reformed theological perspective.

Several years ago, in a paper given at a session on Henry's ethics at the Evangelical Theological Society, I stated that I disagreed with Russell Moore, who has criticized Henry for developing a "generic evangelical" theology out of a desire to build "a sustainable and theologically cohesive trans-denominational evangelical 'movement.'"[13] I responded to Moore's point by saying that I thought it was a good

---

[11] See Timothy George, "What I'd Like to Tell the Pope about the Church," *Christianity Today*, June 15, 1998, 41–42; and Russell D. Moore, "God, Revelation, and Community: Ecclesiology and Baptist Identity in the Thought of Carl F. H. Henry," *Southern Baptist Journal of Theology* (Winter 2004): 27; also R. Albert Mohler Jr., "Carl F. H. Henry," in *Baptist Theologians*, ed. Timothy George and David S. Dockery (Nashville: Broadman, 1990), 530.

[12] Henry, *Christian Personal Ethics*, 203.

[13] Moore, "God, Revelation, and Community," 40.

thing that Henry generally avoided confessional specifics in favor of more generic theological formulations. That was, I am now convinced, a confused response on my part. The truth is that Henry was only selectively generic. Moore is right in saying that Henry did stay generic on ecclesiological questions, but on many other topics Henry quite carefully went "thick"—especially when he had the opportunity to explore theological issues at considerable length. This is certainly the case, I am convinced, on matters of the relationship between theology and ethics.

I'm not going to demonstrate the truth of all of this with a detailed exposition of what Henry says about ethics. Suffice it to point out that in the *Aspects of Christian Social Ethics* chapter that he sees as his contribution to what should basically inform the "structure" of social ethics, Henry defends Barth against Ritschl, and then—in pointing to continuing weaknesses in Barth—he defends Brunner. But Henry then goes on to critique elements in Brunner's own thought, drawing on themes that have been prominent in classic Reformed thought, even quoting the Dutch Calvinist Cecil De Boer in making his own case. And in Henry's interpretation of the moral significance of the Sermon on the Mount, in *Christian Personal Ethics*, he offers a detailed critique of the Anabaptist perspective, turning to what he explicitly labels the "historic Reformed view" as the proper alternative.[14]

All of this leads me to be confident that if Henry had given us a hefty volume on social ethics, he would have provided a Reformed perspective that would have been in careful dialogue with the current theological scholarship of the day. His brief treatment in the *Aspects* book engages in a conversation with many of the same scholarship with whom he interacts in *Christian Personal Ethics*. In each case he is conversant with American liberal theology, the key neoorthodox theologians of Western Europe, as well as other prominent thinkers associated with the conciliar ecumenical bodies.

Today we have somewhat different conversational partners in discussions of Christian ethics. And many of those partners function within the broad evangelical community. Unfortunately, the rich discussion of various historical traditions that engaged many younger evangelicals in

[14] Henry, *Christian Personal Ethics*, 304–8.

the wake of the Chicago Declaration is less visible on the contemporary scene. Insofar as attention is given to historical traditions, much of it is highly selective. Many younger evangelicals engage in a kind of designer theology, a *bricolage* project wherein we find elements drawn from the monastic tradition, alongside some Anabaptist themes, with an atonement perspective that draws heavily on the European post–World War II explorations of the "principalities and powers." There is also a discernible postevangelical trend that features the rejection of the substitutionary atonement along with long-held evangelical convictions about sexual morality.

To be sure, some kind of mixing and matching of elements from various theological traditions is inevitable for those of us who recognize an unnecessary wall building in our own historic camps. When I read, for example, the Stone Lectures that my theological hero Abraham Kuyper delivered at Princeton Seminary in 1898, I frequently bristle at some of his uncharitable comments regarding Catholicism, the Anabaptists, and Lutheran thought. I have learned much from those traditions, incorporating elements of each in my own Reformed theological perspective. But I do see myself as bringing those into a "thick" confessional perspective that has a coherence as a system of thought that differs significantly on key points from those other traditions.

THE CHURCH AS A SOCIAL ETHIC

In the aforementioned paper that I delivered a few years ago at the Evangelical Theological Society, I observed that I could detect some Hauerwasian-type elements in Henry's ethical writings. While I have some serious disagreements with my friend Stanley Hauerwas on ethical matters, I meant the comparison as, at least in part, a commendation. Stanley Hauerwas's writings have influenced many evangelicals these days to emphasize the church's call to be a separated community that nurtures patterns of discipleship that stand over against beliefs and practices of the prevailing culture, thus drawing on Hauerwas's provocative claim that the church does not *have* a social ethic—it *is* a social ethic.[15]

---

[15] Stanley Hauerwas, *Peaceable Kingdom: A Primer in Christian Ethics* (Notre Dame, IN: University of Notre Dame Press, 1983), 100.

We can find a similar emphasis in Henry's writings. And locating these themes in Henry's thought has the special benefit of seeing how they function in the context of a theological perspective that is unimpeachably evangelical. That this is needed can be seen by thinking about what I see as Hauerwas's problematic insistence that it is better for the church to *be* a social ethic than to *have* one. What is going on in this placing of "being" an ethic over against "having" an ethic? A church is called by God to be many things, and they cannot all be simply reduced to a social ethic. The church carries the memories of theological developments in its past. It evangelizes, catechizes, counsels, communicates with other churches, and much more—and most of this cannot be shaped simply by a social ethic that a particular church *is*.

Carl Henry was well aware of the underlying issues at stake here, which is why he insisted in his foundational chapter in *Aspects of Christian Social Ethics* that a correct understanding of the whole range of Christian faith and duty turns on a proper comprehension of divine attributes. How the theologian defines and relates God's sovereignty, righteousness, and love actually predetermines his exposition of basic positions in many areas—in social ethics no less than in soteriology and eschatology.[16]

This makes it clear that the church cannot properly "be" anything without first of all "having" a well-worked-out, biblically sound understanding of who God is.

In the course of his remarks on the overall theological contribution of Carl Henry, Russell Moore rightly observes that it is important to keep in mind, in assessing Henry's thought, that he was very much "a man of his time."[17] This is certainly important for grasping Henry's strong emphasis on the foundational nature of the divine attributes. In insisting that we must be very clear about the nature of divine justice and divine benevolence, Henry was addressing the tendencies of the liberal and neoorthodox thinkers of his day to reduce one to the other, with the liberals treating justice as a form of divine love and the

---

[16] Henry, *Aspects of Christian Social Ethics*, 146.
[17] Moore, "God, Revelation, and Community," 39.

neoorthodox separating the two, but where, in a dialectical manner, justice will ultimately be absorbed into love.

Each option, Henry warned, leads to devastating theological consequences:

> Let it be said . . . that theology that obscures the distinction between justice and grace soon sponsors alien views of social ethics, and any social theory that confounds justice and benevolence will work against a true understanding both of the nature of God and of the character of the Gospel.[18]

And we should be clear about the fact that it really is the character of the gospel that is at stake in our efforts to understand the shape of Christian ethics. One of the most influential works in philosophical ethics during the last few decades of the twentieth century was Alasdair MacIntyre's 1984 book, *After Virtue*. There MacIntyre argued that modern ethics had come to a dead end in the philosophical outlook of Friedrich Nietzsche, in whose writings it became clear that philosophers no longer had any grasp of the proper human *telos*, with the *telos* being the conception of what a fully flourishing human being would be like.[19] The only adequate corrective, MacIntyre argued, was to return to the philosophy of Aristotle, who understood that a true ethic would have to be clear about three things: an understanding of the present condition of human nature, a conception of the human *telos*, and some guidance about how we humans can move from our present condition to what we are meant to be.

This is an excellent framework for understanding the basics of what a robust Christian ethic should address. (And it is worth mentioning that shortly after the publication of *After Virtue*, Alasdair MacIntyre converted to Christianity, becoming a devout Catholic.) Indeed MacIntyre's three Aristotelian requirements lay out nicely the basic ethical concerns that guided Carl Henry in his work in the field.

On one level, the Christian address to the three requirements is easy

---

[18] Henry, *Aspects of Christian Social Ethics*, 171.
[19] Alasdair MacIntyre, *After Virtue: A Study in Moral Theory* (Notre Dame, IN: University of Notre Dame Press, 1984), 148.

to state. The present reality is that we are sinners who fall far short of what we were created to be, and we need divine help to get us from our fallen condition to a state of human flourishing.

But these answers deserve a deep and solid grounding in a theology that is based on fidelity to the supreme authority of the Bible. Yes, we are sinners—but it is urgent that we understand the devastating effects of our sinfulness for all areas of our lives in order properly to grasp what it takes to be rescued from our sinful state. The importance of these connections is nicely laid out by the nineteenth-century Princeton theologian Geerhardus Vos in a marvelous sermon he preached, "Seeking and Saving the Lost," based on Jesus's declaration in Luke 19:10 that "the Son of man came to seek and to save that which was lost."[20] Vos observes that to understand "the inherent logic of the structure of the gospel" is to be clear about the fact that to dilute the meaning of the word "lost" we also must dilute the meaning of what it means "to save."[21] A reduced understanding of our sinful condition inevitably leads to a reduced Savior.

This simple but profound point captures nicely Carl Henry's concerns about the need for an ethic that is "'full-orbed' as Christian theology." Gregory Thornbury appropriately gives the title "Theology Matters" to his chapter outlining the scope of Henry's theological interests.[22] That title states the essence of Henry's work in ethics. Theology matters much in our efforts to understand God's will for human morality.

Henry recognized that our theology of God proper is intimately linked to our grasp of the extent of our sinful condition. This is why, for example, he paid considerable attention in *Christian Personal Ethics* to the theology of the noetic effects of the fall, devoting fifty pages to the relationship of special and general revelation, the image of God, and conscience. In traditional Reformed—and non-Barthian!—fashion, he affirms a continuing "natural content" to the ethical awareness of fallen humanity. The *imago dei* in humankind has not been completely destroyed by the fall. But, he insists, "the content of the moral *imago* is

---

[20] Geerhardus Vos, *Grace and Glory: Sermons Preached in the Chapel of Princeton Theological Seminary* (Edinburgh: Banner of Truth, 1994), 56.
[21] Ibid.
[22] Thornbury, *Recovering Classic Evangelicalism*, 59–115.

apparent to the sinner only in the light which special revelation sheds."[23]
And because this light can be effectively received only by those who
have been transformed by sovereign grace, Henry also devotes considerable attention to those systems that underplay the seriousness of sin's
impact on our fallen consciousness—thus the connections intimately
linking the theology of the divine attributes with both soteriology and
ethics. We are lost sinners, incapable of initiating or contributing to
our own salvation. That fact leads to the all-important question, What
would it take to save us?—a question that in turn leads us to the insistence that, given our desperate condition, our salvation can be brought
about only by a God who is both loving and just.

In articulating all of that, Carl Henry was giving us crucial theo-
logical-ethical counsel for present-day evangelicalism. We serve a God
who so loves sinners like us that he sent the Son to do for us what we
could never do for ourselves—satisfy the just demands of a righteous
Sovereign by bearing the full weight of our guilt and shame on the cross
of Calvary. And having drawn near to us in Jesus Christ, that loving
and just God instructs us in the ways of righteousness—instructions
that we desperately need for our moral lives lest we turn again to our
own sinful ways.

Surely that is an exciting expression of a full-orbed Christian ethic
that we still must strive for in this twenty-first century!

---

[23] Henry, *Christian Personal Ethics*, 157.

3

Carl F. H. Henry's University Crusade

The Spectacular Promise and Ultimate Failure of Crusade University

Owen Strachan

The year was 1949. It was a heady time for evangelicals, a period of institution building, dream hatching, and network constructing. The decade had already witnessed the rise of the National Association of Evangelicals in 1942 and Fuller Theological Seminary in 1947, projects championed by postfundamentalist statesmen such as Harold John Ockenga, Billy Graham, and Carl Ferdinand Howard Henry. The new evangelicals were only just getting warmed up, however. In Cincinnati in December 1949, the first gathering of the Evangelical Theological Society met to discuss key evangelical topics. The press release for the event promised the kind of bold effort that characterized scholarly neo-evangelicalism more generally: "Approximately sixty conservative scholars, coming from every part of the country, gathered at the downtown YMCA in Cincinnati on December 27 and 28 to form the Evangelical Theological Society."

Fuller Theological Seminary theologian Carl Henry was the keynote speaker, addressing the first gathering with a message entitled "Fifty

Years of American Theology and the Contemporary Need." In his message, published later in the *Calvin Forum*, Henry called for distinctly
Christian scholarship:

> *We must also remember that our task is a scholarly task.* This is
> not an attempt to set scholarship over against piety. The two must
> ever go together. Their divorce is also one of the evils that much of
> modern scholarship has fostered. Genuine piety and true scholarship
> must ever go hand in hand. Was it not Warfield who once wrote
> the beautiful sentence: "The systematic theologian should ever rest
> on the bosom of his Redeemer"? But my point now is that the task
> of us theologians in the proposed theological society is not one of
> preaching, of devotional stimulation, or of cultivation of the inner
> life, but primarily a task of scholarly endeavor.[1]

Henry, as later years would show, was not serving up idle talk. In this
period, he and many of his peers warmed to the idea of a renewed intellectual presence in American life on the part of evangelicals. This vision
had institutional shape; numerous educators dared to dream of the establishment of a modern citadel of Christian education, an "evangelical Harvard," as the phrase went.[2] Beginning in the mid-1950s, Henry
began discussing the idea with Billy Graham, whose reputation had
gone global in the preceding years and who had the cachet to pull off
such an endeavor. Over the next several decades, Henry championed the
idea, with Graham waxing alternately hot and cold over it. The largely
untold story of this project is a priceless window into the intellectual
ambitions of the neo-evangelicals of the mid-century period.[3]

The drive to found a great Christian research university began as

---

[1] *Calvin Forum*, February 1950, Henry Papers, Rolfing Library, Trinity Evangelical Divinity School (emphasis original).
[2] Alternately, the "Fundamentalist Harvard." Either way, evangelicals had long set their sights on Harvard.
See M. S. Hamilton, "The Fundamentalist Harvard: Wheaton College and the Continuing Vitality of American Evangelicalism, 1919–1965," PhD dissertation, University of Notre Dame, 1995.
[3] This chapter is a distillation of material from a book project on intellectual neo-evangelicalism cur-
rently under review with several academic presses. It is based on my 2011 doctoral dissertation at Trinity
Evangelical Divinity School, entitled "Re-enchanting the Evangelical Mind: Park Street Church's Harold
Ockenga, the Boston Scholars, and the Mid-Century Intellectual Surge." I had the honor of completing
this dissertation under Douglas Sweeney, John Woodbridge, and George Marsden. My interest in Henry is
not only scholarly but institutional, as I had the distinct privilege of serving under Dr. Sweeney at the Carl
F. H. Henry Center for Theological Understanding at Trinity Evangelical Divinity School from 2008–2010.

many such ventures do: behind the closed doors of power brokers. Henry and Graham shared a conversation in 1955 that shaped the discussion of the project for years to come. This was a heady time for Graham. He had catapulted to megastardom several years earlier through his Los Angeles crusade, which drew the attention of newspaper magnate William Randolph Hearst. Hearst directed his newsroom to "puff Graham," and evangelicalism would never be the same. Traveling all over the world, seeing thousands from all backgrounds come to Christ, Graham discovered a new ability to found institutions from thin air.

Graham and Henry knew one another and shared a common desire to build a great Christian research school. They began a correspondence that shows how capacious and serious their interest in this project was. When Henry wrote to Graham in October 1955, he laid out a grand and thorough vision of the school in question. First, the school could provide an environment "for preparing men professionally and for the pursuit of collegiate and post-collegiate studies leading to higher degrees, in an environment which so articulates evangelical Christianity in relationship to the cultural crisis in all the areas of study that we shall attract students who would otherwise be inclined to go to the big established universities such as Harvard, Yale etc." This would happen through a core curriculum but also "in a specialized way in the various schools, e.g., literature, philosophy, physical sciences, biological sciences, education, etc., the whole proceeding from an emphasis on the Christian concept of vocation."[4]

Such a school required nothing less than outstanding Christian faculty members. "Fundamental to the above is a faculty composed not merely of scholars who have at one time mastered the content of their field, and who have managed to wrest out a respectable Ph.D., but of men who are working up the Christian implications for contemporary issues in their field." These scholars would need "unanimity of conviction in the articulation of their convictions" and would have to possess a common desire to work together "to forge a Christian alternative to the secular interpretations of our day." Only those who were bent on

[4] Letter from Carl F. H. Henry to William Graham, October 8, 1955, Henry Papers, Rolfing Library, Trinity Evangelical Divinity School.

excellence in the classroom and in the research hall need apply. Ideal faculty members would be "dedicated to scholarly earnestness and production (not to outside preaching), restless to supply textbooks in the various spheres of study, and thus productive of students who are fired by the same devotion to scholarship and research (the future Augustines and Anselms and Calvins)."[5]

Henry knew well the lines of tensions he walked. It was of great benefit to many schools and students that many evangelical professors ministered in local churches. He wished for pure scholars, however, academicians who were essentially of the same caliber as Ivy League professors but were resolutely Christian. This brief description of the ideal faculty member, of course, fits what Henry himself sought to do in his own academic career and what many of his fellow neo-evangelical peers pursued.

Graham responded to Henry's letter promptly. He mentioned various conversations with cultural leaders, all of whom indicated support of the idea.

> I have been giving a great deal of thought to the University project. I had a long talk with Harold Ockenga and John Bolten about it. They are extremely enthusiastic. I also talked with VP Nixon, Mr. Sid Richardson, and several other prominent people, including Gov. Dewey and Mr. DeWitt Wallace of *Reader's Digest*. They all feel that there is a definite need in this field. It seems also the feeling of all that I have discussed it with that this University should be definitely in the East, preferably New England. There's something about an Eastern University that has a different prestige, it seems, than one in the West area. This may be entirely wrong, but at least it seems to be the opinion of Harold and others.[6]

This was an exciting letter in Henry's mind. After receiving it, he wrote to Graham one day later. He noted in an exhilarated tone that he had just "gotten a surprising word that you [Graham] join the Gordon

---

[5] Ibid.
[6] Letter from William Graham to Carl F. H. Henry, October 15, 1955, Henry Papers, Rolfing Library, Trinity Evangelical Divinity School.

board, and that a new Christian University is being projected in New England with Gordon as the base, and that you will be throwing your influence and resources behind it."[7] He called this "almost incredible" and a "strategical blunder." Henry urged "procurement of the necessary funds" instead of rushing the idea. At this stage in the drive to create a stellar Christian research university, it is not difficult to peg Henry as the principled curator of the project and Graham as the breezy entrepreneur. The two men operated from different positions from the inception of the plan, with Henry straining valiantly to make it happen and Graham exercising a blend of high-flung creativity and judicious remove at various times.

Henry shifted his tone, sounding as concerned as he was excited. He listed problems he saw with moving quickly with the school: "The problem involved is not merely that of binding creative interest in such a University, on the part of a big donor, to some struggling or half effective project long in existence, although it should be easier to project an entirely new project for which an absolute need exists." These problems paled in light of the greater problem: "The real issue is the fact that such a strategy would blunt the edge of the new and vigorous approach to an evangelical philosophy of education which we so desperately need, and which the present universities lack the insight and vitality to practice. In my previous letter about this . . . I indicated some of these elements."[8]

Henry then expanded upon his contention that the school needed a superstructure that would allow it to transcend many of the difficulties that smaller educational ventures faced. Speaking with awareness of his decided interest in the project, he confessed to Graham that it would "probably frighten you when I speak now about what is needed really to do the job in a proper manner." He unfolded his plans: "The first, and easiest, and indispensable step, is the establishment of a liberal arts college, with all the related departments (e.g., languages, sciences, philosophy, history, social sciences, etc.) with sufficient faculty strength to offer degrees in these spheres right up through the doctorates."

The scary news came next: "My impression is that to project

---

[7] Letter from Carl F. H. Henry to William Graham, October 16, 1955, Henry Papers, Rolfing Library, Trinity Evangelical Divinity School.
[8] Ibid.

buildings, administration, faculty, equipment and other needs, such a venture would involve an investment of $100 million. The present Harvard endowment is 350 million." Once this was in place, "the next step would be the addition of colleges other than liberal arts. Of these, two were the easiest to add—the college of education, and the college of business administration, in that order. Those more difficult to add would be such colleges as engineering, law, medicine, etc., although if a great Christian University were projected, they could not permanently be ignored."[9]

The idea percolated. Conversations continued among the major players and others who professed interest. At one point, Henry enjoyed a correspondence with John H. Strong, son of Baptist theologian Augustus Hopkins Strong, who communicated enthusiasm for the project.[10] Henry later relayed the exchange to Graham and noted how much Strong appreciated the evangelist. There was a historic dimension to this contact, Henry thought; the senior Strong had "enlisted Mr. Rockefeller Senior's support for the idea of a Christian University while pastor of the Rockefeller church in Cleveland," though the plan soon collapsed.[11] Perhaps, mused Henry, things might turn out more auspiciously in their day. For a time, however, the project went quiet.

Several years later, a number of high-profile evangelical leaders and educators met at the Statler Hotel in Washington, DC, on December 29, 1959. The group formally met to discuss "Crusade University" and included Billy Graham, chairman David Baker, Henderson Belk, L. Nelson Bell, Howard Butt Jr., and Paul Harvey, among other evangelical luminaries.[12] Several months before the precipitous meeting, Graham and Henry sent out a special booklet entitled "A Time for Decision in Higher Education: Billy Graham Presents Crusade University." The cover featured Graham smiling in his dazzling way and included an inscription from 1 Samuel 12:23, "I will teach you the

---

[9] Ibid.

[10] Letter from Carl F. H. Henry to John H. Strong, December 16, 1955, Henry Papers, Rolfing Library, Trinity Evangelical Divinity School.

[11] Letter from Carl F. H. Henry to William Graham, December 22, 1955, Henry Papers, Rolfing Library, Trinity Evangelical Divinity School.

[12] Anonymous, "Personnel November 5, 1959 Meeting concerning Crusade University," Henry Papers, Rolfing Library, Trinity Evangelical Divinity School. Attendees are listed as they are recognized in the document.

good way."[13] The booklet is a tremendous window into the ambitions of the evangelicals who wished to start a Christian university.

The school had multiple "objectives," several of which signify a more ambitious program. Crusade University sought several goals at once:

> To provide the highest academic training in the liberal arts and se-lected professional areas for men and women, with a view to train-ing Christian leaders.

> To present the Christian theistic view of the world, of man, and of man's culture in the light of biblical and natural revelation.

> To present the Bible as the word of God, with emphasis on its ab-solute validity.

> To offer areas of concentration in the liberal arts in such profes-sional areas as may be selected.

> To seek to develop habits of Christian citizenship which will enable the student to participate constructively in the life of his community and to recognize his responsibility to the needs of the world.

> To assure physical well-being in a wholesome Christian personality by encouraging student participation in spiritual, social, and recre-ational activities.

> To offer graduate training in theology and such other areas of spe-cialization as will contribute to the well-being of mankind, as rap-idly as such programs can be soundly developed.[14]

The school's objectives include more of the kind of educational theo-rizing offered by Henry to Graham, and there is evidence of Henry's

---

[13] Anonymous, "A Time for Decision in Higher Education," Henry Papers, Rolfing Library, Trinity Evangelical Divinity School.
[14] "Objectives," in ibid.

influence in such phrases as "the Christian theistic view of the world," the "absolute validity" of the Word, and the need for young believers to acknowledge their "responsibility to the needs of the world." The school as charted here displays a preference for the "liberal arts," suggesting that the founders believed that a classical education would better prepare students for redemptive service in the world than the kind of program offered by many fundamentalist schools, which in many places meant classes in the Bible and practical ministry. The visionaries behind Crusade University championed the need to address and work within the broader culture of the country. Ideally, a graduate of the university would "participate constructively in the life of his community" and work for "the well-being of mankind."

Such language signals a shift from the mind-set of previous generations of believers, who focused more on their own communities. The booklet, printed on fine paper and featuring color renderings of the subjects in question—students, buildings, faculty—moved to more esoteric matters. The question of control surfaced next. "The control of the University will be vested in a self-perpetuating board of trustees of 20 members, elected for a five-year term (four to be elected each year). Each member of the board will subscribe to the doctrinal statement of the University and will be dedicated to the cause of Christian education." Outside of major matters, "the academic administration will be in the hands of the president, Deans, and the faculty."[15]

The faculty, a subject of discussion in the Henry-Graham correspondence, came up next. Above a picture of three formally dressed men and three women around a table, the copy read that "Christian teachers with the best training obtainable will be sought for the various departments. Men of proven ability and experience will head the departments and schools, and will be asked to take an active part in recruiting their own staffs."[16] Inasmuch as was possible, "those with a PhD or equivalent training will be sought for the teaching staff."

The venture would not happen so easily. When the parties came together in December 1959, they enjoyed a vigorous discussion over its

---

[15] "Control," in ibid.
[16] "Faculty," in ibid.

nature and vision.[17] The committee, chaired by David Baker and helmed by Graham, had much before them to consider—whom to hire, how to fund the school, where exactly to locate it. These and numerous other issues promised to affect the very nature of the institution, which was a precarious proposition at best. The Crusade University committee was, after all, composed of figures representing existing schools, all of which had their own major needs and goals, and who together sought the establishment of a university linked to no major denomination (and thus no one institutional funding source, or confession) that would, if formed, lead to the plundering of many of the top faculty members from Christian schools and the removal of many Christian scholars from secular environments. Yet this highly complex situation carried great promise as well. The promotion of the kind of full-tilt theological worldview championed by Ockenga and the neo-evangelicals more broadly would have a home.

The first meeting of the parties interested in Crusade University produced what so many such meetings do: committees. Little in the way of a decisive vision was reached, however. What was more, the board found that it did not agree on the matter of campus standards, or the student moral code. In light of such weighty priorities as funding, location, and faculty, this subject may seem quixotic. Yet it engaged the group like no other detail. Discussions spilled over into the summer and led to a second meeting in the fall. In the meantime, attention accrued to the effort. An article by John McCandless Phillips entitled "Protestants Map University Here" appeared in none other than the *New York Times*.[18] Phillips noted in his subtitle on page A5 that "Dr. Graham favors" the idea and reported that "a decision on the project is expected this summer." The initial investment needed would be "about $20,000,000."[19]

Henry used his own bully pulpit in *Christianity Today* to make the public case for the Christian university, a subject that caused no small amount of feedback among a constituency that enjoyed loyalty to many different Christian schools, all of which would be affected by a major

---

[17] For more on the initial meeting, see Garth Rosell, *The Surprising Work of God: Harold John Ockenga, Billy Graham, and the Rebirth of Evangelicalism* (Grand Rapids, MI: Baker, 2008), 208–9.
[18] John McCandless Phillips, "Protestants Map University Here," *New York Times*, May 5, 1960, A5.
[19] Ibid.

new Christian research institution. In October 1960, Henry published his piece, which suggested provocatively that no elite Christian school existed: "It is not proposed to set up just another Christian college (or University, and the larger view) but a University *of the highest academic excellence*. This need is not filled by existing institutions. With full credit to those very few Christian colleges which enjoy the full and well-deserved respect of the world of secular higher education, the fact remains that such academic distinction is definitely the exception." The university Henry proposed would be distinct, "dedicated not only to the Faith but also to the highest and most rigorous academic standards, the University demanding the respect of the secular world of scholarship in the arts and sciences, and in the professions. At the core, solid, dynamic Christian unity; in the branches, solid and creative scholarship."[20]

This was a bold statement to make in the Christian public square. Alumni from schools such as Wheaton, Gordon, and Grove City read the flagship evangelical magazine and would not necessarily have assumed that their alma mater did not represent academic excellence. Henry brooked no compromise in his views, however. He wanted the school to be grounded in "Christian unity" and to produce the strongest "creative scholarship" such that "the secular world" would have to reckon with it. No such university existed, though a "very few" institutions had earned "well-deserved respect." As an educational theorist, Henry was no less shy than he was as a theologian.

Henry's editorial drew a mixed response. Some readers loved it; others expressed concerns. The issue remained on the table for some months until prospective founders of Crusade University met again on November 4–5, 1960. Those in attendance were as follows: Billy Graham (host); Ronald C. Doll, School of Education, New York University; Enoch C. Dyrness, registrar, Wheaton College; Lars I. Granberg, Department of Psychology, Hope College; and numerous other leaders.[21] Henry presided over the meeting.

Discussion waxed hot on the matter of behavioral standards. It is

---

[20] Carl Henry, "Why a Christian University?," *Christianity Today*, October 10, 1960, 24 (emphasis original).
[21] Document entitled "Consultation on a Christian University," Sheraton Park Hotel, Washington, DC, November 4–5, 1960, Henry Papers, Rolfing Library, Trinity Evangelical Divinity School. Attendees are listed as they were identified in this document.

clear from the meeting minutes that nothing so drove conversation as student morality. The following is a brief selection from a much longer discussion of the topic that allows us to see the give-and-take, and the diversity of opinion, operative in the discussion:

> I look upon the inculcation of some of these personal habits not so much as a matter of morality as an opportunity for discipline. (Graham)

> The students at West Point are brought under a very rigid code, and this is later reflected for all their lives. We could ask for strict personal discipline against alcohol, tobacco (though be more open in respect to movies). The people who cracked up under communist pressures in Korea had no firmly held standards. (Doll)

> Why not require spiritual discipline—up at 5 a.m. for an hour of prayer—rather than vacations? (Henry)[22]

This material is only a small swatch of the broader conversational fabric. Though the tone is polite throughout, it is clear that the discussion drew passionate opinions from many of the group's members. Graham and Henry attempted to toe the line in committee, though Graham seemed to lean toward the more conservative side of the discussion, Henry to the left.

The discussion reveals the seriousness with which evangelicals, for better and worse, took campus standards. More than any other matter recorded in the minutes, this topic occupied the committee. Several reasons account for the vigorous debate. First, many of the discussants had grown up in fundamentalist or highly conservative churches. Second, even expressly "evangelical" colleges of the period had stringent moral codes. To *not* have such a behavioral guide would have seemed "liberal" or "progressive" to Christians for whom these labels indicated theological and personal compromise. Indeed, many schools of the liberal

---

[22] Ibid. The order of these comments reflects the order in which they appear in the document, though there are many more such comments in the minutes from this meeting.

Christian tradition had indeed modified or scuttled codes of morality; certainly the broad sweep of colleges and universities founded for the purpose of Christian instruction had done so. Third, the issue truly did merit attention. Would a school merely suggest Christian behavior or, looser still, leave the matter up to students? If Crusade was going to train students to live passionate lives of Christian service, how would it connect the ethics taught in classes to their personal walk with Christ?

The committee broke in early November, the players returning to their ministries, pondering the prospects and perils of a venture like Crusade University. Henry, who had done so much to stimulate conversation at the meeting, made little about the proceedings until nearly two years later. In a letter to S. H. Mullen in September 1962, Henry expressed frustration that nothing had come of the meetings: "Some 20,000 young people of college age made personal commitments to Christ during the Madison Square Garden crusade of Billy Graham, and they were now, as it were, to be 'thrown to the wolves' so far as their collegiate learning was concerned in as much as there was no Christian college in the New York area that had full accreditation."[23] The failure to establish the university had resulted in many college students' falling prey to modernism, as Henry saw things.

At the core of the problem was an overemphasis on a campus morality code. Henry noted his support for such codes while lamenting their centrality in the discussion over Crusade University: "While I have said repeatedly that education without a concern for morality is a sham, it seems to me that such an approach would exclude from the faculty of the Christian University representative scholars" of varying denominations. These included "Scottish Presbyterian, Anglican, Dutch reformed, German Lutheran, Swiss Presbyterian, French Presbyterian, and other evangelical bodies—and if we are to have a Christian University what we need is the best evangelical minds."[24] Henry was surely right. In the age of unprecedented evangelical institution building, it was the campus ethical code that served as the destroyer of intellectual vision, the archangel wielding a heavy sword against neo-evangelical strategy.

---

[23] Letter from Carl Henry to S. H. Mullen, September 25, 1962, Henry Papers, Rolfing Library, Trinity Evangelical Divinity School.
[24] Ibid.

The problems with the establishment of Crusade University were not limited to those suggested by Henry. The school had trouble enlisting help from major donors such as John Bolten, who financed many of Ockenga's projects, including Fuller; and J. Howard Pew, whose money drove efforts such as Grove City College and *Christianity Today*. Many of the most wealthy evangelicals had long-standing ties with other schools; Garth Rosell has shown that though Bolten initially had interest in funding a university, he eventually lost interest due in part to a concern that secular schools would lose what little evangelical leaven they then had.[25] It may have been such lack of interest that allowed the project to crash on the rocks of the campus morality code; that is, perhaps if the major players—both financiers and statesmen like Graham—had felt more strongly about the effort, the division over behavior might have mended itself. Daniel Poling, son of one of the men around the meeting table in 1960, later wrote that Graham's businessmen bet strongly against the project and advised him accordingly.[26] They saw it as a potential quagmire for a man whose career had taken off like a rocket.

Other problems arose as well. Henry wrote to William Schmidt Jr. in November 1962 and suggested, "While there remains a good deal of interest in the matter of a Christian University, the question of location is still as indefinite as ever—if not more so—and the matter has not moved to a point where any decision in this area is likely to be made in the immediate future."[27] Three years later, Henry appealed to Graham again, seeking to resuscitate the idea that had once captivated their conversation. "Although no immediate prospect of a Christian University is in view," he began, he had a thought:

Suppose we three (who are rather well-known to the broad inter-denominational constituencies) serve as a committee guaranteeing the integrity of a fund called Friends of Christian University, and we open a bank account under the name in American Security Bank and Trust Company. Suppose then we get a movement started—for

---

[25] Rosell, *Surprising Work*, 210–11.
[26] Daniel Poling, *Why Billy Graham?* (Santa Fe, NM: Sunstone Press, 2008), 70–72.
[27] Letter from Carl Henry to William Schmidt Jr., November 12, 1962, Henry Papers, Rolfing Library, Trinity Evangelical Divinity School.

each evangelical in the USA to send one dollar more for this fund, and to invite one other person to give one dollar more, with the understanding that 1) if the University eventuates, the list of donors goes into the cornerstone; 2) if it doesn't break ground by 1975, the funds will be equally divided between BGEA [Billy Graham Evangelistic Association], *Christianity Today*, National Association of Evangelicals, and American Bible Society (to attract evangelicals in the ecumenical context). If we reported at the end of the first year that 5000 persons are interested, we might get a movement rolling. Does the idea have merit?[28]

Graham did not respond to Henry with any definite direction. He had been willing to entertain and even promote the idea in past years, but he had never approached the prospect of a research school with Henry's zeal. Graham clearly valued evangelical education and had given generously of his time to schools such as Fuller. He had, moreover, served as a college president for a number of years. What ardor he once had for the project appears to have cooled, however.

Unlike his friend, Henry continued his quest. He responded to detractors, attempted to rally leading evangelicals, and presented his pitch to potential donors. In a letter written in August 1965 to Alan Bell, he laid out the possibilities of such a school, observing that "for 10 years and more some of us have been contemplating the possibility of a great Christian University, located near one of America's major cities accessibly to a major airport in nearby facilities of a large prestigious secular campus."[29] He then opined, "In this decade we have already lost an educational opportunity to prepare thousands of young leaders. The need has increased rather than decreased."

The promise of a great university was still great: "The pervasive scientific skepticism calls for a dedicated cadre of young intellectuals thoroughly grounded in evangelical perspectives, equipped to challenge alien views, and trained to penetrate and permeate the secular institu-

---

[28] Letter from Carl F. H. Henry to William Graham, February 23, 1965, Henry Papers, Rolfing Library, Trinity Evangelical Divinity School.
[29] Letter from Carl Henry to Alan R. Bell, August 20, 1965, Henry Papers, Rolfing Library, Trinity Evangelical Divinity School.

tions of our age. Meanwhile Oral Roberts, on a narrower base than ours, has raised more than \$12 million for a somewhat related project in Tulsa."[30] Henry then suggested possible donations that could reverse this trend: first, the school could use \$25 million for a campus, liberal arts college, and graduate schools of "education, theology, communicative and creative arts, and philosophy."[31] This magnificent level of funding never materialized.

The Institute for Advanced Christian Studies (IFACS) did begin, however, in 1967. Led by Henry, it sought "to enunciate the Christian world-view in order to contain the secular tide that engulfs contemporary culture."[32] The official press release for the group signified an auspicious start: "Proposals for an Institute for Advanced Christian Studies got solid support recently during an important consultation on higher Christian education held on the campus of Indiana University." Buy-in for the project was diverse: "The two-day meeting, sponsored by the Lilly endowment in the Indiana University foundation, was attended by more than a dozen faculty members from prestigious secular institutions as well as academic representatives of various evangelical institutions."[33] The project began promisingly, with directors from Indiana University, University of Michigan, Massachusetts Institute of Technology, and University of Illinois. Henry was the fifth inaugural director and the engine behind the institute until it was shuttered in 2002.[34]

As of March 1967, IFACS had begun. The quest for a great Christian research university continued apace, however, for Henry. He had corresponded with Ockenga one year earlier about the idea of locating the school in Amarillo, Texas, and had gone so far as to talk to Graham about it. In February 1966, he reported to the pastor that Graham worried that they "would run into direct hostility from Southern Baptists in that area," and that "while funds might be available from some sources, this advantage would be outweighed by the hostility of the Southern Baptists, since their enthusiasm should be conserved if the University

---
[30] Ibid.
[31] Ibid.
[32] Carl F. H. Henry, *Confessions of a Theologian: An Autobiography* (Waco, TX: Word, 1986), 341.
[33] "Educators Endorse Institute Plan: Action Committee Named to Project Institute for Advanced Christian Studies," *Christianity Today*, February 17, 1967.
[34] See "IFACS Dissolves," *Conference on Faith and History* 8 (2003): 8.

were located elsewhere."[35] Other sites also failed to interest the evangelist: "Billy's interest in Orlando is once again in low gear, since the party that seems to have the necessary funds to create a university *ex nihilo* has turned out to be the owner of some invisible corporations."[36]

The quest continued. A meeting in August 1968 at the Seven Continents restaurant at O'Hare Airport considered the possibility of a "cluster college campus" in the Pacific Northwest. In the proposal for the idea, the presidents of several colleges announced their "plans for a cluster of Christian colleges in the Northwest. We propose, therefore, that the time is now come for action! After three years of operation in the associated Christian colleges of Oregon, George Fox and Warner Pacific are ready to implement this new concept in Christian higher education."[37] Quaker theologian D. Elton Trueblood spoke at the meeting, which seemed like many such affairs to inspire significant interest in the idea of some form of a meta-school, but Henry did not involve himself in such a plan in future days.

Henry's pursuit of the Christian university persisted into the 1980s, when he was in his seventies. Henry was asked to give a presentation in June 1983 at the Mayflower Hotel in Washington, DC, on the need for an international Christian graduate university. The theologian did not hold back on the subject. His recollections provide a window into how he viewed the frustration of the formation of a research institution: "Twenty-five years ago American evangelicals missed an opportunity to plant a Christian University in a major metropolitan center, a liberal arts campus with graduate schools of theology, medicine, history, philosophy of science, literature and the arts—the whole spectrum." Henry continued the point: "For $10 apiece we could have done it—there are over 30 million adult evangelicals in the United States. But we didn't and we have paid a high price."

In terms resonant with Harold Ockenga's 1947 Fuller address, Henry argued that America had suffered spiritually as a result of the church's inability to effectively answer secular challenges: "Secular hu-

[35] Letter from Carl F. H. Henry to Harold J. Ockenga, February 16, 1966, Henry Papers, Rolfing Library, Trinity Evangelical Divinity School.
[36] Ibid.
[37] Anonymous, "A Proposal for a Cluster College Campus," Henry Papers, Rolfing Library, Trinity Evangelical Divinity School.

manism continues to snipe at the supernatural, to undermine God's revealed truth and his moral commands. We have good evangelical colleges, even some universities in the making, but we haven't fully fazed modern secular culture with the Christian worldview." He closed with a peroration showing that his zeal for his grand plan had not waned:

> Let there be scientists who behold God's glory and nature and not only impersonal processes; anthropologists who affirm the image of God is man and not only an animal ancestry; philosophers who stress that fear of God is the beginning of wisdom rather than the beginning of mythology; moralists who emphasize God's commandments rather than the tolerances of modern culture; artists who set *agape* to music and poetry and who will capture our now wicked world of words for whatever is good and godly; let us have intellectual leaders who offer life and hope to civilization that has missed the way and needs to be alerted again to the incomparable greatness and grace of Jesus Christ.[38]

Three decades after his initial conversations with Graham, the potential of a school still captivated Henry, as his comments show. The ideal graduate schools envisioned by Henry had shifted (as they had in previous communiqués), this time to "theology, medicine, history, philosophy of science, literature and the arts."[39] The failure to found such a school by evangelicals rankled Henry; he believed that the movement had "paid a high price" as a result. As he saw it, the school could have provided a counter to "secular humanism," filled as it would have been with scholars grounded in the rich theological resources of Christianity yet engaging on the front lines with secular academicians to testify to the "incomparable greatness and grace of Jesus Christ." Henry surely admired many scholarly peers who worked with similar burdens, but he believed that a university could have enhanced and magnified such scholarship for the greater good of Christianity and the country more generally.

---

[38] Carl Henry, presentation given on June 23, 1983, at the Mayflower Hotel in Washington, DC, Henry Papers, Rolfing Library, Trinity Evangelical Divinity School.
[39] Ibid.

The preceding body of material reveals in fresh detail the great ambitions of the neo-evangelicals in general and the Boston scholars in particular. As is apparent from the documents he left to posterity, Henry cast a bold vision for a Christian research university. To his statesman peers, big-money businessmen, beguiled *Christianity Today* readers, conferences of academics, and many more, Henry spun his vision of a grand institution founded on the kind of worldview thinking that drove Fuller Seminary and other postwar evangelical ventures. It is not too much to say that the elite Christian university was the prevailing hope—if not the occupation—of Henry's adult life.

Henry worked on many projects, publishing over thirty books, including the landmark six-volume work *God, Revelation, and Authority*, held professorships of one kind or another at multiple evangelical schools, and found time to involve himself in numerous social justice causes.[40] On a level reached by no other evangelical except for Graham and Ockenga, Henry was an evangelical statesman and the most significant conservative evangelical theologian of the postwar period.[41] His life was ferociously busy, and it would be a misnomer to suggest that the formation of a great academy consumed him. But the idea inspired Henry for most of his life and never sat far from his thoughts, regardless of what discouragement he faced.[42]

Kenneth Kantzer confirmed this in 1993 when he reflected in *Chris-*

[40] For more on Henry's life and thought, see Henry, *Confessions of a Theologian*; Bob Patterson, *Carl F. H. Henry*, Makers of the Modern Theological Mind (Waco, TX: Word, 1983); G. Wright Doyle, *Carl Henry—A Theologian for All Seasons: An Introduction and Guide to Carl Henry's* God, Revelation, and Authority (Eugene, OR: Pickwick, 2010); Owen Strachan, "Carl F. H. Henry's Doctrine of the Atonement: A Synthesis and Brief Analysis," *Themelios* 38/2 (2013); Paul R. House, "Remaking the Modern Mind: Revisiting Carl Henry's Theological Vision," *Southern Baptist Journal of Theology* 8/4 (2004): 4–25; R. Albert Mohler Jr., "Carl F. H. Henry," in *Baptist Theologians*, ed. Timothy George and David S. Dockery (Nashville: Broadman, 1990), 518–38; and a number of the more personal essays in Carl F. H. Henry, *Gods of This Age or God of the Ages?*, ed. R. Albert Mohler Jr. (Nashville: Broadman, 1994). The Southern Baptist Theological Seminary devoted its entire Winter 2004 edition to Henry. For insight into Henry's social justice work, see David Swartz, *Moral Minority: The Evangelical Left in an Age of Conservatism* (Philadelphia: University of Pennsylvania Press, 2012).

[41] For more on Henry's theological and philosophical contributions, see Gregory Alan Thornbury, *Recovering Classic Evangelicalism: Applying the Wisdom and Vision of Carl F. H. Henry* (Wheaton, IL: Crossway, 2013). The capstone work of Henry's theological career is *God, Revelation, and Authority*, 6 vols. (Waco, TX: Word, 1976–1983). The six volumes (all reprinted by Crossway in 1999) in order of original publication: vol. 1, *God Who Speaks and Shows, Preliminary Considerations* (1976); vol. 2, *God Who Speaks and Shows, Fifteen Theses, Part 1* (1976); vol. 3, *God Who Speaks and Shows, Fifteen Theses, Part 2* (1979); vol. 4, *God Who Speaks and Shows, Fifteen Theses, Part 3* (1979); vol. 5, *God Who Stands and Stays, Part 1* (1982); vol. 6, *God Who Stands and Stays, Part 2* (1983). In conjunction with Crossway, R. Albert Mohler Jr. oversaw the reprinting of these volumes.

[42] For more on the intellectual aims and insecurity of the neo-evangelicals, see Molly Worthen, *Apostles of Reason: The Crisis of Authority in American Evangelicalism* (New York: Oxford University Press, 2013).

tianity Today on Henry's career. Kantzer reported, "From his student days, Carl dreamed of a great Christian university modeled after sixteenth-century Wittenberg or Geneva."[43] From an early period until the close of his career, "he dreamed of drawing the best and brightest young minds, preparing them, and sending them out to win the minds and hearts of men and women to the gospel and an unequivocal evangelical faith." Kantzer followed with a cautious assessment of the great plan: "Perhaps the idea was ill-advised. Augustine taught us a millennium-and-a-half ago that Christianity is best understood not high in an ivory tower, but in the roaring thoroughfares of real life. In the radical pluralism of the modern world, a thousand rays of light may penetrate better than a single beam from a lighthouse."[44] The point is worth considering, as is the way the pursuit of a university by Henry and others sheds light on the paradoxical nature of the neo-evangelical movement.

We must not miss the ironic nature of Crusade University. The project, to put it plainly, did not succeed. But the push for such a momentous institution signaled that something unusual was afoot in the neo-evangelical era. Henry and others moved away from an isolated, defeated mentality, embracing a bold, restless, ambitious vision for the future of their movement. This meant founding new institutions such as *Christianity Today*, the Evangelical Theological Society, Fuller Theological Seminary, and the National Association of Evangelicals—all successes from the start. It also meant trying to start others, like Crusade University, and failing.

The quest, however chastened, yet lives in our day. Recent decades have witnessed the quest of a number of major Christian schools to become large-scale, nationally impactful institutions. Often these schools have been led by figures who knew or were influenced by Henry. Baylor University famously traversed this course under statesman Robert Sloan until various elements derailed the project, which came as a major disappointment to many onlookers, due to the promise of Sloan's educational enterprise. Sloan is now building a similar program on a smaller scale at Houston Baptist University.

---

[43] Kenneth Kantzer, "The Carl Henry That Might Have Been," *Christianity Today* website, April 5, 1993, accessed January 22, 2014, http://www.christianitytoday.com/ct/2003/decemberweb-only/12-8-15.0.html.
[44] Ibid.

Schools such as Gordon College, under president D. Michael Lindsay; Wheaton College, under President Philip Ryken; Biola University, under President Barry Corey, and others continue to provide strong academic training for young Christian intellectuals. Union University in Tennessee has ramped up its efforts considerably in recent years, efforts that began under former president David Dockery; Dockery will likely expand the vision of Trinity Evangelical Divinity School, where he now serves as president, and capitalize on the institution's reputation and promise. The King's College in Lower Manhattan is led by Gregory Thornbury, a protégé of Henry, and has a solid chance of establishing a serious evangelical institutional presence in New York, the city that first drew Henry's eye as the ideal site of an elite Christian school.

With these good efforts under way, though, we must stop and ask: Why have Christians not yet succeeded in building a great evangelical research university? Does the vision not speak for itself? Surely it would require massive fundraising from Christians, who already give generously to the promotion of the gospel of Christ's kingdom through missions and evangelism. But the idea still has moxie. Imagine that many of Henry's fulsome hopes had been met, including a massive endowment that would allow the drawing of top faculty members, the creation of a large doctoral program, and a large campus in a major urban center. How many top-flight PhDs might the school have graduated or sent on to secular schools with strong credentials? How many books might have been funded by faculty members accustomed to high loads and the pleasant burdens of student development? What might be the output of several elite centers answering the key economic, historical, philosophical, and sociological questions of the day? What exactly would such a school mean to evangelicalism? If grounded in a strong confessional statement and abiding by that statement, is it possible to conclude that it could have meant a great deal to the broader evangelical movement?

There are reasons why Crusade University never materialized. It is difficult to pull faithful donors from existing schools, to pull top faculty members from their current positions, and to sell evangelicals on long-term projects not directly related to missions. It is clear that some possible backers of the scheme thought it onerous to pull off and knew that if they shifted their giving to Crusade University, their other beneficiaries might suffer. One wonders if Graham himself saw this possible problem. After all, his globe-trotting ministry required substantial financial support from some of the very same big-ticket financiers who might have become backers of the school.

The rather tricky nature of who would run the school and what kind of cast it would have was also vexing to the participants. Put simply, a common vision for leadership never materialized. To be sure, in the face of an increasingly secular culture, the school would have found itself walking a tightrope in terms of academic respectability and confessional fidelity. Would scholars, for example, feel pressure to give up on biblical and creedal doctrines so as not to commit intellectual suicide? How would the school have run the rapids between intellectual inquiry on the one side and doctrinal rigor on the other? The fact that Crusade never was attached to a denomination only increases the difficulty of this maneuver. Though much of the story behind the institution-that-never-was is buried and gone, we can surmise that the lack of a clear theological base only made founding it more challenging. Lastly, as highlighted in the preceding narrative, the much-debated ethics code proved not a footnote in the triumphant story of a great enterprise, but the destroyer of evangelical dreams. Whatever else was in play, the parties interested in Crusade University found themselves caught between a dancing policy and a hard place when it came to launching their great effort. The evangelical movement was the worse for this impasse.

There are many reasons, then, why such a school never took shape and form. But there are always good reasons for failure. Carl Henry, a theologian of the highest rank and one worthy of respect and honor, knew this, but he pressed on with his goal throughout his life. We who have come after Henry and his neo-evangelical confreres must not dodge this aspect of his legacy. As those who care about Christian education, are we right to talk ourselves out of grand and ambitious projects because they seem hard? Do we subscribe to a kind of spiritual pragmatism when it comes to funding priorities? Is it possible that in coming days we might establish an institution that could be a major aid to the cause of our gospel-preaching local churches, a school like Calvin's academy, the Puritans' Oxbridge, Mather's Harvard, Edwards's Yale, or Kuyper's Free University?

Whatever our next steps may be, it is clear from the preceding material that the neo-evangelicals, led by Carl Henry, dreamed big. Sometimes they attempted great things and succeeded, as in the formation of Fuller, the now-thriving Evangelical Theological Society, and *Christianity Today*. It is not only in the projects that succeeded that we see the capacious intellectual ambitions of Henry and his fellow neo-evangelicals. Ironically, their failures—specifically, their inability to found Crusade University despite much plotting and planning—show us just how big the vision was, how grand the hopes were, and how fragile the evangelical movement proved to be.

4

Carl F. H. Henry

A Biblically Faithful Theologian Evangelist

John Woodbridge

One afternoon in 1954, Dr. Carl F. H. Henry sauntered through the streets of London toward Hyde Park, famous for the high-octane rhetoric of its soapbox orators at Speaker's Corner. Whereas Billy Graham was a public figure who had preached the gospel of Jesus Christ to some 1,750,000 persons over twelve weeks during the Greater London Crusade of 1954, Henry realized that few English would recognize who he was, ambling into Hyde Park.[1] Henry wanted to listen to verbal crusaders pitch their various ideological wares.

After enduring a number of political rants, Henry spied a father-and-son team of evangelists perched on the top of a lofty stepladder. They were urging passersby to get right with God. Henry offered an encouraging comment to them, only to have the father say to him, "Do you have a word for your Lord?" The father promptly invited Henry to mount the stepladder. Henry reluctantly climbed up one rung after another. The father introduced him to the people below as "an American

---

[1] For Henry's full account of this episode, see Carl F. H. Henry, *Confessions of a Theologian: An Autobiography* (Waco, TX: Word, 1986), 133. On Billy Graham's London Crusade of 1954, see Billy Graham, *Billy Graham: The Autobiography of Billy Graham* (San Francisco: HarperSanFrancisco, 1997), 207–38.

visitor." Henry looked at the raucous crowd and said, "Right now . . . if you will repent and receive Christ as Savior, God will forgive your sins, too, and give you new life!"

Feigning to accept Henry's gospel invitation, one man dramatically fell to the ground as if under conviction and cried out, "God, be merciful to me a sinner." Others shouted unpleasantries up at Henry. Somewhat chagrined, Henry "discretely" descended the ladder, listened to the father and son a little longer and tried to meld into the anonymity of the crowd, only to overhear two men blurt out, "That blooming American didn't have very much to say, did he?" Henry thought to himself: "[Billy] Graham's calling and mine, are very different and I was willing to leave it that way."[2]

If we rely solely on this one anecdote drawn from Henry's autobiography *Confessions of a Theologian*, we might conclude that he viewed the calling of the theologian and the calling of an evangelist as very distinct. However, this would be a serious mistake to make. Why so? Our interpretation is specifically countermanded by Henry's own later words delivered at the World Congress on Evangelism in Berlin in 1966—a congress Henry chaired for none less than the evangelist Billy Graham.

In his opening address, "Facing a New Day in Evangelism," Henry highlighted the present need for evangelists and theologians as well as for biblically faithful theologian evangelists. He specifically urged the twelve hundred congress delegates from around the world to embrace the vocation of a biblically faithful theologian evangelist: "In these next years we must strive harder to become theologian evangelists, rather than to remain content as just theologians or just evangelists."[3] He was convinced that any genuine advance of major import for the evangelical movement would be led by theologian evangelists.

The central purpose of this study is to discern the reasons Dr. Henry, evangelicalism's premier theologian of the second half of the twentieth century, came to believe both theologians and evangelists should strive to become biblically faithful theologian evangelists. First, we will offer

---

[2] Henry, *Confessions*, 133.
[3] Carl F. H. Henry, "Facing a New Day in Evangelism," Berlin World Congress on Evangelism, 1966 (Wheaton College, Billy Graham Center Archives), 2. See esp. Collection 14. For Henry's account of the Berlin congress, see Henry, *Confessions*, 252–62.

examples of Henry's engagement in evangelistic activities to demonstrate his own commitment to evangelism as a theologian. Second, we will note briefly the insightful ways Henry related the preaching of the gospel to issues such as the protection of human dignity, the preservation of human rights, and the pursuit of social justice. Third, we will explore Henry's rationale for urging theologians and evangelists to embrace the vocation of a biblically faithful theologian evangelist. As a postscript, we will propose that Henry's life work and ministry as a biblically faithful theologian evangelist present us with spiritually uplifting modeling and compelling reminders of how we should bear witness for Christ in today's world.

Before proceeding any further, please permit me to offer a personal tribute to Dr. Henry, the Christian man. I met Henry and his wife, Helga, for the first time when I was nine years old. Henry was the founding dean of Fuller Theological Seminary in 1947 and served as a professor of theology. My father, Charles Woodbridge, had just joined the faculty of Fuller in 1950. Pasadena/Altadena, California, was a splendid place to grow up in the early 1950s. Orange groves still visibly lined stretches of Route 66 before it entered Pasadena as Colorado Boulevard. One of my first Technicolor memories of Pasadena was attending a large Easter sunrise service at the Rose Bowl. Sometime later, I learned that Carl F. H. Henry, my father's theologian friend and colleague who, I thought as a youngster, used such big words, was the organizer of these services. Henry's initiative permitted thousands of Southern Californians to gather and celebrate Christ's resurrection. In those days it did not appear especially unusual that Henry, a highly trained evangelical theologian, could also be committed to serious evangelistic outreach. Theologian pastors of the 1950s such as Harold Ockenga of Park Street Church, Boston, and Fuller's president in absentia, also spoke evangelistically and evidenced a "burden for souls." As a boy, I had heard Ockenga preach in this manner at evangelist Jack Wyrtzen's Word of Life camp in Schroon Lake, New York.

My bias in favor of Dr. Henry was enhanced in part by my experience of growing up as a so-called Fuller brat. I have very fond personal memories of the Henry family and other Fuller families such as the Everett Harrisons, the Gleason Archers, the Wilbur Smiths, the Elton Ladds, and others. These happy memories elicit from me more positive feelings for and a different understanding of the gestalt of community life at early Fuller than that found in certain well-written, coolly clinical histories.[4] This literature sometimes portrays early Fuller faculty members as independently minded star professors competing with each other and tending to pull in different directions. Undeniably, a divisive side of early Fuller existed as a number of faculty members did entertain differing, principled perspectives on important theological matters. My father, who in time became a second-degree separationist, participated in some of those controversies. Nonetheless, another evangelistically alive, missionary-minded, and warm, collegial side of early Fuller community life existed. Its merits are often not sufficiently highlighted and celebrated.

Along with Fuller and Ockenga, Henry exercised an especially important role in creating early Fuller's attractive ambience—one he believed was theologically robust, evangelically ecumenical, and evangelistically committed. Henry's assessments as an observer-participant and founding dean should be added to any serious historical reconstruction of community life and the theology of the school. He indicated that early Fuller was "broadly Calvinistic and stressed the importance of intellectual credentials and theological integrity above practical skills."[5] Henry noted that faculty members collectively supported evangelism: "Although a graduate school, Fuller Seminary was unapologetically committed to the importance and necessity of evangelism. The Rose Bowl seemed an excellent setting which to combine academic and evangelistic forces."[6] Henry also pointed out that "the founding faculty was determined to avoid the seminary's [theological] dilution. From the founding in 1947 it discussed the need for a clear statement of faith."[7] On January 31, 1950, Fuller trustees and faculty members adopted a statement of faith affirming biblical inerrancy and other doctrines as a "sacred trust" and "sacred commitment."[8]

As for the quality of the students at early Fuller, Dr. Henry had

---

[4] See, e.g., George Marsden, *Reforming Fundamentalism: Fuller Seminary and the New Evangelicalism* (Grand Rapids, MI: Eerdmans, 1987).
[5] Carl F. H. Henry, "How to Lose a Seminary," address delivered at Fourth Presbyterian Church, 1988, Bethesda, MD.
[6] Henry, *Confessions*, 125.
[7] Henry, "How to Lose a Seminary."
[8] Ibid., 123–24.

nothing but praise: "No seminary faculty ever faced a student body more eager and dedicated than that group of pioneer seminarians."[9] Many early Fuller students such as John Winston, a member of the first graduating class, became leading evangelical pastors, missionaries, and educators across the world. Winston helped found the Free Faculty of Evangelical Theology of Vaux-sur-Seine outside Paris, France.

Students at early Fuller greatly admired Dr. Henry. Trinity Evangelical Divinity School Professor Emeritus David Larsen (Fuller class of 1956) remembered:

In the epochal early days of Fuller Theological Seminary . . . students began coming from around the globe to join an outstanding faculty in the new venture encouraging the evangelization of the world and the upbuilding of the Church which is Christ's body. We experienced joyful excitement in our school which upheld the highest view of Scriptural reliability and supernatural salvation. . . . Carl F. H. Henry's inspired defense of propositional revelation (in the face of dialectical theology's onslaught), his unwavering loyalty to the fundamentals of historic Christianity, his espousal of social conscience and his avoidance of cultural isolation or exaggerated ecclesiastical separatism set the pace.[10]

Larsen indicated that when his church burned down, including his library, Henry invited him into his office and said, "David, here's my library; take the books you need." Larsen recounted that after a class in which Henry had given a magnificent lecture on an aspect of philosophy of religion, he saw Henry out in the hallway gently witnessing to a mailman who had just delivered the morning's mail.[11]

In a 1988 speech in Washington, DC, Dr. Henry, as a firsthand observer, disputed the validity of Professor George Marsden's thesis that posited "in its beginnings Fuller seminary was unfortunately fundamentalist in its commitment to a fully trustworthy Bible."[12] Henry, as

---

[9] Ibid., 118.
[10] Personal letter from David Larsen to John Woodbridge (2013).
[11] Ibid.
[12] Henry, "How to Lose a Seminary."

founding dean, disagreed with this characterization, and for good reason. Though an inerrantist, he did not self-identify as a fundamentalist in the late 1940s. In fact, like Ockenga, he had become well known as one of the principal architects of the new evangelical movement. Henry's *Uneasy Conscience of Modern Fundamentalism* (1947) had provided conservative Protestants with a telling critique of the deficiencies of fundamentalism. By contrast, in 1948 Henry extolled the strengths of the new evangelicalism in a series of articles entitled "The Vigor of the New Evangelicalism," published in the journal *Christian Life and Times* (January–April 1948): "The new evangelicalism voices its plea for a vital presentation of redemptive Christianity which does not obscure its philosophical implications, its social imperatives, its eschatological challenge, its ecumenical opportunity and its revelational base."[13]

My own admittedly impressionistic perception of upbeat personal relations at early Fuller was based on sustained contact with many of the school's professors. I spent time in their homes and went to Sunday school classes, Fuller parties, and snow camps with their children. I did not sense that the faculty members of early Fuller, whatever idiosyncratic traits a few may have manifested, were especially cranky or socially standoffish. Any viewing of Edward Carnell's home movie of Henry, Smith, Fuller, and other early Fuller faculty with their wives at a Christmas party dispels a sense that they were generally a dour, overly competitive lot.[14] They were genial, kind, and committed to serving Christ faithfully in their respective churches.

One way I gained a firsthand appreciation of the spirit of camaraderie of Fuller faculty members was to caddy for some of them at the nine-hole Altadena country club. Watching individuals play golf often provides genuine insights into character and conviviality. I had ample opportunity to watch the reactions of these men with each other after one of them made an especially awful shot, missed a short putt, or whiffed the ball. Later, less flattering depictions to the contrary, Harold

---

[13] Cited in Henry, *Confessions*, 117.
[14] John Carnell, the son of Edward Carnell, possesses a copy of his father's "Christmas movies." These movies provide visual testimony to the sometimes playful and friendly ways various Fuller professors interacted with each other.

Lindsell appeared to be a fun-loving and amiable man in real life. It is true that he was not quite ready for the professional golf circuit. A lefty in golf, he was encumbered with quite a wicked hook that took the ball he shot in most unpredictable directions. This circumstance provided ample scares for golfers in adjoining fairways. Mrs. Lindsell, a gracious lady, hospitably entertained our church high school group at her home on a number of occasions.

Indeed, early Fuller hospitality could engender cordial fellowship between members of the Fuller faculty family. For example, the Woodbridges and the Ladds shared Thanksgiving dinners. Sometimes, however, this hospitality did not include special programming for children. I fell asleep underneath a piano in the living room of the great Elton Ladd during an after-dinner slide show of the Holy Land. Undoubtedly Ladd's commentary was scintillating, but an avalanche of slides induced sleep. As a youngster, I thought the generosity of the famous Bible teacher Wilbur Smith, with his inimitable voice, was nothing short of amazing. He won my enduring affection and loyalty by giving me twenty-five cents for an ice cream cone during a Fuller faculty retreat up at Mount Herman, California. Whatever disagreements my father and Smith may have had regarding competing perceptions of 1930s Northern Presbyterian history, I knew Smith was a fine man, given that twenty-five cents. My favorable impression of Smith had been easily purchased, and it remained permanent.

Regarding Dr. Henry, I loved the fact that he displayed a wry sense of humor and could put on a fantastic magic show. Moreover, his son Paul and I became members of the same class at Wheaton College.

As an adult, I was struck by Dr. Henry's urbanity, broad sense of fair play, humanity, personal kindness, and grace. He and his wife, Helga, a marvelous missionary-minded writer, became true, caring friends. I found Henry, along with Kenneth Kantzer, to be one of the most godly, humble, and gracious men I ever knew. Plus he was a man of deep prayer and great faith. He told me that he would sometimes walk into my father's office at early Fuller and say, "Charlie, we need to pray for such and such a student." Then the two men would fall to their knees and pray for the student by name. Once, in an almost grandfatherly fashion, Henry took me aside and indicated he had submitted my father's name to Ockenga to become the president of Fuller.[15] Henry correctly surmised that for various reasons, I did not know this and other things about early Fuller that he shared with me. Henry also poignantly described to me the grief he and Helga experienced when their beloved son Paul became ill and then passed away. The faith of the Henrys remained unshaken despite their deeply felt loss. So, as you can see, I am really biased toward speaking well of Carl F. H. Henry. How wonderful it was that we, and many of my fellow contributors to this volume, together celebrated Henry's one hundredth birthday.

But did this great evangelical theologian actually possess an evangelistic heart? To make that claim might seem problematic. Did he not affirm that his calling was "very different" from that of evangelist Billy Graham after he, Henry, unceremoniously climbed down from a lofty perch on a stepladder in Hyde Park, London, in 1954?

Numerous pieces of evidence reveal that Dr. Henry was thoroughly committed to supporting and engaging in evangelistic outreach. First, Henry's heart for evangelism was impacted dramatically by his own life-changing conversion experience, accompanied as it was by the immediate evangelistic commission he received to share the good news of the gospel. We remember that a frightened Martin Luther, exposed to a lightning-bolt storm, made a promise to Saint Anne to enter a monastery if she would protect him. He survived the storm and thereafter entered a monastery. Henry, a tough, pagan, New York City/Long Island newspaperman before his conversion, underwent his own terrifying lightning-bolt experience. Henry recalled that while sitting in a car in 1933 waiting for a storm to pass by,

> a fiery bolt of lightning, like a giant flaming arrow, seemed to pin me to the driver's seat, and a mighty roll of thunder unnerved me. When the fire fell, I knew instinctively the Great Archer had nailed me to my own footsteps. Looking back, it was as if the transcendent Tetragrammaton wished me to know that I could not save myself and that heaven's intervention was my only hope.[16]

---

[15] Henry, *Confessions*, 140.
[16] Ibid., 45–46.

Soon after, Gene Bedford, a University of Pennsylvania alumnus who had witnessed to Henry, invited him to pray the Lord's Prayer. Upon doing so, Henry indicated that he had "inner assurance hitherto unknown of sins forgiven, that Jesus was my Savior, that I was on speaking terms with God as my Friend. . . . I now knew God to be the King of my life. Had he dispatched me, I would have gone that very day to China or anywhere else in his cause."[17] Bedford then advised Henry: "If you have good news to share, Carl, don't hoard it from others. Ask God to show you with whom to share it."[18] From the first moments after what he later called a "blinding" conversion, Carl F. H. Henry was "all in" and never doubted the truthfulness of the Christian faith thereafter. He was willing to share the gospel of Jesus Christ and to go to foreign mission fields if the Lord so bid him.

The second piece of evidence is Henry's consistently expressed deep appreciation for the vocation of evangelists. By the late 1930s, the reputation of revivalists and evangelists had fallen on hard times in the United States among Protestant, liberal, mainline churchmen. They repudiated revivalism, associating it with manipulative, emotion-laced altar calls offered by fire-and-brimstone evangelists like Billy Sunday. They argued that experiencing Christian education and receiving the ordinances of the Christian churches provided better avenues for persons to become Christians than "walking the sawdust trail." Sinclair Lewis's depiction of a sleazy, hypocritical evangelist in the novel *Elmer Gantry* (1927) fed their disdain for the vocation of a revivalist and evangelist.[19]

Henry the theologian was likewise disturbed about some evangelists' unsavory practices. Nonetheless, he appreciated the Spirit-empowered revivals he had experienced as a student at Wheaton College and regularly prayed for a national awakening. In 1942 Henry wrote an impressive paper celebrating the ministry of Charles Finney in preparation for a "Finney Sesquicentennial Memorial Conference."[20] He indicated that Finney was "prominent as a theologian no less than as a revivalist."[21]

---

[17] Ibid., 46.
[18] Ibid., 46–47.
[19] See Joel Carpenter, *Revive Us Again: The Reawakening of American Fundamentalism* (Grand Rapids, MI: Eerdmans, 1997).
[20] Carl F. H. Henry, "Charles Grandison Finney: His Life and Ministry," Wheaton College, Billy Graham Center Archives, Carl F. H. Henry 1913–2003 Memorial Page.
[21] Ibid., 1.

Henry acknowledged that Finney's theological views "have not all found general acceptance, except in the small denominations which propagate Finney's theology."[22] Nonetheless, Henry indicated that "the revivalism for which Finney stood is the life purpose of conservatives in every denomination who are warring in prayer for spiritual awakening in the world today."[23] Henry proposed that because Finney had experienced a gripping conversion, he was "equipped for an evangelistic ministry of passion and power."[24] Henry also emphasized the fact that Finney upheld an "orthodox" view of Scripture such that "Scripture was infallibly secured from all error."[25] He claimed that Finney was one of the greatest evangelists of all time.

Third, Henry evidenced a concern for evangelistic outreach by his tireless promotion of and support for Easter sunrise services and inner-city missions. In 1940 Henry's beloved mother passed away. While mourning her death, Henry reflected upon the significance of Christ's resurrection for believers as described in 1 Corinthians 15. This scriptural reading greatly comforted him. He knew that his mother was now with the Lord. He wrote:

> To minister to the bereaved would no longer be the intimidating dreaded task it once seemed; it would be a wider opportunity to display the truth of the gospel of grace, even as I had experienced it in my own and my family's time of need. It should then have surprised no one that when invited I shared eagerly in activities of the Soldier Field Easter Sunrise Service committee in Chicago, and later spearheaded the Pasadena Rose Bowl Easter Sunrise Service committee in California.[26]

In 1963 the city of Pasadena formally honored Dr. Henry for having "conceived the idea of the world-famous Pasadena Rose Bowl as a setting to proclaim Christ's Resurrection from death, bringing eternal life to all, thereby instituting the annual Rose bowl Sunrise Ser-

---

[22] Ibid., 7.
[23] Ibid.
[24] Ibid., 3.
[25] Ibid., 7.
[26] Henry, *Confessions*, 100.

vice. . . . Dr. Henry's influence has been felt throughout the Southern California community and the world, which is better for his having been among us."[27]

As for inner-city missions, in 1942, while serving as a Northern Baptist Seminary theology professor, Henry published his first book, *The Pacific Garden Mission: A Doorway to Heaven.* It consisted of the stories of changed lives, such as those of Billy Sunday and Mel Trotter. The two men had been converted through the gospel ministry of the Pacific Garden Mission in Chicago.[28] To research this study, Henry—ever the newspaper investigative reporter—dressed up as a bum so that he would understand firsthand what it felt like to come off the gritty streets of Chicago and go into a city mission for a warm meal and for a bed, often earned by required attendance at an evangelistic meeting. Henry's quest for authenticity in reporting hit a snag, however. He wrote about the evangelistic meeting he attended:

> With wide, sweeping gestures the song leader that night beat out the hymns as if he were conducting some massive choir. Finally came testimony time. Here and there someone rose to speak a hesitant word for Jesus, until a crescendo of voices took up the witness. I, too, ventured a word of anonymous gratitude that Christ had changed my life since first he became my Savior and Lord. At that, the song leader unwittingly blew my cover. "Now you know," he said, "why I've been so nervous all evening. That man, who just gave his testimony, is one of my professors at Northern Baptist Seminary." It was the first—and last—prayer meeting out of which I walked as soon as heads were bowed.[29]

Harry Ironside, the well-known pastor of Moody Church in Chicago, wrote a marvelous foreword for Henry's *Pacific Garden Mission* that captured well Henry's passion for and confidence in the power of the gospel to transform lives:

[27] Ibid., 120.
[28] See Carl F. H. Henry, *The Pacific Garden Mission: A Doorway to Heaven* (Grand Rapids, MI: Zondervan, 1942).
[29] Henry, *Confessions*, 102.

In a masterly way the gifted author has presented a panorama of regeneration—a moving picture of the redeeming value of the blood of Christ and the life-giving energy of the Holy Spirit, manifested in the salvaging of human wreckage and the new creation of utterly lost men and women—transforming drunkards, gamblers and criminals of all types into devoted servants of God and hard-toiling servants of the Lord of glory, whose delight is to bring others to know Him who has wrought so mightily on their behalf.[30]

Today, we sometimes view theology as a discrete academic discipline separated one hundred miles distant from actual evangelistic engagement. By contrast, Carl F. H. Henry, the leading evangelical theologian of the second half of the twentieth century, did not. He devoted his very first book to telling the story of stunning conversions to Christ through evangelism. He also promoted National Tract Week in 1942.

The fourth bit of evidence is that other Christians, such as Billy Graham, recognized that Henry was committed to evangelistic outreach. Graham tapped him to lead major conferences, such as the Berlin World Congress on Evangelism in 1966. Henry had met Graham at Wheaton College and appreciated Billy's evangelistic fervor and gifts. Henry was thrilled by the results of Graham's evangelistic efforts in Los Angeles in 1949. He appreciated the dignity and respect Graham brought to evangelism—a healing balm for the wounds inflicted by the blemished practice of Elmer Gantry–style revivalism. For three months Henry devoted himself to preparing Billy Graham's Mid-Century Rose Bowl appearance in 1950. A crowd of fifty thousand attended the evangelistic outreach—one of the largest gatherings of its kind west of the Mississippi until its day.

Billy Graham deeply esteemed Dr. Henry's commitment to evangelism. In fact, Graham indicated that one key reason he thought Henry would be an excellent choice to serve as the founding editor of *Christianity Today* was Henry's commitment to evangelism. In a letter to Nelson Bell dated June 5, 1955, Graham wrote: "I do not know any man in evangelical circles with whom I could agree theologically more than

---

[30] H. A. Ironside, foreword to Henry, *Pacific Garden Mission*, 7.

with Carl Henry. I do not believe that we could find a more dedicated, yielded, Spirit-filled, gracious man of God than Carl. I have profound respect for him. He has a great love for evangelism."[31] On August 18, 1955, Henry, in replying to Graham's queries, wrote about his commitment to evangelism: "I have no personal reputation for bitterness: my friends have included men in all theological brackets. But in an evangelistic and missionary thrust, I have one uncompromisable zeal—that Christ be known in his total claim upon life."[32]

Fifth, if it counts at all as evidence of his commitment to evangelism, Henry assumed the guise of an actor by playing the role of evangelist Charles E. Fuller during a service at a railroad mission in Edinburgh, Scotland. The presiding elder of the service had mistakenly announced to the crowd of seventy, "How delighted we all are to have with us tonight Dr. Charles E. Fuller of the Old Fashioned Revival Hour." Then the audience sang "Heavenly Sunshine," a regularly featured song on Charles Fuller's radio broadcast. Henry explained what happened next. Because none of the audience had ever seen Charles Fuller, he, Henry, decided he would have to assume the evangelist's identity:

> To have corrected the mistaken identity at this stage would have ruined the service. I prayed for special unction. Some of the worshipers may have thought that the wireless [radio broadcast from America] somewhat distorted my normal voice but many, I suspect, until this day think they heard the great radio evangelist, and that he was not nearly as impressive at close range as at a distance.[33]

We see, then, that Henry as a theologian was thoroughly committed to biblically faithful, evangelistic outreach.

CARL HENRY, EVANGELISM, AND SOCIAL JUSTICE

The second segment of this chapter focuses on the ways Dr. Henry related the vocation of the biblically faithful theologian evangelist to

---

[31] Henry, *Confessions*, 141.
[32] In his letter of August 18, 1955, Henry indicated that he would not accept the editorship of the new magazine unless from the outset it "combined an irenic spirit with theological integrity." Ibid., 147.
[33] Ibid., 136.

gospel proclamation and concerns for the dignity of man and social justice. In *The Uneasy Conscience of Modern Fundamentalism*, Henry had magnificently explained the relationship between gospel preaching—our primary task, reiterated Henry—and social responsibility and engagement: "The evangelical task primarily is the preaching of the Gospel, in the interest of individual regeneration by the supernatural grace of God, in such a way that divine redemption can be recognized as the best solution of our problems, individual and social."[34]

In his address "Facing a New Day in Evangelism," given at the congress in Berlin, 1966, Henry provided specific examples of the ways Christ's gospel impacted different arenas of life. He brilliantly and persuasively made the case that Christianity rather than atheism is the true font of human rights. He cited the huge deficits of non-Christian approaches to human rights:

> The clamor for human rights is a hallmark of our times. But atheistic naturalism cannot sustain the case for enduring and universal rights. Communist theory suspends all human rights on the sanction of the totalitarian state, thus substituting the absolute state for the sovereign God. But only the divine image as a creation legacy and redemption latency supplies an adequate support for human dignity, endowing man with universal rights even against the totalitarian state.[35]

Then Henry sagely related the gospel to the claim that the God of the Bible is the God of justice and justification:

> But the Gospel of Jesus Christ does not remind men in a congratulatory way of their personal dignity and worth; it upholds the dignity of man by offering a recovery of his squandered destiny through the forgiveness of sins and a new life. The God of the Bible is the God of *justice* and of *justification*. The Christian evangelist has a message doubly relevant to the modern scene: he knows that justice is due

---

[34] Carl F. H. Henry, *The Uneasy Conscience of Modern Fundamentalism* (repr. Grand Rapids, MI: Eerdmans, 2003), 88–89.
[35] Henry, "Facing a New Day in Evangelism," 4.

to all because a just God created mankind in His holy image, and he knows that all men need justification because the Holy Creator sees us as rebellious sinners. The Gospel is good news not simply because it reinforces man's lost sense of personal worth, and confirms the demand for universal justice on the basis of creation, but, also, because it offers rebellious men as doomed sinners that justification and redemption without which no man can see God and live.[36]

Dr. Henry then gave this stern warning about secularism: "Lack of vital faith in the supernatural Creator and Redeemer sooner or later means the terrible loss of human dignity, of social justice, and of personal salvation. Outside a rediscovery of the Gospel of grace there now remains no long-range prospect for the survival of modern civilization, but only a guarantee of its utter collapse."[37] In this context, Henry called upon the delegates at the Berlin congress to give themselves afresh to a new initiative to fulfill the Great Commission: "Is it too much for men devoted to Jesus Christ to pledge their hearts and lives to a bold new effort to give every man on earth in our time the opportunity to accept or reject the Redeemer?"[38]

HENRY'S VISION FOR THEOLOGIAN EVANGELISTS

The third segment of this chapter seeks to identify the reasons Dr. Henry formally urged delegates at the Berlin conference of 1966 to strive to become biblically faithful theologian evangelists. Obviously, Henry knew there sat in front of him accomplished Christian leaders who viewed themselves solely as theologians and others who viewed themselves solely as evangelists. In his address, he joked that some of the theologians and evangelists did not think the others belonged at the congress. He indicated that he had received letters from evangelists who "wrote that the theologians have no business here, since few of them know how to lead souls to Christ; others wrote that the evangelists by themselves would quickly derail the Congress into doctrinal confusion."[39]

---

[36] Ibid., 4–5 (emphasis original).
[37] Ibid., 5.
[38] Ibid.
[39] Ibid., 2.

He urged delegates to "accept each other as we are, justified but not glorified, knowing only in part but rejoicing that we know Christ and have the light of His inspired Word to correct us."[40] Henry's appeal reenforced the congress's theme, "One Race, One Gospel, One Task."

Henry provided a number of reasons to explain his advocacy of the calling of a biblically faithful theologian evangelist. First, Henry reminded his audience that all Christians, not just evangelists, are called to engage in evangelistic witness: "The question that must haunt the conscience of every evangelical believer is this: In view of the Great Commission, what does the Risen Lord expect right now from me and from my local church?"[41]

Second, Henry observed that evangelical advances in the world had often been stymied by the fact that large numbers of evangelical Christians were relegating the task of evangelism to others, specifically professional evangelists. Many Christians were apparently absolving themselves by claiming they were neither called nor gifted by the Lord to engage in Christian witness and evangelism. Henry declared: "One major weakness of modern Christianity lies in its abandonment of the heavy burden of evangelism to a small company of professional supersalesmen."[42] For the evangelical movement to advance, theologians as well as everyone else, for that matter, needed to engage in Christian witness and evangelism.

Third, Dr. Henry proposed that evangelistic outreach not nurtured by faithful biblical theology could end up in doctrinal confusion. Those who came to Christ might not be discipled nor grounded well in Scripture. They might slip away from biblically based evangelical beliefs. Given the very real downsides of evangelists remaining solely evangelists, and of theologians remaining solely theologians, Henry urged the delegates at the Berlin congress to strive to become biblically faithful theologian evangelists.[43] This recommendation constituted a pivotal heartfelt plea of Henry's opening address, "Facing a New Day in Evangelism."

Some evidence suggests Dr. Henry's perception of German church

---

[40] Ibid., 3.
[41] Ibid., 1–2.
[42] Ibid., 1.
[43] Ibid., 2.

life had prompted him to promote the vocation of the biblically faithful theologian evangelist at Berlin in 1966. In a letter dated April 26, 1972, written to the Right Reverend A. J. Dain, Henry weighed the level of success his efforts had achieved at the 1966 Berlin conference in urging theologians and evangelists to become biblically faithful theologian evangelists. Billy Graham and others had chosen Dain to serve as the chairman of the forthcoming 1974 International Congress on World Evangelization. In his 1972 letter Henry cited a German illustration of evangelistic efforts ending in doctrinal confusion owing to the fact that those pursuing evangelistic outreach had lacked sufficient theological and doctrinal understanding:

> As I look back upon Berlin 1966, the evangelical community has in the intervening years rather forfeited its opportunity for coordinated theological leadership, for evangelical ecumenism, and for a clearly-defined social thrust. Out of Germany has come a concern for the theology of missions, and that is to the good. (What is not fully appreciated by evangelicals generally is that this concern, rooted in the confessionally-oriented churches, sees that the defection to Bultmann on the Continent was much more prominent in pietistic circles—preoccupied with evangelism and the new birth—than among confessionally-oriented believers interested in theological-philosophical issues as well.) Without evangelical precision and involvement at these other levels—of a stand vis-à-vis the world religions, modern secularity, and shaping theological concepts—I think those who hope that some unified evangelical para-ecumenical movement will arise simply out of evangelistic concern are likely to be disappointed.[44]

In the same letter Dr. Henry indicated that his appeal for delegates at Berlin in 1966 "erected a rather successful built-in program bridge between evangelism and theology merely as a prefatory liaison that never has been followed up."[45]

---

[44] Letter from Carl F. H. Henry to Right Reverend A. J. Dain, April 26, 1972, Wheaton College, Billy Graham Archives, Carl F. H. Henry 1913–2003 Memorial Page.
[45] Ibid.

Dr. Henry encouraged Reverend Dain to tackle among other concerns the issue of bringing theology and evangelism together in the forthcoming conference: "So an immense task is left to the International Conference if it is going to be concerned at once with truth and grace, and with justice as well."[46]

In sum, Dr. Henry made a superb case in Berlin to the effect that evangelistic outreach should be shaped by biblically faithful theology for it to have maximum spiritual and social impact upon a particular culture. For him, theologian evangelists were especially well suited to launch significant bold advances for the evangelical movement. Henry's Berlin appeal about the need for theologian evangelists echoed the very wise counsel James Denny, the Scottish theologian, had expressed years earlier: "If evangelists were our theologians or theologians our evangelists, we should be nearer the ideal church."[47] In our world in which we often "study" theology and "practice" evangelism as two distinct endeavors, Henry's plea is one we need to reflect upon and heed perhaps more than ever.

The inspiring story of Carl Henry's life provides us with a marvelous example of the power of the gospel of Jesus Christ to transform a life. In this instance a hardened pagan newspaper reporter from New York City became a gracious servant of the Lord, willing to dedicate his all, including his genius-like skill sets, to the service of Christ and his kingdom.

Reflecting upon Dr. Henry's life can refresh our spirits in many ways, among others reminding us of biblical principles and practices we too should embrace as we live out our Christian lives. Following are a number of those reminders.

Reminder 1: The need for each one of us to engage in bearing faithful witness for Christ. As noted above, in his Berlin address Dr. Henry declared: "The question that must haunt the conscience of every evangelical believer is this: In view of the Great Commission, what does the Risen Lord expect right now from me and from my local church?"

Reminder 2: The need for each one of us to depend wholly upon

---

46 Ibid.
47 James Denny, *The Death of Christ* (London: Hodder & Stoughton, 1902), 7.

the Lord's strength and not our own in ministry. In the closing comments of his 1966 address "Facing a New Day in Evangelism" in Berlin, Dr. Henry indicated to the delegates that "we shall do little" if we do not have "the full cooperation of evangelical Christians around the world." But then Henry added a strong coda to the effect that we will do "nothing at all" if we depend on our own strength in ministry. Henry declared:

> Let me note in closing, however, that without the Great Commissioner we can do nothing at all. If we take the great Commission seriously, we must take the Great Commissioner just as seriously: "He that believeth on me, the works that I do shall he do also. . . . Abide in me, and I in you. As the branch cannot bear fruit of itself, except it abide in the vine; no more can ye, except ye abide in me. . . . Without me ye can do nothing" (John 14:12, 15:4–5). It is tragic when men who profess to serve Christ, in effect forsake the duty of evangelism; it is equally tragic when disciples who proclaim a devotion to the Great Commission try to "go it alone."[48]

Reminder 3: The need for each of us to remember that it is the gospel, not the gospel plus one more thing, that is the power of God unto salvation (Rom. 1:16). Dr. Henry repeatedly indicated that it is the gospel of Jesus Christ by itself that has the power to transform lives, whether that of a pagan newspaperman from New York City like him, or a rough-hewn baseball player like Billy Sunday converted in the Pacific Garden Mission, or a brilliant college student atheist like the young Kenneth Kantzer.

Reminder 4: The need for each of us to base evangelistic proclamation upon Holy Scripture. In the very first fascicle of *Christianity Today* (October 15, 1956) Henry published Billy Graham's marvelous article "Biblical Authority in Evangelism." In this piece Graham explained how his commitment to the total trustworthy character of Holy Scripture affected the impact of his preaching during the famous 1949 Los Angeles crusade: "During that crusade I discovered the secret that

---

[48] Henry, "Facing a New Day in Evangelism," 6.

changed my ministry. I stopped trying to prove that the Bible was true. I had settled in my own mind that it was, and this faith was conveyed to the audience. Over and over again I found myself saying 'The Bible says.' I felt as though I were merely a voice through which the Holy Spirit was speaking."

Reminder 5: The need for each of us to work out the social implications of the gospel in caring for our neighbors and in addressing pressing societal problems. As already noted, in *The Uneasy Conscience of Fundamentalism* Dr. Henry wrote: "The evangelical task primarily is the preaching of the Gospel, in the interest of individual regeneration by the supernatural grace of God, in such a way that divine redemption can be recognized as the best solution of our problems, individual and social."[49] In this light, we can understand better why Henry so esteemed the ministry of Chuck Colson and served on the board of Prison Fellowship.

If Dr. Henry were with us today, what would he say? My guess is that he would repeat with deep Christian warmth his valedictory remarks, "If I Had to Do It Again." These familiar comments capture well Henry's life as a biblically faithful theologian evangelist, and so it seems altogether fitting to end with them:

> From the outset of my Christian walk I have treasured the Book that speaks of the God of ultimate beginnings and ends, and illumines all that falls between. . . . An evangelical Christian believes incomparable good news: that Christ died in the stead of sinners and arose the third day as living head of the church of the twice-born, the people of God, whose mission is mandated by the scripturally given word of God. The term evangelical—whose core is the "evangel"—therefore embraces the best of all good tidings that on the ground of the substitutionary death of Christ Jesus, God forgives penitent sinners and he shelters their eternal destiny by the Risen Lord who triumphed over death and over all that would have destroyed him and his cause. That good news as the Apostle Paul makes clear, is validated and verified by the sacred Scriptures. Those

---

[49] Henry, *Uneasy Conscience*, 88–89.

who contrast the authority of Christ with the authority of Scripture do so at high risk. Scripture gives us the authentic teaching of Jesus and Jesus exhorted his apostle to approach Scripture as divinely authoritative. There is no confident road into the future for any theological cause that provides a fragmented Scriptural authority and—in consequence—an unstable Christology. Founded by the true and living Lord, and armed with the truthfulness of Scripture, the church of God is invincible. Whatever I might want to change in this pilgrim life, it would surely not be any of these high and holy commitments.[50]

---

[50] Cited in John Woodbridge, "Evangelical Self-Identity and the Doctrine of Biblical Inerrancy," in *Understanding the Times: New Testament Studies in the 21st Century: Essays in Honor of D. A. Carson*, ed. Andreas J. Kostenberger and Robert W. Yarbrough (Wheaton, IL: Crossway, 2011), 137–38.

5

The Compleat Christian

The Massive Vision of Carl F. H. Henry

D. A. Carson

On the occasion of Carl Henry's eightieth birthday, John Woodbridge and I edited a volume of essays in his honor, under the title *God and Culture*.[1] In that volume, in an essay of appreciation, Kenneth Kantzer wrote: "In the good providence of God, through [Carl's] speaking, teaching, witnessing, and personal encounters, he has woven his life into the warp and woof of the lives of millions. The entire evangelical church looks up to him, and I share richly in this heritage."[2] The broad sweep of that life is readily accessible in many surveys, both paper and digital, and especially in his theologically rich autobiography, *Confessions of a Theologian*. Yet a bare ten years after his death a decade ago on December 7, 2003, many a young systematician has never read even one of the forty books he wrote; many an ethicist knows him only through secondary surveys; many a pastor is largely unaware of the ways in which that pastor's own thinking has been shaped by Henry;

---

[1] D. A. Carson and John D. Woodbridge, eds., *God and Culture: Essays in Honor of Carl F. H. Henry* (Grand Rapids, MI: Eerdmans, 1993).
[2] Kenneth Kantzer, "Carl Ferdinand Howard Henry: An Appreciation," in Carson and Woodbridge, eds., *God and Culture*, 377.

many younger Christian leaders who talk incessantly of missional Christianity and who think they are tying together Christian confessionalism and social concern for the first time in the modern era, are painfully and embarrassingly unaware that a giant charted this landscape before they were born; and many Christian educators, both in seminaries and in universities, have little idea of Henry's visionary commitment to excellence, faithful scholarship, engagement, and influence in the worlds of ideas and tertiary education.

Part of this, of course, is nothing more than the brutal effects of the passage of time. Most people are largely forgotten in a generation or two, or at most three—even by their own families. It is given to very few to be cherished in the memories of peoples and nations—and even when it does occur, the memory is often seriously distorted. The person has become a beloved but somewhat distorted icon. Many people revere the name of Wesley or Calvin without ever reading a single book they wrote and with only a hazy knowledge of when they lived. The picture Scripture casts up in this regard is plainly true: we human beings are like grass, or, at best, like flowers growing in the grass—but the season ends, the grass withers, the flowers fade, and only the word of our God endures forever (Isa. 40:8). It is good for our humility to be reminded that the most prominent of us will, should the Lord not return first, be utterly or at least almost entirely unknown in a hundred years.

Nevertheless a public memory that does not seem to be able to survive for even ten years is somewhat surprising. Worse, some who happily call themselves evangelicals seem more intent on debunking Henry than on learning from him, eager to demonstrate that Henry's magisterial *God, Revelation, and Authority* is nothing more than a theological relic that has passed its "sell by" date.

We must not overlook what a towering figure Carl Henry was. His reign as editor of *Christianity Today* helped to establish his intellectual leadership. In the 1970s Richard Ostling of *Time* magazine called him evangelicalism's leading theologian. Some of his works were paradigm shifting, not least his 1947 volume *The Uneasy Conscience of Modern Fundamentalism.* His six-volume magnum opus, to which I have already referred, *God, Revelation, and Authority,* published between

1976 and 1983, showed he was far more than a scribbler of journalistic articles and occasional books. Timothy George has argued that in the mid-twentieth century, Billy Graham and Carl Henry were the most important shapers of contemporary evangelicalism. Not a few of today's senior evangelical systematicians, such as Millard Erickson, Gordon Lewis, and Bruce Demarest, affirm the shaping influence Henry had on them, not to mention some young ones such as Russell Moore and Gregory Thornbury. Doctoral students sometimes write dissertations on Henry's life and thought, including the executive director of The Gospel Coalition, Ben Peays, a PhD graduate of Trinity Evangelical Divinity School and contributor to this volume. Carl Henry was one of several young leaders who worked together to start the National Association of Evangelicals. His international influence multiplied during the years after he was appointed lecturer-at-large for World Vision (1974). His mentoring of Chuck Colson and his subsequent work with Prison Fellowship were largely behind the scenes, but no less influential for that. During his career he taught in several institutions that helped shape American evangelicalism, including Fuller Theological Seminary, Eastern Baptist Theological Seminary, and Trinity Evangelical Divinity School. In 1966 Henry and Graham were the primary movers and shakers behind the World Congress on Evangelism, held in Berlin. The friendships and networks established there led directly to the 1974 International Congress on World Evangelization held in Lausanne. Often referred to as Lausanne I, that congress is organically tied to the most recent Lausanne Conference, held in South Africa in 2010. The figure of Carl Henry towers over the landscape.

Mercifully, now marking over a century since Carl Henry's birth, a handful of scholars are doing their best to prevent the dissipation of the Henry legacy, let alone the fading of his memory. Not least is Gregory Alan Thornbury, whose important book *Recovering Classic Evangelicalism: Applying the Wisdom and Vision of Carl F. H. Henry* is neither biography nor lament but an appeal to build on Henry, especially his epistemological foundations, to recapture and build up what he calls "classic evangelicalism." The 2013 conference sponsored by the Henry Center at Trinity Evangelical Divinity School explored numerous facets of Henry's thought, including his subtle grasp of the importance of history in biblical revelation; his hermeneutics; his sophisticated rationalism in which he distinguishes, in Keith Yandell's words, between incomprehensibility and ineffability: it is possible to know and articulate literal truths concerning God, even if this infinite God outstrips all human knowing; and his ambitious plans for a Christian research university, which, because Henry was a man of his own times, was sometimes dubbed "Crusade University." Along with another Henry conference at the Southern Baptist Theological Seminary in Louisville, these conferences will doubtless result in published papers—such as this book—that will play their part in informing a new generation to whom Joseph means nothing (see Ex. 1:8).

Before I come to the point of this chapter, it might be helpful if I list three reasons why some Christians have sought to marginalize Henry— quite apart from the universal tendency I mentioned at the beginning of this talk, viz. the tendency toward remarkably rapid forgetting once a thinker has gone to his reward.

1) Not a few critics have focused rather negatively on one element of Henry's thought without attempting a broader (and necessarily more positive) evaluation of the man. I could not begin to count how many times I have read that Henry was a Christian rationalist, or a philosophical modernist, or, worst of all, an epistemological foundationalist—usually uttered with the same dismissal one reserves for charging someone with an addiction to pornography or pedophilia. To take but one example, this one from a normally reputable source, Alister McGrath dismisses Henry's understanding of revelation, labeling it "purely propositional," stemming from Henry's regrettable enslavement to the rationalism of the Enlightenment.[3] This sort of criticism has two serious flaws.

First, it is not more than labeling. As far as I know, the foundationalist label was first applied to Carl Henry by Hans Frei, when the latter was ticked with Henry because of Henry's review of Frei's book *The Eclipse of Biblical Narrative.* Over against classic, liberal, destruc-

---

[3] Alister E. McGrath, *A Passion for Truth: The Intellectual Coherence of Evangelicalism* (Downers Grove, IL: InterVarsity, 1996), 106.

tive source-criticism, Frei was right to emphasize the inherent power of biblical narrative and its importance for interpretation, and many of his contributions were extraordinarily helpful. But Frei wanted to maintain this stance while continuing to adopt the conclusions of the earlier liberal criticism, even if he rejected their methods. Henry rightly saw that issues of truth are at stake, propositional truth. If all that Frei read of Henry was that one review article, I can see why he might have inferred, wrongly, that Henry was an unreconstructed foundationalist and simplistically addicted to a view of truth as exclusively propositional, but I find it difficult to imagine that any intelligent critic who has actually read Henry extensively would make the same mistake. Regardless of the reasons, that label and its associates stuck, even at the hands of Henry's fellow evangelicals who should have known better, had they taken the time to delve into Henry more probingly. It is an axiom of the best of academic debates not to apply to one's opponents labels that the opponent would himself disavow. That courtesy has not been extended to Henry.

Second, much of the criticism of Carl Henry has focused on this one issue—epistemology. Almost completely overlooked, however, have been Henry's zeal for evangelism, his vision casting, his call for a research university, his understanding of personal and social ethics, his christology, his theology proper, his attempts to interact with a secular world, his commitment to historic evangelicalism, and much more. Carl Henry has often been neglected on all these issues because he has already been dismissed due to his ostensible old-fashioned foundationalism.

I suppose I should say something about the substance of the epistemological issue. Although Henry repeatedly insists on the truthfulness of the Bible's propositions, it is a serious misreading of Henry to imagine he thought that all revelation is nothing but propositions, or to suppose that access to such propositions rests on the rationalist presuppositions of the late Enlightenment. On this point, as far as I can see, Thornbury has Carl Henry exactly right:

[Henry] stressed the absolute dependence of human knowledge upon divine disclosure, whether natural or particular. In other words, according to Henry, we know what we know because God wills both the possibility and the content of that knowledge. . . . God circumscribes and determines what can be known. Nonetheless, the world remains knowable because God himself is an intelligent Deity. Contrary to the trajectory of rationalism, no autonomous standard for reason can be offered since reason itself loses meaning apart from the divine character. Since the divine discloses himself as a person, revelation is personal in nature and can therefore speak to all of humanity. Consequently, revelation both coheres and corresponds to reality because God is one. It is not a truism to say, therefore, that divine revelation is communication that we can trust. . . . Every condition of knowledge (i.e., justified true belief), therefore, stems from an allowance of either common or particular grace to the end that we live in the world God has actually created, and glorify the agent of said creation, even Jesus Christ.[4]

Or, in the words of Henry himself:

In a sense, all knowledge may be viewed as revelational, since meaning is not imposed upon things by the human knower alone, but rather is made possible because mankind and the universe are the work of a rational Deity, who fashioned an intelligible creation. Human knowledge is not a source of knowledge to be contrasted with revelation, but is a means of comprehending revelation.[5]

Thus God, by his immanence, sustains the human knower, even in his moral and cognitive revolt, and without that divine preservation, ironically enough, man could not even rebel against God, for he would not exist. Augustine, early in the Christian centuries, detected what was implied in this conviction that human reason is not the creator of its own object; neither the external world of sensation nor the internal world of ideas is rooted in subjectivistic factors alone. Or again, Peter Hicks has Henry right when he says:

[4] Gregory Alan Thornbury, *Recovering Classic Evangelicalism: Applying the Wisdom and Vision of Carl F. H. Henry* (Wheaton, IL: Crossway, 2013), 52–53.
[5] Carl F. H. Henry, *The Drift of Western Thought* (Grand Rapids, MI: Eerdmans, 1951), 104.

Henry's central thesis is that God reveals and speaks. There is no reason why we should limit God to one form of revelation (through either a person or a book, through either encounter or concept). God reveals and speaks in a number of ways, in his creation, in general revelation, and supremely in Christ, the incarnate Word. But, additionally and foundationally, he is able to formulate and communicate truth in an epistemic word, in which he articulates truth verbally through "intelligible disclosure"; and this, in sovereign grace, he has chosen to do.[6]

In short, Henry's epistemology is in line with the Augustinian/Reformed heritage, with some wrinkles of his own. Henry absolutely refused to think of epistemology from the bottom up; he began with God. Shouldn't all Christians begin with God? His suspicion of narrative criticism was called forth by the work of Hans Frei, whose wobbly stance on Scripture's truth claims made Henry uneasy. Since Frei's day, the expression "narrative criticism" has been applied to a broader set of readings than that espoused by Frei, some of them entirely compatible with Henry's understanding of the nature of Scripture. Others have focused more attention on the diverse uses of language, not least in Scripture itself. Nevertheless, a sympathetic reading of Henry, rather than a reductionistic reading of him, will enrich and reestablish his central points about the nonnegotiability of the Bible's central truth claims for all those who tremble at God's Word.

2) One of the reasons Henry is not better known is that he has written so much, and much of what he has written is not particularly easy to read. It is not quite fair to say that Henry's prose is turgid (though that has often been said). Rather, Henry presupposes that his readers enjoy the same mastery over eight-cylinder words that he does. Moreover, his cultural background infiltrated enough of his thought processes that the length and structure of his sentences often achieve almost Germanic magnificence. Those who enjoy skimming their theology will not find Henry very palatable. Similarly, although Henry preached quite often, he was always more of a lecturer than a preacher.

---

[6] Peter Hicks, *Evangelicals and Truth* (Leicester, UK: Apollos, 1998), 89–90.

3) One of the overlooked reasons Henry is not widely read today is that when he wrote, he thought like the journalist he was trained to be. This means that he was constantly interacting with the thought leaders and cultural trends of his own time. That is part of what made Henry so influential when he was alive: he was clearly abreast of the thinkers and writers who swirled through the century, especially the early and middle parts of the twentieth century. But for exactly the same reason, that makes his books seem out of date today. Even when his ideas are important and have the potential for crossing generations, Henry, journalist that he was, carefully tied them to whatever was going on in his own time. The six thick volumes that constitute *God, Revelation, and Authority* can be summarized in fifteen theses. The substance of those theses Henry unpacks, of course, but a very great deal of his space is devoted to unpacking those theses while interacting with scholars and other writers whom none but experts read today, so Henry's work sounds more esoteric and dated than it is. This is true of almost all of Henry's books. His *Uneasy Conscience* was prophetic in 1947 and is still worth perusing (not least because it is one of his shorter volumes), but it is cast not so much as a biblical-theological essay serving as a textbook for several generations of students, but as a tract for the times grounded in an urgent "Thus says the Lord!" Of his substantive books, perhaps the one best cast as a textbook is his *Christian Personal Ethics*. Thus, Henry's relevance and power in his own day, carefully tied to the most influential tides of his time, are precisely the things that make him sound dated today.

So at last I come to the nub of my argument. Why should we esteem Carl Henry so highly today? What in particular does he have to teach us that we are ill-advised to ignore? Who was Carl Henry? I shall take three steps.

I. A SUMMARY STATEMENT

1) Henry was a trained theologian with a ThD from Northern Baptist Theological Seminary (1942). Until his closing years, his breadth of reading was prodigious: he was a theologian who kept reading, not only within his first discipline, but across a very wide area of interests. I'll briefly return to this point.

2) He was a philosopher with a PhD in the subject from Boston University (1949). The kind of philosophy that was taught at the time helped to ensure that he was perpetually interested in the big picture, in how diverse strands of thinking did or did not cohere. His dissertation, which traced personal idealism in Strong's *Theology*, ensured he was bringing his academic disciplines together.

3) All his adult life he was a writer, an editor, and, for parts of his life, a journalist. The latter ensured an outward-looking stance. He was never interested in philosophical and theological ideas constructed for other specialists alone. He could see what ideas *meant* and desired to work them out in the world at large.

4) All his life he was interested in ethical questions—not only in an academic sense (his *Christian Personal Ethics* was one of the more challenging books I read as an MDiv student) but in a prophetic sense. This was not only a function of his comprehensive vision of the outworking of the gospel but a function of his knowledge of Christian views in earlier generations and his own compassion for the poor and the oppressed.

5) Everywhere and all the time, he was an evangelist and interested in those whose calling it was to be vocational evangelists. Not for a moment did he think that his massive learning and considerable responsibilities exempted him from the obligation to be a faithful, joyful witness. In retirement in Watertown, Wisconsin, he found a way to start a city-wide Easter sunrise service where the gospel was preached. He found ways to share his faith with ordinary folk who had no idea of the mind inside the kind man who was talking to them about Jesus and his cross.

6) His travels made him a world Christian. In their later years, when Carl and Helga lived in Watertown, Joy and I tried to drive up to see them, about two hours away, every six weeks or so. Our conversations were wide ranging, but sooner or later he would ask where I had been recently. Almost always he had intelligent observations about the country or city in question, often attached to questions about the state of the church there, whether such-and-such a leader was still serving, and the like, even though it may have been a quarter of a century or more since he had been there. His faith was never merely local, still less jingoistic. He was a world Christian.

7) He was an educator, not only in the sense that he taught at several institutions of higher theological learning and wrote to inform and instruct, not entertain, but also in the sense that he longed to see established a great evangelical research university, willing and able to engage with the intellectual and social currents of the day. This dream has not been fulfilled; it is not yet close to being fulfilled. We are still wrestling with questions about the conditions needed, under the good hand of God, to bring such a dream to fulfillment. It would be useful to weigh in on such conditions, but that of course would transmute this address into something else, so I refrain. But if the dream is no longer thought to be quite as unattainable as it once was, that is due, in no small part, to Carl F. H. Henry.

8) He was interested in history—not with the technical eye of the professional historian, where Henry had few skills, but with two foci. First, his evangelicalism was never the stuff of the last twenty years, or the last fifty years, or the last two hundred years. He wanted to be in touch with the church of the last two thousand years, the church that was devoted to and controlled by the evangel, the gospel of Jesus Christ. It is worth remarking, in passing, that one of the troubling features of many young theologians today is their lust for the novel. Mature Christian faith may well try to articulate that faith freshly in the light of new cultural profiles, but it will *also and always* demonstrate its dependence upon and organic connection with "the faith that was once for all delivered to the saints" (Jude 3). Second, he saw, more clearly than many, how the *historical* claims of the gospel are essential to any true and cogent grasp of the gospel. For example, for him there was no space for fuzzy notions about the real, space-time event of the resurrection of Jesus. Jesus's resurrection was miraculous, but that was not reason to assign it to the noumenal world, divorcing it from the phenomenal world.

9) He was an entrepreneur. Scholar and writer though he was, it took an entrepreneur to envisage and then begin *Christianity Today* and to bring the Berlin congress of 1966 into being.

10) He was a family man. My own connections with Carl and Helga were fairly distant when their son Paul was still alive. Eventually I got to know them well, and toward the end, when their own

decline was well advanced, their daughter was diagnosed with cancer. So I never witnessed their family dynamics firsthand, and I therefore refrain from speaking of what I do not know. But I must add that those I have known who knew Carl and Helga longest testify to the quality of their home.

11) He was a mentor to many. His interest in individual students was hugely respected by successive generations. Of course, some held themselves distant from "the great man," for in his public persona he was equipped with the gift of intimidation, not least because of his encompassing mind and fulsome vocabulary. But those who managed to get to know him found him to be humble, eager to encourage, thoughtful, often other-oriented, and remarkably free of pretensions. When Carl Henry was in his early eighties, one of our students picked him up at O'Hare airport, driving him to Trinity Evangelical Divinity School where he was slated to teach a modular course. In awe of the great man, the student directed Henry's attention to the large words on one wing of our library, "The Carl F. H. Henry Resource Center," and asked him what it felt like to have his name on a large building. Carl replied with typical humor: "It feels like I should be dead."

12) Above all, he was simply a Christian. At the age of seventy, he was asked what he treasured most. He replied, "Jesus Christ as personal Savior and Lord. . . . Into the darkness of my young life he put bright stars that still shine and sparkle."

II. A PATTERN FROM THE BEGINNING

Carl Henry was one of a most remarkable group of young evangelicals who pursued doctoral studies at Harvard and Boston Universities at the same time. The group included John Gerstner, Roger Nicole, Samuel Schultz, Harold Kuhn, Harold Greenlee, George Turner, Paul Jewett, Edward Carnell, George Ladd, Stanley Horton, Lemoyne Lewis, Kenneth Kantzer, and others. Yet in some ways, Carl Henry was the leader of this "club." Kantzer has written:

> Carl did not know as much Old Testament as Sam Schultz, who was completing his work in Old Testament under Charles Pfeiffer. He did not know as much New Testament as Harold Greenlee and George

Ladd, both studying under Henry Joel Cadbury. He did not know as much of the history of doctrine as did Paul Jewett and I. And he did not know as much philosophy as Harold Kuhn, who was assistant to Arthur Darby Nock, chairman of the department. But on all crucial points, he knew enough to argue intelligently toe to toe with any of us. In short, he already had the makings of a first-rate evangelical theologian leaning toward philosophy of religion. No evangelical theologian who bases his or her understanding on the norm of Scripture and seeks to communicate that faith effectively to the world of scholarship around us can ignore any of these fields. Not least, Carl Henry knew what was going on in the world. . . . Carl, moreover, was never afraid of new ideas. . . . His emphasis was always on the big picture. Above all he sought to think clearly and effectively, consistently and comprehensively about the total Christian world and life view. From the very first he exhibited an impassioned desire to serve God with the mind.[7]

This combination of concerns, in my judgment, is the key to Carl's life and ministry.

III. INTEGRATION

The problem with the picture I have just sketched is that it may give the impression of bits and bobs. But Carl was not, as it were, a theologian *and* an educator *and* an entrepreneur, and so forth. He forged these strengths into one life, one Christian life devoted to his Lord and Savior. He was, in the best sense, a "compleat" Christian. For all that we need thinkers and leaders who carry specialist strengths, the church cries out for pastors and teachers who join these many strengths together in the service of the King of kings. In the twentieth century, it is hard to think of a better model than Carl F. H. Henry.

---

[7] Kenneth Kantzer, "Carl Ferdinand Howard Henry: An Appreciation," in Carson and Woodbridge, eds., *God and Culture*, 371.

6

Hope, Discipline, and the Incarnational Scholar

Carl F. H. Henry's Motives, Methods, and Manners

Paul House

The conference held in Louisville in 2013 honoring the centennial of Carl Henry's birth was a happy occasion. It brought together scholars, pastors, students, friends, and family members to honor the memory of Carl and Helga Henry. Recollections were shared, and not a few tears were shed. In keeping with Henry's own desire to seek truth and thereby forward gospel work in general and the evangelical expression of it in particular, there was also a good bit of formal and informal theological discussion and vision casting. Henry was always combining theology, editorializing, and the gentle (or not so gentle) unsettling of consciences. He spoke and wrote to persuade, not simply to transfer data.

This chapter seeks to honor the Henry spirit of friendship, inquiry, encouragement, and conscience prodding (mine included).[1] I will argue that Henry was a theologian motivated and heartened by hope, armed

---

[1] This chapter was originally an oral presentation, and it still bears some of the marks of its origins even after my rewriting for this venue.

with a disciplined method, and possessed of a manner that demonstrated high standards for incarnational education and fellowship. I will also offer applications for current theologians that will focus primarily on three important subjects: Henry's example of the character of a theologian, Henry's high standards for theological research and writing, and the proper form and substance of theological education today. The necessity of high-level academic preparation and the necessity of a biblical-theological basis for the form education takes are particularly contested subjects in evangelical circles. All these topics mattered to Henry.

To be more specific, I will state that young theologians ought to adopt Henry's academic rigor and accompanying work ethic and that senior evangelical leaders ought to support fully face-to-face education and oppose online and hybrid courses if they wish to embrace Henry's incarnational legacy. To make this case I will share personal recollections that inform my understanding of Henry's character and include pivotal aspects of Henry's biography. Henry called evangelicals to higher personal, theological, and educational ground. This chapter seeks in a small way to do the same.

THE CHARACTER OF A THEOLOGIAN: PERSONAL RECOLLECTIONS OF CARL HENRY

Candor requires writers to divulge personal relationships when writing about another person. I make no secret of my appreciation for Carl Henry, especially since I was privileged to know him for a few years at the end of his life. My first contact with Henry occurred in 1983. I was vice president of a new student group at the Southern Baptist Theological Seminary called the Student Evangelical Forum. Among other things, we invited evangelical speakers to campus to help balance our educations. John Woodbridge was our first guest, and he gave a fine talk about his recently published book *Biblical Authority: A Critique of the Rogers/McKim Proposal*, which remains a noteworthy and commendable work.[2] One evening Tim McCoy, our president; Phil Roberts, our faculty sponsor; and I surrounded a telephone (as we did in those

---

[2] John Woodbridge, *Biblical Authority: A Critique of the Rogers/McKim Proposal* (Grand Rapids, MI: Zondervan, 1982).

days) to call and invite Carl Henry to speak to our group. He agreed and eventually came the next academic year.[3] Fellow group member Mike Tucker served as Henry's student host for that visit and framed Henry's thank-you letter.

In 1996, I was tasked with being founding editor of *The Southern Baptist Journal of Theology*. In that capacity I contacted Henry about being a contributor to our "Theological Forum" segment. He kindly accepted and served ably alongside Scott Hafemann, Timothy George, and Don Carson. I then began to correspond with him.

In January 1997, Ben Mitchell, Greg Thornbury, and I visited Dr. and Mrs. Henry at their apartment in Watertown, Wisconsin. Within minutes of meeting Thornbury, Henry asked the nervous PhD student to open an upcoming summer seminar at Trinity with a paper on Hans Frei.[4] We then carried on a lively conversation about theological method, stoked by the warmth of the subject and by the fact that Mrs. Henry had the thermostat in the room set so high that we visitors were sweating through our shirts.[5]

During the conversation we asked Henry to tell us who owned publishing rights to *God, Revelation, and Authority*. We asked because his six-volume magnus opus had never been sold together as a set. Moreover, the books were out of print, a situation several of us hoped to rectify. He assured us that not only did he own the copyright but he also had the printer's plates. At the time of our visit I lacked volume 5 to complete my own set. Hearing this, Henry disappeared into another room and then reentered with a copy of volume 5 and sold it to me for twenty dollars, signature and inscription included. Carl Henry embraced financial reality.

In January 1998 Henry made a memorable visit to the Southern Baptist Theological Seminary (SBTS) to give lectures to faculty and students. Thornbury references these addresses in his book, and SBTS has video copies of the presentations.[6] This event was among the last of this kind of assignment Henry attempted. He struggled physically to complete his task. At the end of one long day he told me that modern medi-

---

[3] Carl F. H. Henry, *Confessions of a Theologian: An Autobiography* (Waco, TX: Word, 1986), 379.
[4] In a letter dated May 19, 1997, Henry wrote, "Greg's paper to the class was well received—it accomplished just what I hoped it would."
[5] Family members attending the Louisville meeting assured me that I had given an accurate account of Mrs. Henry's typical winter temperature setting.
[6] Gregory Alan Thornbury, *Recovering Classic Evangelicalism: Applying the Wisdom and Vision of Carl F. H. Henry* (Wheaton, IL: Crossway, 2013).

cine guarantees we will perish only from the worst diseases. I thought of his comment a few years later when he lay dying in Watertown.

Steps were soon taken to republish *God, Revelation, and Authority*. Lane Dennis, whose father, Clyde, was a friend of Henry's, kindly committed Crossway to publish the volumes if interested parties could come up with (as I recall) fifteen thousand dollars to help with expenses. This amount was raised with help from individuals, churches, and SBTS. Many people helped relaunch *God, Revelation, and Authority* at Southern Seminary's bookstore on January 22, 1999, Henry's eighty-sixth birthday. Pictures of Henry at the book signing reveal a happy man on a very good day.

During Easter weekend of 2000, Greg Thornbury, Ben Mitchell, Richard Bailey, Molly House, and I went to Watertown to visit the Henrys and to attend their community's annual Easter sunrise service.[7] Henry was the chairman of the event. During his Fuller Seminary days Henry had organized similar services in the Rose Bowl. Service, not venue and numbers, mattered most to Henry. I never saw Henry again, though we continued to write to one another.

I share these and other very situated memories because they influence my conclusions about Carl Henry's character. Though the list could be extended, I think the following three characteristics stand out. First, he was a serious Christian and a serious theologian. Second, because he was a serious Christian and a serious theologian he was a hospitable man, a caring husband, an encourager of younger people, a constant witness of the resurrected Christ, and a very hard worker. Third, he was also almost incurably hopeful, for he never stopped learning, conversing, teaching, and planning for more and better work to be done. In these and other ways, his character serves as an excellent example to other believers in general and to other theologians in particular.

THE HOPE OF GLORY:
HENRY'S THEOLOGICAL MOTIVE

Some may question the assertion that Carl Henry was a hopeful man. After all, many of his later writings sound alarms about the death of Western civilization facilitated by the decline of Christian commitment

---

[7] Mitchell was one of the speakers.

and church vitality.[8] He also makes critical statements about modern theology in *God, Revelation, and Authority* and, in his autobiography and other writings, about evangelicalism.

His sober statements actually help make the point. Henry saw very clearly what could lie ahead, but he did not see darkness as *inevitable*. Therefore, he worked on (and on), believing God in his mercy could remake secular and secularized modern and postmodern minds into Christian minds. He warned and worked in love, always fueled by a confident assurance of his own salvation by God's grace alone and the certainty that history will culminate in Christ's victory over Satan, sin, and death. I once asked him about the most important thing to teach seminarians. He responded, "Never let them forget the glory of a soul saved."

Henry certainly never forgot the glory of *his* soul saved. As his autobiography recounts, he grew up on Long Island.[9] His parents had an uneven marriage and eventually separated. His father was a hard worker but also a regular drinker with a violent streak. The Henry children attended Sunday school at the local Episcopal church, but Henry was not a believer in Christ. Coming of age during the Great Depression, he earned money in high school by becoming a newspaper reporter.

After high school he advanced in the newspaper business, becoming an editor by 1933. Henry learned to love words. As he recalled, "Writing had now become, as it were, not only my bread and butter, but my very being."[10] This love of words never faded, which provides key background information for some of his theological positions, especially those on the authority and inspiration of the Bible. His passion for journalism never diminished either, which helps explain some of his later career decisions and his writing style.[11] But at age twenty he had not yet come to love Jesus, and his general unfamiliarity with *God's* words at this time allowed him to experience firsthand many truths he expressed later in detailed theological studies.

For instance, during the summer of 1933 Henry professed faith in

---

[8] See, e.g., *Evangelicals at the Brink of Crisis: Significance of the World Congress on Evangelism* (Waco, TX: Word, 1967); *Christian Countermoves in a Decadent Culture* (Portland, OR: Multnomah, 1986); and *Twilight of a Great Civilization: The Drift toward Neo-Paganism* (Wheaton, IL: Crossway, 1988).

[9] Henry, *Confessions of a Theologian*, 15–40.

[10] Ibid., 40.

[11] I owe this observation to a comment D. A. Carson made in a personal conversation in November 2013.

Jesus through the efforts of a godly woman and a young man affiliated with the Oxford Group, which stressed the trustworthiness of the Bible, evangelism, and seeking God's guidance in Christian living.[12] Henry knew very little about the Christian life. Basically, everything about Christianity came to him as an unfolding revelation for some time. By 1935 Henry decided to go to Wheaton College. But just before time to depart for Illinois, he came down with acute appendicitis. Doctors recommended surgery, but the procedure would delay his entry into college. He prayed for guidance, and to the doctor's surprise Henry got better immediately. Henry thereafter believed that God had healed him and sent him to Wheaton on schedule.[13]

It is interesting to note how well these early events illustrate some of the core beliefs in *God, Revelation, and Authority*. Volume 2, published over forty years after Henry's conversion, outlines fifteen theses that shape the whole project. Consider thesis one in light of what Henry experienced in 1933: "Revelation is a divinely initiated activity, God's free communication by which he alone turns his personal privacy into a deliberate disclosure of his reality."[14] Henry eventually knew by studying the Bible, philosophy, and theology that this was true; but he *experienced* it first. He never claimed he was seeking God in 1933; rather, he claimed God was seeking him.

Or consider the second thesis's emphasis on God's personal work with human beings: "Divine revelation is given for human benefit, offering us privileged communion with our Creator in the kingdom of God."[15] Henry notes that God was not *required* to offer this communion.[16] He then adds that God's "revelation is not some impersonal mass media commercial or routine news report. . . . It is, rather, a personal call and command to each individual."[17] He subsequently stresses that this *personal* redemption places believers among God's people and gives each one "a place in God's kingdom."[18]

---

[12] Henry, *Confessions of a Theologian*, 45–46.
[13] Ibid., 52, 57–59.
[14] Carl F. H. Henry, *God, Revelation, and Authority*, vol. 2, *God Who Speaks and Shows: Fifteen Theses, Part 1* (1976; repr. Wheaton, IL: Crossway, 1999), 8.
[15] Ibid.
[16] Ibid., 30.
[17] Ibid., 31.
[18] Ibid., 33.

This place in the kingdom entails personal and communal gospel work to do now, on earth, in current days.[19] Believers undertake these good works (see Eph. 2:9–10), Henry asserts, knowing that "we move daily nearer that day when human law will no longer dangle on the whim of tyrants or the will of a fickle majority or the compromises of political puppets, that day when the command of God and the righteousness of Christ will prevail in every sphere of life. Although now only partly disclosed, Jesus in his rule is himself the kingdom of God until at 'the end of the days' he will reign as King of the world and of all worlds."[20] As Henry puts it in thesis fifteen, "The self-manifesting God will unveil his glory in a crowning revelation of power and judgment; in this disclosure at the consummation of the ages, God will vindicate righteousness and justice, finally subdue and subordinate evil, and bring into being a new heaven and earth."[21]

Henry could not have written with anything resembling this level of theological acumen in 1933. Yet he already considered nothing too hard for God, for God had healed him of appendicitis when doctors urged hospitalization and had sustained him during the early years of the Great Depression. Kingdom hope filled him early on, and later it sustained him through losses of various sorts: personal loss through the deaths of his mother and his son, professional loss of the editorship of *Christianity Today*, and the physical losses associated with the deterioration of his health. Henry's obedient example underscored his belief that a properly motivated Christian theology flows *from* the promises of God in the Word of God, *through* men and women redeemed by the blood of Jesus Christ, *by* Holy Spirit–inspired hope, *for* work in the world. In short, his personal view of the Christian life was as simple and as complicated as the gospel itself.

THE REMADE MIND: HENRY'S DISCIPLINED THEOLOGICAL METHOD

Motives are essential to a theologian's work, but motives lie fallow without a method of embodying them. Henry's theological method

---

[19] Henry, *God, Revelation, and Authority*, 2:36.
[20] Ibid., 37.
[21] Ibid., 16.

was hammered out over decades of serious study and practice. He entered Wheaton College in 1935 and never stopped reading, learning, and writing. He took the Reformation motto of "always reforming" to apply not just to the church but also to his own mind and actions. From the start he wanted to learn about and tackle big issues: the nature of God, revelation, and authority; the connection between science and faith; the purpose and shape of history; and the intersection of kingdom hope and ethical behavior. He believed that Christian faith rightly understood and thus applied could remake the modern mind. He set out to discern and deliver a theological method that could provide the essentials of this transformation.

How he did so is daunting to contemplate and to imitate. Therefore, it inspires and constantly points to new horizons. As his autobiography and many published works attest, Henry desired to present what he discovered as God's truth in personal and rational language. To this end he absorbed as much biblical, philosophical, theological, and ethical writing as possible to gain the basis for drawing foundational theological principles. He then explicated the nature of these principles in writing by conversing with ancient and modern writers to shape minds into conformity with the mind of Christ, the *logos*, the substance of reality. He believed that the Bible provides a gauge of truth.

His determination to explicate truth and thus reality reveals a remarkable linking of discipline and hope.[22] Indeed, his life shows that, as Wendell Berry observes, "Corrupt or false means must inevitably corrupt or falsify the end. There is an important sense in which the end *is* the means."[23] Henry knew there are no shortcuts in kingdom theology because there are no shortcuts in good work.

Graduate theological students should particularly consider how relentlessly he pursued gaining knowledge in the biblical sense of "understanding shown through character." From college days on, Henry knew that degree requirements reflect minimum standards, not lifetime achievement awards. He received BA (1938) and MA (1941) degrees

---

[22] On the inextricability of these two traits see Wendell Berry's excellent essay "Discipline and Hope," in Wendell Berry, *A Continuous Harmony: Essays Cultural and Agricultural* (San Francisco: Counterpoint, 2012), 83–161.

[23] Ibid., 88 (emphasis original).

at Wheaton, and bachelor of divinity (1941) and doctor of theology (1942) at Northern Baptist Seminary. But these were not enough for him. Henry gained solid philosophical training from Gordon Clark at Wheaton College,[24] but he knew he needed more history of philosophy. He gained some good basic theological and biblical training at Northern,[25] but he understood that he needed better methods of integrating philosophy, theology, and Scripture. He also knew that receiving a doctorate in theology at Northern for writing a dissertation entitled *Successful Church Publicity* was frankly absurd. Thus, he subsequently took courses at Indiana University[26] and eventually gained his PhD at Boston University, mainly in summers while teaching.[27]

Completing degrees did not end his drive to learn. While teaching at Northern, Fuller, Eastern, Trinity, and Hillsdale, he read widely and deeply in ancient and modern philosophy and theology. He did the same while editor of *Christianity Today* from 1956 to 1968, an era in which he interviewed and collaborated with numerous theologians.[28] Throughout his lifetime he strove to understand other theologians from their own writings, not from secondary sources, so he could treat other authors fairly.

Next, consider how relentlessly he pursued presenting his findings in early print and oral presentations. His earlier books indicate his concern for integrating philosophy, theology, history, ethics, and Scripture. Note the following titles: *Remaking the Modern Mind* (1946); *The Uneasy Conscience of Modern Fundamentalism* (1947); *Notes on the Doctrine of God* (1948); *Giving a Reason for Our Hope* (1949); *The Protestant Dilemma* (1949); *The Drift of Western Thought* (1951); and *Christian Personal Ethics* (1957). Volumes produced during the *Christianity Today* years, such as *The God Who Shows Himself* (1966) and *Evangelicals at the Brink of Crisis* (1967), likewise demonstrate his growing world vision and his knack for turning oral presentations into book chapters.

As was stated above, Henry loved the written word, and content mattered most to him. These early books demonstrate a growing, care-

---

[24] Henry, *Confessions of a Theologian*, 66–67.
[25] Ibid., 89–113.
[26] Ibid., 111.
[27] Ibid., 121–23.
[28] See ibid., 114–251.

ful, and exploring mind disciplined by wide reading in general and by a commitment to the intellectual tradition of conservative confessional Christianity in particular. His prose in these and later works falls flat when he tries to use trendy jargon. But it marches when he pursues an argument using clear, powerful terms. At its best his prose features "the momentum of clarity," a phrase Wendell Berry uses to describe Wallace Stegner's writing.[29]

Next, consider the comprehensive nature of Henry's mature, seasoned, and well-crafted theology in *God, Revelation, and Authority.* Note how his philosophical studies lead to theses such as number three, "Divine revelation does not completely erase God's transcendent mystery, inasmuch as God the Revealer transcends his own revelation";[30] and number four, "The very fact of disclosure by the one living God assures the comprehensive unity of divine revelation";[31] and number five, "Not only the occurrence of divine revelation, but also its very nature, content, and variety are exclusively God's determination."[32] His philosophical studies also led him to contend in thesis ten, against subjectivist views of inspiration and authority, that "God's revelation is rational communication conveyed in intelligible ideas and meaningful words, that is, in conceptual-verbal form."[33]

His biblical and theological studies helped him see the necessity of confessing the faith in strong Trinitarian and incarnational terms. Thesis eight claims, "The climax of God's special revelation is Jesus of Nazareth, the personal incarnation of God in the flesh; in Jesus Christ the source and content of revelation converge and coincide,"[34] while thesis nine states, "The mediating agent in all divine revelation is the Eternal Logos—pre-existent, incarnate, and now glorified."[35] Theses eleven and twelve highlight the Holy Spirit's superintending role in the communicating, interpreting, and protecting from error of Scripture.[36]

---

[29] Wendell Berry, *Imagination in Place* (San Francisco: Counterpoint, 2010), 39–44.
[30] *God, Revelation, and Authority,* 2:47.
[31] Ibid., 69.
[32] Ibid., 77.
[33] Carl F. H. Henry, *God, Revelation, and Authority,* vol. 3, *God Who Speaks and Shows: Fifteen Theses, Part 2* (1979; repr. Wheaton, IL: Crossway, 1999), 248.
[34] Ibid., 9.
[35] Ibid., 164.
[36] Carl F. H. Henry, *God, Revelation, and Authority,* vol. 4, *God Who Speaks and Shows: Fifteen Theses, Part 3* (1979; repr. Wheaton, IL: Crossway, 1999), 7, 129.

Thesis thirteen underscores the Holy Spirit's role as giver of life, and thesis fourteen stresses that the Holy Spirit is the giver of power and joy to the church, God's kingdom in miniature.[37]

Finally, though his theological vision is comprehensive, consider how much room it leaves for further study. For instance, Henry told me more than once he was sorry he never wrote a volume on public ethics. He continued to explore Christology,[38] and he commented to me that evangelicals should give ecclesiology more attention. Because he deals with perennial issues, he leaves us much space to develop his ideas on authority, inspiration, and inerrancy—the subject of *God, Revelation, and Authority*, volume 4—or to explore further the nature of God—the topic of *God, Revelation, and Authority*, volume 5. This latter subject is an especially vital one in light of current claims of world religions and their role in political upheaval.

In a fallen world it will always be necessary to contend that revelation from the one living God is personal, rational, available, written, and relevant to every person on earth. Happily, eventually people return to these matters, for they are the connective tissue of human existence. It is possible to build on Henry's legacy if the next generation will catch his vision. But it is necessary to consider the cost of doing so. Such theological work is exciting, but it is hard work. Carl Henry *toiled*. He probably did not watch a lot of television and most likely did not spend hours surfing the web. He had an old-world German work ethic, one shared by his marvelous, beloved wife, Helga, a child of German-speaking missionaries to Africa.[39] He enjoyed life and clearly loved Helga and their family, but he did not waste a lot of time.

Perhaps the following quotation from Henry best summarizes the challenge that must be faced and the work that must be done: "The most influential theological scholarship will doubtless continue to be that of devoted individuals who earnestly grapple with the problems of the day. . . . The present crisis in theology . . . calls qualified evangelicals to invest their fullest energies to produce serious theological,

---

[37] Ibid., 494, 542.

[38] See his *The Identity of Jesus of Nazareth* (Nashville, TN: Broadman Press, 1992).

[39] For a description of her background consult Helga Bender Henry, *Cameroon on a Clear Day* (Pasadena, CA: William Carey Library, 1999).

philosophical, and biblical literature in the entire spectrum of theological controversy and engagement."[40] The work will not be easy, and it never has been.

THE INCARNATIONAL SCHOLAR: HENRY'S THEOLOGICAL MANNER

Motives and methods alone do not make a theologian. Manners, the way one operates, play a huge role. Henry's manner was incarnational and apostolic, as one might expect from a theologian who stressed God's personal redemptive work revealed in an inerrant written revelation. Though one could demonstrate these traits in a number of ways, I will do so by sketching his ministry as lecturer-at-large for World Vision, the Henrys' hospitality, and his ministry of encouragement through letter writing.

Henry left *Christianity Today* in 1968. Though Henry's son was happy his father was no longer beholden to the evangelical establishment,[41] at the relatively advanced age of fifty-six Henry needed a job. His brother-in-law helped him land a position at Eastern Baptist Theological Seminary,[42] where he taught from 1969 to 1974. Henry's autobiography reveals that he found this experience lacking in many key regards, including in academic rigor.[43] Consequently, after his first year at Eastern, Henry taught at least one term a year at Trinity Evangelical Divinity School. Trinity was clearly his most enjoyable seminary teaching experience. He loved Trinity and taught there periodically through 1997.

At the even more advanced age of sixty-one Henry severed ties with Eastern and accepted a position as lecturer-at-large for World Vision. World Vision gave Henry a salary and expenses to lecture around the world.[44] He had already traveled extensively and had become known internationally through *Christianity Today* and by serving as chair of the 1966 World Congress on Evangelism. Yet the World Vision ministry took him to a remarkable number of new places on a rather dizzying

---

[40] Carl F. H. Henry, *Evangelicals in Search of Identity* (Waco, TX: Word, 1976), 79–80.
[41] Henry, *Confessions of a Theologian*, 275.
[42] Ibid., 313–14.
[43] Ibid., 323–33.
[44] Ibid., 353.

schedule.[45] Mrs. Henry often accompanied him, at their expense.[46] He lectured to thousands of people around the globe. Though he could have allowed his books, translations of his books, and tapes of his lectures to do this work, he carried a face-to-face ministry to place after place. During a tour of Asian nations in 2003 I met many people who still remembered Henry's visits to Singapore, Taiwan, and Malaysia. His presence contributed greatly to the impact his theology had there.

When at home the Henrys hosted a wide variety of people. Their meticulously kept guest book, presented to them by friends when they left Pasadena for Washington in 1956, illustrates the Henrys' hospitality and influence. For example, Ben Mitchell and I were examining it once and came upon a date on which several Christian college presidents had signed their names. We asked Henry the occasion, and he replied, "Oh, there was a controversy we were trying to help mediate." The Henrys welcomed people into their home for such face-to-face conversations aimed at fellowship and reconciliation, for people mattered to them.

Henry's correspondence likewise proves his concern for others.[47] It was conducted on paper, and it was massive. He typed many letters on an old portable typewriter. Many letters he wrote by hand. I do not know why he chose to do one or the other. But I know his letters to me were encouraging, challenging, chastening, and always welcome.[48]

Henry's intentional incarnational approach to Christian education invites probing of the theological basis and the practice of theological education today. The same is true of other major twentieth-century theological educators, including Dietrich Bonhoeffer, who was a theological teacher longer than he was a pastor or university professor.[49] Both Henry's and Bonhoeffer's lives and writings reveal that personal, face-to-face, incarnational, sacrificial, intentional, and challenging education is biblical, not just preferable. More importantly, the life and practices of Jesus of Nazareth reveal the same.

Henry knew that Christian education in the home, church, univer-

---

[45] Ibid., 354–62.
[46] Ibid., 354–55.
[47] His letters and papers are housed at Trinity Evangelical Divinity School.
[48] On this point see this chapter's conclusion below.
[49] See Paul R. House, *Bonhoeffer's Seminary Vision: A Case for Costly Discipleship and Life Together* (Wheaton, IL: Crossway, 2015).

sity, and seminary is by definition incarnational and sacrificial, since God the Son became flesh and died on the cross. Henry understood that Christian education cannot be merely a transfer of data, much less a selling of credits or a conveying of credentials, for it serves a personal God. Rather, Christian education is a lifelong Spirit-filled, embodied bestowing of the blessings of knowledge and wisdom from and to members of the body of Christ. Christian teaching is a gift of the Holy Spirit, and Christian learning results in maturity and wisdom. As Bonhoeffer wrote in *The Cost of Discipleship*, if something has no physical body, if it remains abstract, it is not the church.[50] As my colleague Timothy George said to me in a personal conversation, God sent his Son, not a video.

Thus, studying Henry's life and writings has some very practical implications for today's theological educators, seminary students, seminary trustees, and churches. I have written elsewhere about the high standards Henry had for students, faculties, administrators, and trustees, so I will not repeat that material here.[51] I will simply note that the most basic implication is that it is impossible to meet biblical standards for formational Christian education by offering, teaching, and taking for-credit online classes. These exempt faculty and students from embodied contact, an approach in direct conflict with the Bible's examples of formative education. The same is true of "hybrid" classes that put faculty and students face-to-face with fellow students and teachers only very briefly. To be clear, the same is likewise true of large and impersonal, or even small and impersonal, on-campus classes. Human beings are made in the image of God—Father, Son, and Holy Spirit—and are thus made for more personal ventures. The body of Christ requires human contact to mature and to minister.

Henry's 1947 volume *The Uneasy Conscience of Modern Fundamentalism* is arguably his best-known book. As I talk with many evangelical theological college and seminary educators and students around the world, I discern an uneasy conscience. This uneasy conscience stems

---

[50] Dietrich Bonhoeffer, *The Cost of Discipleship*, trans. R. H. Fuller and Irmgard Booth (New York: Touchstone, 1995), 248.
[51] See Paul R. House, "Making Christian Minds: Carl Henry and Christian Higher Education," *Renewing Minds: A Journal of Christian Thought*, 1/1 (Spring 2012): 67–79.

from the growing use and advocacy of impersonal forms of education that view students as consumers and teachers as delivery systems. It stems from making nonembodied courses routine, not aids in an emergency. It stems from having no strong theological justification for offering them. It stems from marketing these and other courses as commodities, and doing so to outflank other seminaries. It stems from faculty members overseeing online courses because they need the money, though they think such courses unsuitable for preparing ministers. It stems from administrators justifying these courses because constituents want them, or because the classes help with needed cash flow, though their heart is simply not in them. It stems from acquiescing to a massively reductionist view of preparation for church service, not persevering in Jesus-style incarnational shaping. It stems from having a less biblical view of education than people holding a lower view of God's revealed truth. It stems, then, from not caring for our brothers and sisters as we ought.

Administrators, faculty members, and students often substitute talk of marketing and money for theological discourse in these discussions. They often comment that there is no need to fight the disembodied trend in education because it is "inevitable" that education will go this route, and in any case it is what the churches and denominational bodies are demanding. Meanwhile, students reflect the advertising they have seen on the seminaries' websites. They stress that the courses are "convenient."

Perhaps a look at the past will help. Theologians examine the Bible, and they consult the communion of the saints. Even a cursory review of the Bible will indicate that it contains no promise of convenient, abstract, easy, or cheap ministry formation in the Old or New Testaments. To cite our highest example, Jesus called his disciples out of their livelihoods in a most inconvenient way for them and for their families. A similar quick review of recent church history related to the Henry events held in 2013 yields the same conclusion.

The 2013 Henry conferences were hosted at the Southern Baptist Theological Seminary and Trinity Evangelical Divinity School. James P. Boyce, Southern Seminary's founder, kept the institution going against incredible physical and financial odds after the Civil War, a conflict, it must be noted, his own beliefs fostered. He and his colleagues refused to accept the seminary's demise as inevitable, and there was nothing convenient about this commitment. Ken Kantzer, a major architect of Trinity's rise in justified influence, sacrificed his own considerable scholarly potential to lead the institution's advance. He made choices that demonstrated his unwillingness to accept an easy path or to doubt that Trinity could reach the levels he desired.

As for seminary students and what is convenient, it is worthwhile to consider the testimony of Southern Seminary's first African-American graduates: Garland Offutt, Jesse Bottoms, Benjamin Miller, and Claude Taylor. In post–World War II segregation days they could not sit in classes with white students because the commonwealth of Kentucky did not have the commonwealth of brains and integrity to know these were *men*. So they sat outside classroom windows and in hallways to hear lectures, took instruction in brave professors' studies, and persevered through a variety of indignities to get an education. They followed in the heritage of the original apostles and perhaps exceeded Peter and his fellows in this regard.

The 2013 conferences were also sponsored by Fuller Seminary. Carl Henry left Northern Baptist Seminary in 1947 to be one of the four founding faculty members there. Henry and his colleagues, all now deceased, greeted thirty-nine students, taught in rented quarters, purchased houses hurriedly, faced opposition from their denominations for teaching at an interdenominational seminary, and dealt with the many difficult tasks associated with beginning a new institution.[52] The students risked their futures at a new and (in the beginning) unaccredited institution. Henry wrote concerning the students,

> No seminary faculty ever faced a student body more eager and dedicated than that group of pioneer seminarians. . . . Difficulties, whether academic or denominational, only seemed to challenge and motivate these early students all the more. When denominations thwarted Fuller graduates from church posts, they opted gladly for service instead on distant mission fields or in small homeland parishes that soon prospered.[53]

---

[52] Henry, *Confessions of a Theologian*, 114–18.
[53] Ibid., 118–19.

Prison Fellowship was also a sponsor of the 2013 Henry conferences. Henry was a longtime board member and was a great encourager of Prison Fellowship's founder, Charles Colson. The scope of that organization's ministry has not been determined by what is convenient or what seems inevitable, when one considers the likely outcome of most prisoners' lives. It has, rather, thrived as it has taken on great challenges.

The dead have left their words and examples, and the living must decide what to stand for and what to oppose. Carl Henry was hopeful when it came to education, and there is reason to have hope for seminaries. Evangelical seminaries exist, and they have capable, dynamic, and committed personnel. It is *not* too late for seminary education to make good educational decisions grounded in sound theology and sound governing practices. It is not too late to build on the evangelical heritage of personal, engaged, mentor-driven, affordable, and rigorous education. It is possible to challenge Christians to give generously to this worthy project, as Ralph Waldo Beeson did to open Beeson Divinity School of Samford University, yet another conference sponsor.

It is possible for evangelicals to be leaders in personal education in which technology is a vital handmaid. By all accounts such education will occur in the future, for the debate about the future of education has been joined and will continue for some time.[54] I believe incarnational education will endure because God wills it. But maybe we will be forced to follow Bonhoeffer's example and offer quality face-to-face education in rural settings until there is no way to proceed, or to take such face-to-face education on the road, as Henry did when working for World Vision. Regardless, it is possible to clear our conscience. The price of *not* doing so is too high.

Again perhaps it is best to let Henry have the final word on the importance of the personal touch that is best for churches, students,

---

[54] For a volume that questions the current trend of idolizing web-based solutions to education and other issues, consult Evgeny Morozov, *To Save Everything, Click Here: The Folly of Technological Solutionism* (Philadelphia: PublicAffairs, 2013). For a discussion of university education in a digital age consult Frank B. McCluskey and Melanie L. Winter, *The Idea of the Digital University: Ancient Traditions, Disruptive Technologies, and the Battle for the Soul of American Education* (Washington, DC: Westphalia Press, 2012).

seminaries, and denominations. He writes in *Evangelicals in Search of Identity* that evangelical renewal requires:

> [the] recovery of the larger sense of evangelical family in which fellow-believers recognize their common answerability to God in his scripturally given Word and their responsibility for and to each other within the body of faith. Unless the new society gains visibility as an identifiable fellowship of holy love, righteousness, and joy, Christians will speak to the chaotic fragmentation of national life only in terms of an isolated individual faith that needlessly forfeits the corporate vitalities of the regenerate community. In short, evangelical Christians must repent of the radical independency that aligns believers against believers in a spirit of competition and even of suspicion and judgment.[55]

CONCLUSION

Carl Henry was both an exemplary theologian and a fine human being. He fit Herman Witsius's definition of a true theologian, which is "one who, imbued with a substantial knowledge of divine things derived from the teachings of God himself, declares and extols, not in words only, but by the whole course of his life, the wonderful excellencies of God and thus lives entirely for His glory."[56]

This does not mean Henry had no flaws. For example, I believe he placed too much stock in large movements and contributed to evangelicals' naïve embrace of unbiblical marketing of gospel work. In these ways he was a man of his times. Furthermore, like all of us he could have been more thoroughly biblical at some points. Sometimes he was guilty of overwriting, or of turning a theological work into a journalistic piece. Nonetheless, he contributed mightily to the evangelical intellectual tradition that we build upon when we are at our best. He combined orthodox theology, compassion, joy, and a keen sense of embodied reality, as hopefully the following concluding recollections illustrate.

During 1998 I suffered a severe personal setback. I informed Henry

---

[55] Henry, *Evangelicals in Search of Identity*, 73–74.
[56] Herman Witsius, *On the Character of a True Theologian* (1877; repr. Greenville, SC: Reformed Academic Press, 1994), 27.

of this in a letter before he came to Louisville for the *God, Revelation, and Authority* launch described above. He responded January 12, 1999. He noted his anticipation of the book launch, writing, "January 22 will indeed be a memorable day, made so by the grace of God rather than by any deserving of my own." He expressed his sorrow over my situation and gave advice about the future. Then he concluded, "Thank you for all the kindnesses you have shown me. Hold your head high and may your bearing reflect the joy and victory of the Lord as He works out undreamed of and yet transcendent alternatives. Your brother in Christ, Carl Henry."

He then added a postscript, "I shall have a travel charge of $25 each way . . . and I surely hope someone covers your Louisville-Cincinnati double trip." Carl Henry cared about all aspects of reality. Therefore, he was a hopeful, disciplined, incarnational theologian, who now enjoys "undreamed of and transcendent" realities, the joys of a soul saved.

7

Vain Philosophy?

Carl F. H. Henry's Plea for a
Philosophically Informed Ministry

Gregory Alan Thornbury

The centennial celebration of Carl F. H. Henry was something of an irony because he was a humble and very modest man. He lived in a modest apartment and gave generously to the institutions he loved, and even though he was perhaps the most well-known and influential evangelical theologian of his generation, he never pulled rank. Marvin Olasky once recounted to me one particularly illustrative story that shows this kind of humility and the irony of all the celebrations of Carl. Late in his life, Henry wrote op-ed columns for *World* magazine. Every couple of weeks Olasky would receive a three-page article in the mail, typed out on Henry's trusty old typewriter. Enclosed with each article Henry included a stamped, self-addressed postcard. The card, written in Henry's own hand, contained two simple options for Olasky's editorial pen: "Accept" or "Reject." Marvin thought that was remarkable, and I do too. Henry never presumed upon his editor, even though he was an editorial legend. With every article he submitted to *World*, Henry wanted to know if Olasky liked it or did not like it. Of course, Olasky admits he never once returned a single submission to Henry marked with a rejection. But Henry wanted feedback; he wanted to grow as a writer and as a scholar, which is an amazing testimony to his humility.

Henry was dispirited at times, I think, that his work had not achieved the popularity he would have liked to see during his life. For example, *God, Revelation, and Authority* never appeared as a printed set during his lifetime. But he said several times to many of us who knew him that in a previous generation Albrecht Ritchl's work had not been approved of and taken up until the generation after his passing. He left it to us to celebrate his work, and that's what we are doing in this volume.

In this essay, I intend to focus on a very narrow slice of what Carl Henry was about, a theme I discuss in my own little volume on his life and work. That slice regards the issue of Henry's scholarship and the importance he placed upon philosophical literacy in his written corpus. Carl Henry held several academic posts throughout his career, but whereever he was, he flew under the banner of "philosopher." Philosophy was a discipline he cared so deeply about that he went back to graduate school at Boston University in order to earn a second PhD in the field. He wrote his dissertation about personal idealism and A. H. Strong's theology as an outworking of the influences of Borden Parker Bowne.[1]

In interviews I have given on the Henry legacy, I have pointed out that I feel personally indebted in all this. I went through something of a dark night of the soul when I was in college. I was under the sway of a very articulate, Oxford-trained biblical studies professor who introduced me to a high dose of higher criticism. For me, it was something very close to a Bart Ehrman scenario. I nearly gave up on my confidence in the authority and trustworthiness of the Bible. My godly father, a faithful pastor and scholar in his own right, said, "Find Carl Henry and his volumes in your library and read them before you give up the faith."

I remember walking down that long staircase at my college, sitting down on the floor in the stacks, and pulling out *God, Revelation, and Authority*. My faith began to reawaken. The reason Henry pulled me

---

[1] Carl F. H. Henry, *Personal Idealism and Strong's Theology* (Wheaton, IL: Van Kampen Press, 1951).

back in, however, had something to do with the fact that he was doing more than just tit-for-tat responding to higher critics as to why the Bible is historically reliable. He did that, but he went further—he brought philosophical gravitas to *God, Revelation, and Authority*. His focus was not narrow. He encompassed epistemological concerns, which were my primary concerns as an undergraduate student studying philosophy. Humanly speaking, I came within a whisker of losing my faith. But because Carl Henry was a philosopher defending biblical authority, I rallied.

PHILOSOPHY, EVANGELISM, AND THE LIFE OF THE MIND

Throughout my teaching career, I frequently get the following question, usually from those preparing for church-related ministry: "Didn't the apostle Paul tell us to beware of philosophy?" My response is always that the adjective is all-important in Paul's admonition to the Colossians. Paul did not want us to avoid the noun, *philosophy*, but only a particular kind, the empty sort of philosophy, one based upon human tradition and the elementary principles of this world, rather than on the foundation of Christ (Col. 2:8).

For a while, I thought that the bias against philosophy was limited to a few ministry candidates here and there, but now I think this sentiment is shared a bit more broadly. I vividly recall friends returning from a major evangelical conference several years ago at which R. C. Sproul gave an address in part on the significance of Hegelian philosophy.[2] While I was not in attendance at the conference, my friends—many of them ministers—returned admitting their surprise at the subject of the address and to having effectively zoned out during its duration. But I think R. C. Sproul understands what Carl Henry believed: that understanding philosophical movements and trends is the new preevangelism. It is a discipline we need to relearn in evangelical ministry preparation.

Consider, for example, Slajov Žižek, the apoplectic Slovenian philosopher who today is every bit as recognizable on the world stage as

---

[2] R. C. Sproul, "The Defense and Confirmation of the Gospel," paper presented at Together for the Gospel conference, Louisville, Kentucky, April 2010.

Bertrand Russell was in the mid-twentieth century. When Žižek talks, legions of young people listen. And when they attend his lectures, read his books, and watch his films, what is he talking about? Hegelian philosophy. Žižek's twelve-hundred-page magnum opus, *Less Than Nothing: Hegel and the Shadow of Dialectical Materialism*, is about how Hegel, Marx, and Lacan have reshaped the worldview of the West. Žižek revels in this Hegelian notion that history is a total fabrication, our way of compensating for the fact that reality really is less than nothing. History is a series of meaningless accidents to which we try to attach a narrative. Against the materialist (Darwinism and deconstruction) and spiritualist (new age and Heideggerian existentialism) accounts of modernity, Žižek points to something missed in atheist/agnostic theories of modernity: a Freudian/Lacanian death drive, which is the negation of all negation.[3] In other words, the picture is more stark than previous generations of ministers ever dreamed.

As we try to reach this generation for the gospel and find ourselves frustrated because young intellectuals are cynical and hard to reach, we need to ask ourselves this important question: how many of us love them enough to read the texts they read—not to read them just to dismiss the texts, or to cherry-pick them for the things we think are wrong with them, but to really have a conversation with them and those who read them? That is what Carl F. H. Henry did. Sadly, while it has become commonplace in modern evangelicalism to convene conferences that are long on Bible exposition and contend admirably for orthodoxy, these same conferences are largely silent on the great ideologies that grip the hearts of those whom we are most desperately trying to reach in our culture today.

Carl Henry understood in the immediate aftermath of the Second World War that evangelicals needed to compete in the realm of ideas. A case in point: in the May 9, 1960, edition of *Christianity Today* his lead editorial was, "Why We Need a Christian University in New York City." In the piece, Henry talked about denominational colleges that had gone adrift by the 1960s and lamented the way in which a gen-

---

[3] Slavoj Žižek, *Less Than Nothing: Hegel and the Shadow of Dialectical Materialism* (New York: Verso, 2012), Kindle edition, loc. 358 of 26195.

eration of young people were being taught philosophy in a context in which skepticism was not answered with the gospel. He said:

> Even churched colleges have a disappointing history; many have lost their early Christian vision, and evangelical conviction often struggles for expression and even survival on campuses to which it once imparted life. Among approximately 600 of the 750 liberal arts colleges in the United States that are church-related, some have not attained high academic ideals, but many more neglect the implications of the Christian faith. The founders have had a great vision, churchmen and laymen had given sacrificial support, the campus has a great beginning and tradition. But often when professors in these same schools today close the classroom doors to lecture, they resurrect Aristotle and Hegel and Darwin and Dewey, Kant and Kierkegaard, only to leave Jesus Christ hanging on the Cross, unrecognized and unwanted.[4]

What was Henry saying here? He was saying that the university cares about ideas. Specifically, it cares about philosophy. And, he said, here we are, sending our young ones, whom we train at church, to these secular universities or "Christian" colleges and universities that are adrift and have a crush-everything-in-your-path attitude toward disassembling any biblical background a young person may have. And yet we are content to stand by and watch the philosophers capture the hearts of our children and carry them away from Jerusalem in captivity.

It is also instructive to note something else that was contained in that 1960 issue of *Christianity Today*. The next article was by Gordon Clark, in which he laid out a survey of philosophy in the 1960s, explaining instrumentalism, John Dewey, existentialism, and logical positivism and their influence in contemporary culture.[5] The next article was by Dirk Jellema, of what is now Case Western University, talking about the rise of the postmodern mind. Jellema charted how social theories move away from a patterned reality concept of the world. That was *Christianity*

---

[4] Carl F. H. Henry, "Evangelical Advance: Do We Need a Christian University?" *Christianity Today*, May 9, 1960, 5.
[5] Gordon Clark, "Philosophy in the Sixties," *Christianity Today*, May 9, 1960.

Today, the leading evangelical magazine, in the 1960s: three or four of the articles in that issue had to do with the importance of philosophy and its influence on society. Henry and his peers were less concerned with internecine evangelical squabbles than they were with the world of ideas that competed with the Christian truth claim. We need to get back to that. In a book that Henry edited in 1978, called *Horizons of Science*, he described himself as "a scholar who maintains a keen interest in the reconciliation of theology, philosophy, and science."[6] That's who he was to his core as a scholar. Some of that same élan would do us good today.

HENRY AND THE MODERN MIND

We talk a lot about *The Uneasy Conscience of Modern Fundamentalism*, and for good reason. But there was an important earlier book: Henry's *Remaking the Modern Mind*, published in 1946. In it, Henry contended for a new philosophical literacy that must be the mandate for the new evangelicalism. He followed this with *The Uneasy Conscience of Modern Fundamentalism*. We have to remember, Henry said, that the order is important. He first covered the entire history of philosophy in the West with *Remaking the Modern Mind* before moving to socio-political and cultural critique with *Uneasy Conscience*. He dedicated *Remaking* to three of his teachers—Gordon Clark, W. Harry Jellema, and Cornelius Van Til—with the following inscription: "'Three Men of Athens' G.H.C–W.H.J.–C.V.T. Who have sharpened my convictions, by action and reaction, in delightful philosophic interchange."

In *Remaking the Modern Mind* Henry traced the influence of the pre-Socratic philosophers, of Plato and Aristotle, and of Spinoza and Hume, on the West's thinking about the uniformity of nature and the possibility of theism, while juxtaposing them to the concepts in the Hebrew Christian revelatory pattern.[7] He considered the impact of Kantian and Hegelian idealism in Western history alongside close readings of Nikolai Berdyaev, Reinhold Niebuhr, Étienne Gilson, and Paul Tillich. Despite later characterizations of Henry as some sort of hopeless rationalist, he subjected Descartes to withering critique in *Remaking*

---

[6] Carl F. H. Henry, ed., *Horizons of Science: Christian Scholars Speak Out* (San Francisco: Harper & Row, 1978), 87.
[7] Carl F. H. Henry, *Remaking the Modern Mind* (Grand Rapids, MI: Eerdmans, 1946).

the Modern Mind. He considered the influence of Henri Bergson and Samuel Alexander decades before anybody thought it might be worthwhile to revise the doctrine of God along the lines of process theism. Carl Henry was talking about issues of contemporary interest in 1946, though apparently not many evangelicals were listening.

Henry's work paved the way for an entire generation of philosophically informed theologians. It is impossible to imagine the rise of scholars like Norm Geisler and E. J. Carnell, Colin Brown, and Millard Erickson, without the work Henry did to lead the way. The same thing is doubly true for Francis Schaeffer, who borrowed liberally from thinkers such as Van Til, often without attribution. In sum, Henry understood that the greatest threat to world evangelization was ideology. Consider his final paragraph in *Remaking the Modern Mind*:

> The modern ideology needs to be remade—that is admitted today by those who have shaped it as well as those who have opposed it. But its effective remaking can be accomplished only in a philosophic framework in which rebirth is something more than a change of human temperament, in which indeed it is a divine reversal, a work of regeneration. If the modern mind is not reborn, but merely exchanges one mood for another, we stand only a generation from the fruit of atheism: the pessimism of despair.[8]

And thus he ended his book. Now that's a prophetic word.

In the weeks and months after I wrote my book on applying Henry's thought to current theological problems, people asked, "If you learned one thing from Carl Henry, what was it?" My inevitable reply was that we must distinguish between the gospel and ideology. The gospel is the one transcendent, ahistorical, never-changing truth claim. It encompasses every culture and yet is not bound to any one ideology or culture. The foundation for Henry's confidence in the authority of Scripture was not blind faith. It came from his having read so deeply in the history of philosophy that he was confident there was no more satisfying account of reality other than Christianity, no other viable alternative.

---

[8] Ibid., 307.

His confidence in the creed was not sheer will to power, but a rational conclusion born out of analysis. Henry believed that there was no viable option for Western culture other than biblical theism. He thought that it was impossible to outflank the genius of Christianity as a platform for human flourishing. As he remarked in his 1951 monograph *The Drift of Western Thought*, Christian theism created the climate in which modern science arose, contrary to the charges of naturalism:

> The uncompromising monotheism of the Hebrew-Christian tradition, coupled with the insistence upon a divine creation of the universe, so that the entire structure of finite being finds its rationale in an orderly, benevolent, and sovereign divine Mind, furnished the background for the modern confidence that science, wherever it penetrated, would find the universe to be meaningful.[9]

The follow-up to *Uneasy Conscience* was a book called *The Protestant Dilemma*. In it, Henry reflected upon the key moment the neo-evangelical movement faced as the West emerged from the post–World War II environment. Again, Henry saw an opening for a new philosophical point of view. In this book he talks about a key turning point, similar to the post–World War II environment, in Plato's *Republic*:

> What the mid-twentieth century crisis demands most is a method with implications for both the philosophic and the moral failure of our age, a message with more self-evidence about it than the problematic postulations of the recent mind, a message with an authoritarian self-authentication not found in merely speculative groanings. . . . What modern man longs for in his deepest moments is some voice from beyond, some self-disclosure of the spiritual-moral sphere, some initiative which God—if there be a deity—shall take in the present plight of humanity's lostness.

A similar longing to that of our culture is found at a high point in Plato's *Republic*. The great Greek thinker, foreseeing that the prevail-

---

[9] Carl F. H. Henry, *The Drift of Western Thought* (Grand Rapids, MI: Eerdmans, 1951), 44.

ing moral instability would lead to the downfall of the nation, urged his contemporaries to become explicit about the spiritual moral universe. Plato then proposed an outline for an ideal state that would function with reference to an eternal good, an eternal truth, and an eternal beauty. At that point, very practical questions arise: How are the multitudes to be prevailed upon to undertake the change from the old world in order to receive the new? To what compelling sanction can appeal be made such that people will dedicate themselves to their proper roles?[10]

Plato's answer was to devise one grand lie, at which point he talked about the tiered structure of the philosopher king, and then the military class, and then the servant class. The "Noble Lie" is to be framed by making an appeal to God, Plato said. God proclaims the first principles to the rulers and above all else that they should anxiously guard it. And here are Plato's words: "Such is our tale. Is there any chance of making our citizens believe it?"[11]

Henry said the following about this enervating aspect of Plato: "For all of its brilliance, there is no more pathetic moment in Plato's *Republic*. For here Plato, who would have been the last to concede that an eternal spiritual moral realm was merely a postulation of his own mind, would nonetheless ride the conviction into the hearts of the multitudes by anchoring it to pure mythology."[12] Henry strongly objected to the idea that the best-case scenario is Plato. Yes, it is true that Justin Martyr, Origen, and Clement of Alexandria all told us that of all the pagan philosophers, Plato is the best. And yet, at the end of the day, all Plato was able to offer his culture was something deeply cynical or only randomly historical. If Žižek were here, he would say that Plato drowns in a Hegelian-Lacanian abyss of the negation of negation at this point. Plato admitted that his mythology was not to be taken seriously. It was a "just so tale" devised to control the polis.

Henry's confidence in biblical theism comes as a result of philosophical searching. Although Henry loved to tell his testimony of how he came to faith in the risen Lord Jesus, his meme as an evangelical scholar

---

[10] Carl F. H. Henry, *The Protestant Dilemma* (Grand Rapids, MI: Eerdmans, 1948), 36.
[11] Ibid., 37.
[12] Ibid.

came from his being a philosopher first. If God does not disclose himself in intelligent sentences and paragraphs, as Henry repeatedly argued, we are lost in the cosmos. In the face of the threat of pure ideology, Henry wanted the American evangelical movement to demonstrate that the gospel is up to the challenge.

READING TEXTS AND SAYING NO

For his part, throughout his scholarly life's work, Henry did his best to live up to his own expectations. When one picks up and reads his massive six-volume *God, Revelation, and Authority*, what one appreciates is the breadth of Henry's scholarship. Biblical studies, contemporary theology, sociology, psychology, history, and politics are all represented in his research. Henry was interested in trying to bring the disciplines together. He headed up the Institute for Advanced Christian Studies (IFACS), the mission of which is to coordinate interdisciplinary conversations. He modeled for us what to read, how to read, and why to read. The most important aspect of this modeling was that he was interested in a *critical* reading of philosophical texts.

Perhaps the most important thing about the way Henry read these texts is that he taught us that it is not only acceptable but actually incumbent upon us to say at key points this word to the philosophers: no. This is a discipline that I fear some evangelical theologians have forgotten. Evangelicals too often look for support for their ideas in philosophies that will never converge with Christian theology. In my book *Recovering Classic Evangelicalism,* I defined evangelicalism in the following way: "Anything you can do we can do later. We can do anything later than you."[13] In other words, evangelicals take up with a philosophical tradition just as it gets past its sell-by date in the academy. We find a philosophy appealing precisely at the moment it is going out of fashion everywhere else in critical theoretical thought. Ignored and forsaken are the fathers of the faith. We need to memorize 1 Corinthians 4:15 afresh: "For though you have countless guides in Christ, you do not have many fathers."

---

[13] Gregory Alan Thornbury, *Recovering Classic Evangelicalism: Applying the Wisdom and Vision of Carl F. H. Henry* (Wheaton, IL: Crossway, 2013), 22.

These philosophers and intellectuals in most circumstances would not be impressed if they thought we were appropriating them for these purposes. We pay lip service to authorial intent when it comes to biblical texts, but we seem unwilling to extend that same grace to the philosophers we cite. Here I would adduce C. S. Lewis's support in this connection when he simply stated, "Christians and pagans have more in common with one another than Christians have in common with the post-Christian mind."[14]

Henry was happy to be *contra mundum* in response to the philosophers. He was willing to take them at their word. If the theorist claimed that his position was alien to the Hebrew Christian conception of the world, he believed them. He would not try to shoehorn them in the company of Zion. This conviction stemmed from the fact that the author of *God, Revelation, and Authority* believed that the great theological horse race of our time was in hermeneutics. That's why the two largest volumes of *God, Revelation, and Authority* take up this subject.

In my opinion, the most fascinating chapter in all of *God, Revelation, and Authority* is chapter 13 of volume 3, in which Henry adjudicates a conversation between Schleiermacher, Dilthey, Heidegger, von Harnack, Barth, Bultmann, and Gadamer. Henry gently agrees with Barth that we are never able to free ourselves from prejudice and philosophical presuppositions when interpreting a text. Prejudice is our self-preempting of the right reading of a text. But what I want to point out here is that Henry is always ready to both agree and disagree. He can say both yes and no simultaneously to the philosophers. In this case, Henry is unwilling to accept Gadamer's conclusion that we are so historically determined that we cannot develop an imaginative sympathy with a text, as both Schleiermacher and Dilthey claimed. And so he gently works through, with Gadamer, the reality that we have these concepts of tradition and of repetition and horizon fusion. One does not have to say that the only meaning of a text is the meaning for today. It is possible for a text to have a definitive meaning: yesterday, today, and forever.[15]

---

[14] C. S. Lewis, a review of "*De Descriptione Temporum*," *Time*, May 2, 1955, 94.
[15] Carl F. H. Henry, *God, Revelation, and Authority*, vol. 3, *God Who Speaks and Shows: Fifteen Theses, Part 2* (Waco, TX: Word, 1978), 203–15.

Henry was optimistic in his outlook. He modeled for us the cardinal virtues of an evangelical scholar by keeping himself abreast of philosophical conversations. I once asked Henry what should be added to the present seminary curriculum. He said two semesters of history of philosophy and a course on logic. Historically, many seminaries considered this, or something even more robust, to be standard preparation. A quick survey of theological curricula in evangelical seminaries today, however, suggests that Henry's preferences are not widely shared.

To be sure, Henry would not want theological education to be the province of only hoary-headed academics and scholars. He wanted philosophy to be something that pastors and church leaders and laypeople could engage too. It is the ministry of the church to engage in this way. Henry knew when to say yes and when to say no. He was happy to give ground to philosophical ideas where they connected with biblical theism, but he was also willing to say no if the philosophical idea did not fit in with biblical theology. He had a keen sense for the ephemeral, vain, and vacuous; light, cynical, or ideological. In sum, Carl Henry was characterized by wisdom in his scholarship, and he encouraged people in ministry to engage this material.

Allow me to lay out what will surely be the most unexpected illustration in this book. I'm going to compare Carl Henry to John Lennon. When John Lennon met Yoko Ono, he was at his lowest point. He met Yoko at a gallery exhibit, where he saw one of her expositions: a ladder going up to the ceiling. At the top of the ceiling there was a little latch door. He climbed up and opened the latch, and inside was a message that said, "Yes." Lennon absolutely loved it, because everything else in his life up to that point had been a no. Everything had been no, everything had been dark, but here was Yoko, saying yes. John got down the ladder and started saying yes to Yoko Ono. He had to say no to a lot of other things, including the Beatles and, although it was a struggle, other women.[16]

This is essentially the same point that Carl Henry makes to us. We say yes to the gospel. We say yes to the bridegroom presented to us in John's Apocalypse. We humble ourselves and put our story into that

---

[16] Jann S. Wenner, *Lennon Remembers* (New York: Verso, 1971), 37–38.

story. But we should also be happy to say no to things that threaten that story. Carl Henry, unlike a lot of his heirs, was not afraid to go to Yale and debate with Hans Frei on the issue of narrative theology. He did not ask Hans Frei to come to the Evangelical Theological Society or to convene somewhere in "safe" territory. He went to Yale and had the conversation on Frei's home ground.[17]

We cannot underscore enough that a vital part of Carl Henry's legacy, that gentle man we are honoring in this book, was that his humility and modesty were paired with an impressive philosophical gravitas. It was the combination of those two things—the head and the heart—that made Carl Henry the man we are honoring.

I want to end with a story that comes from an episode on the campus of Southern Seminary. I was participating in a theological studies colloquium on contemporary theology. Carl F. H. Henry came at the beginnings of the seminary's Henry Institute and spoke on a number of occasions. After he arrived on campus and was mingling with the students, we had a lunch meeting with participants in the contemporary theology doctoral seminar. We were talking about Pannenberg's newly released third volume of his systematic theology, and an astute PhD student posed this question to our distinguished guest: "Dr. Henry, what do you consider to be the most pressing question in modern theology?" He did not bat an eye but immediately replied, "Have you met the risen Lord?" It was the right question with the right answer.

---

[17] Readers will want to note that Trinity Evangelical Divinity School has recently made the full audio of the Frei-Henry exchange available to the public: http://henrycenter.tiu.edu/category/carl-henry-2/.

8

The Modern Mind and the Uneasy Conscience

Carl F. H. Henry and Postwar Evangelical Social Ethic

Ben Peays

It was an unusual proposition, but it worked. In 1947 Carl F. H. Henry wrote a short book entitled *The Uneasy Conscience of Modern Fundamentalism*. No one would have expected a short book on intra-Christian social engagement to sell over one hundred thousand copies, but Henry's little text caught fire. As a result, it is considered to be one of the catalysts for the development of American evangelicalism during the past sixty years.

Henry, just thirty-four years old at the time of its publication, was full of spirit when he wrote *Uneasy Conscience*. He wrote in the mold of a prophet, seeking to diagnose the current state of fundamentalism as related to the church's mission. This was not all, however. Henry penned his text to unsettle, to awaken, and to call the church to fulfill its intellectual and cultural obligations to a fallen society. Convinced it was essential for the church to be both culturally and intellectually engaged, Henry set out to create a more "open evangelicalism that would transcend the barriers that had been erected by a separatistic mentality."[1]

Uneasy Conscience sits on the shelves of a good number of pastors and students. Few people, however, know of the book's backstory. A recently discovered collection of personal letters between Henry and his peers from 1946 and 1947 provides valuable insight into both the mindset that yielded Henry's *cri de coeur* and the reception that the book's early form and final form provoked among the author's peers. This is the special focus of this chapter: in telling the story of the creation of *Uneasy Conscience,* we zero in on reception history. The responses that Henry's work received from his peers offer rich historical perspective on the period. These epistolary exchanges further reveal how bold Henry's vision was, how fractured the conservative American church was in the late 1940s, and, ultimately, just how much it needed a book like *Uneasy Conscience.*

THE FIRST USAGE OF "UNEASY CONSCIENCE" BY HENRY

In June 1941 Carl Henry was pastoring a small, elderly congregation of about thirty people at Humboldt Park Baptist Church in Chicago. He was twenty-eight years old but was well into his academic training. Henry had recently earned a BA (1938) and an MA (1940) from Wheaton College, and a BD (1941) from Northern Baptist Theological Seminary; he would finish his ThD from Northern the following year. While he pastored, Henry taught courses at Wheaton College and served as a news stringer for local Chicago outlets such as the famed *Tribune.*

This was a heady time in world affairs. In this same month, the European Axis launched the largest military attack in human history on the Soviet Union, code named "Operation Barbarossa." Reichschancellor Adolf Hitler used an estimated four million soldiers, six hundred thousand vehicles, and 750,000 horses to try to conquer the Soviet Territories. It was a terrifying time of total warfare characterized by

---

[1] Carl F. H. Henry, *The Uneasy Conscience of Modern Fundamentalism* (Grand Rapids, MI: Eerdmans, 1947), x.

the German blitzkrieg, a mode of attack that featured multipronged assaults from air, ground, and artillery.

Following these events from afar, Henry decided to contextualize this military concept for the dear souls of his Humboldt Park congregation. On September 7, 1941, Henry preached a sermon titled "How to Run a Blitzkrieg," based on Ephesians 6. Henry said:

> There is a rising tide of reaction in Fundamentalism today—a reaction born of an uneasy conscience and determined no longer to becloud the challenge of the Gospel to modern times. It is a reaction to which the best minds of evangelicalism are bending their effort these days, convinced that no synthesis is more relevant than modern frustration and Biblical redemptionism.[2]

The world was seized in 1941 by the contest between light and dark, good and evil. As Henry surveyed the world scene, his conviction deepened: the world's frustration with social and moral evil could be satisfied only with the redemptive message of the cross. The culture was a battleground with territory to be gained or lost for the kingdom. The gospel needed to be preached and advanced into society, and the church must be its vehicle. A young Henry preached:

> "Put on the whole armor of God," warns St. Paul. You have enlisted in the divine blitzkrieg against Satan. Christ has armed His servants for the fight. Two kingdoms divide the world—the kingdom of heaven and the kingdom of Satan. It is a fight to the finish—and in the end, the right will prevail and the wicked will be vanquished.[3]

Henry picked up these themes in later sermons as well. On October 22, 1942, Henry preached a message titled "The Divine Invader," saying:

> Beneath the superficial placidity of our modern society there is an uneasy conscience, and with the creation of this uneasiness the

---

[2] Ibid., 24.
[3] Carl Henry, "How to Run a Blitzkrieg: Ephesians 6," unpublished sermon, September 7, 1941, Carl F. H. Henry Papers, Rolfing Library, Trinity Evangelical Divinity School.

Christian gospel has had very much to do. The great shadow on the conscience of the modern West is the shadow of the cross.[4]

Henry then read a portion of English poet Francis Thompson's (1859–1907) "The Hound of Heaven," which talks of God being in pursuit of his children. Henry concluded the sermon saying:

> Now this hidden canker of an uneasy conscience is in itself our greatest scathe and scourge, and for that only our own disobedience is to blame; yet it is but the reverse side of our most precious blessing, and for that we must thank God as for nothing else that has come to us. For it means that however much we try to keep to ourselves, yet He will not leave us to ourselves. It means that He invades even our "ultimate heart's occult abode." It means that His love has claimed us from the beginning, and that to the end He refuses to let us go. It means that the Hound of Heaven is still on our traces.[5]

The quotation is notable for that memorable phrase, the "uneasy conscience" of mankind, which Henry recognized had no rest in its natural state. Years before he titled his most famous book with the formulation of the Reformer Martin Luther, Henry was testing the phrase in a small and unknown Chicago pulpit. Soon, the entire evangelical movement would have it on their lips.

HENRY'S DEVELOPING CONVICTIONS

During the next few years, Henry continued teaching even as he increased the amount of his preaching to a punishing level. In 1943, he spoke eighty-four times in forty-six different locations. That number increased to ninety-eight times in forty-three different locations in 1944. His personal preaching log indicated that he usually received between five dollars and twenty-five dollars for a sermon, and congregations most often ranged from one hundred to two hundred people. In churches and in a range of academic settings, Henry test-drove his

---

[4] Carl Henry, "The Divine Invader," unpublished sermon, October 22, 1942, Carl F. H. Henry Papers, Rolfing Library, Trinity Evangelical Divinity School.
[5] Ibid.

burgeoning convictions about the intellectual and cultural deficiencies of conservative American Christianity.

During the summer of 1944, Henry took graduate classes in philosophy at Indiana University under the direction of W. Harry Jellema and Henry Veitch. These men played a significant role in helping Henry formulate the philosophical elements of ideas found in *Uneasy Conscience*. They took special interest in ontology and epistemology while at the same time placed an interest in moral philosophy and spiritual reality. This meant, on the one hand, maintaining Christian world-life intellectual convictions while, on the other, promoting a Christian perspective.

On June 19, 1944, Henry first gave the talk titled "Remaking the Modern Mind" to 150 people at the historic Cataract Hotel in downtown Sioux Falls, South Dakota. The aim was to do just that—remake or reshape the predominant intellectual thinking of the day. Henry was passionate about combating modernism because he believed modern thought, by definition, prevented belief in the true God. The god of modernism was under the restrictions of the space-time universe, and as a result, that god was limited in existence and operation. On July 27, 1944, Henry first put the ideas into print, publishing "Remaking the Modern Mind" in the Baptist magazine *Watchman Examiner*.[6]

In 1945 Henry was elected president of the alumni association at Wheaton College. In his presidential speech, he publicly set forth his challenge for fundamentalism to better engage society. This was a subject that he was well acquainted with, as the previous citations show. Henry's pastoral and journalistic experience wedded with his philosophical and academic training to give him a unique perspective on the American church's cultural shortcomings. This speech was the starting point for developing the ideas behind what he would later call "the uneasy conscience of modern fundamentalism."

ADVENTURES IN PUBLISHING: THE GENESIS OF *REMAKING THE MODERN MIND*

On Saturday May 24, 1946, Henry had breakfast with William B. Eerdmans to discuss the possibility of publishing his thoughts concerning the

---

[6] Carl F. H. Henry, "Remaking the Modern Mind," *Watchman Examiner*, July 27, 1944, 732–33.

unfortunate state of fundamentalism. Eerdmans proposed that Henry write a series of eight articles to appear in their publication *Religious Digest.*

The arrangement was straightforward, though the results were altogether unpredictable. The journal would run one article per month beginning with the September 1946 issue and ending with the April 1947 issue. Eerdmans further suggested that the articles be published into book form with a release date set for the summer of 1947. Henry was offered one hundred dollars to write the articles, plus an additional 10 percent royalty on the retail price for each copy of the book sold. The first article due date was set for July 1, 1946. After the meeting, Henry went to work on drafts of the articles and then sent them to a small set of peers for feedback.

While he worked on these short pieces, Henry experienced the frustrations many young authors face while working on another book project entitled *Remaking the Modern Mind.* This text featured some similar themes to the material that Henry would develop in *Uneasy Conscience. Modern Mind*, however, was more expressly philosophical, which caused consternation for the publisher, Scribner's Press. Editors there sat on it for a period of time before expressing their simultaneous admiration and concern. The manuscript was impressive, but the publisher was concerned it was "directed towards a more serious reader" than they hoped to reach.[7]

After six weeks of waiting, Scribner's editors finally wrote Henry to say there was too much indifference over *Modern Mind* at the editorial level, and they were mailing the manuscript back.[8] A frustrated Henry wrote to Don Norman, general manager at the Wm. B. Eerdmans Publishing Company, to gauge their interest. Norman responded enthusiastically and promised to have it on the market within three months after receiving the manuscript, giving it priority over twenty-two other books already on the schedule.[9]

Such a generous offer led Henry to reconsider the option of sending

[7] Letter from Carl Henry to William H. Savage, May 15, 1946, Carl F. H. Henry Papers, Rolfing Library, Trinity Evangelical Divinity School.
[8] Letter from William H. Savage to Carl Henry, June 3, 1946, Carl F. H. Henry Papers, Rolfing Library, Trinity Evangelical Divinity School.
[9] Letter from Carl Henry to Elwyn A. Smith, August 21, 1947, Carl F. H. Henry Papers, Rolfing Library, Trinity Evangelical Divinity School.

it to other publishers. He noted to Norman that "the quality of books on the Eerdmans list, plus the priority assurance given," was an "attractive incentive to send the manuscript directly to you, without first trying Harpers and Macmillan; I don't like to think of a 2-month delay with each set of readers. Consequently, as soon as railway express delivers it here, I shall forward it."[10] Within days, the returned manuscript finally arrived from Scribner's. Henry told the deliveryman to wait at the door while he opened the envelope and repackaged it in a new envelope for Eerdmans. Henry's quick-handed turnaround was surpassed only by his publisher's: six months later, on January 1, 1946, Eerdmans published *Remaking the Modern Mind* as a 309-page book.

PROMOTIONAL STRATEGY

Henry was a man who always had many irons in the fire. Even as he launched *Modern Mind* into the world, he worked closely with Eerdmans to build interest in his articles for the *Religious Digest*. Near the end of June 1946, Norman traveled from Grand Rapids to Chicago to talk promotional strategy with Henry. Norman had the idea to create a special year-end promotion that offered the *Uneasy Conscience* book for one dollar with a new subscription to the *Religious Digest*. Henry had the additional idea to send the October issue of the magazine and *Uneasy Conscience* to a key prospect list of about thirty pastors, professors, and other Christian leaders. These were all strategic men that Henry believed "for one reason or another interact in a conspicuous way with Fundamentalism, and will enlist interest for the volume."[11] These names included men such as Cornelius Van Til of Westminster Theological Seminary, Wilbur Smith of Moody Bible Institute, Harold J. Ockenga of Park Street Church in Boston, and John Walvoord of Dallas Theological Seminary. They also decided to send copies to key outlets including the bookstores at Moody, Wheaton, Houghton, and Gordon colleges, and Northern and Eastern seminaries. Henry was hopeful that he could get fellow National Association of Evangelicals

---

[10] Letter from Carl Henry to Don Norman, June 3, 1946, Carl F. H. Henry Papers, Rolfing Library, Trinity Evangelical Divinity School.

[11] Letter from Carl Henry to William B. Eerdmans, April 9, 1947, Carl F. H. Henry Papers, Rolfing Library, Trinity Evangelical Divinity School.

constituent Ockenga to write a full review of the book in *United Evangelical Action* and possibly also secure a review from John Bradbury in the *Watchman Examiner*.

Eerdmans was particularly interested in getting the book into the hands of an up-and-coming generation. Henry offered to approach InterVarsity Christian Fellowship Director Stacey Woods about a possible special book edition for college students that could be distributed through their campus outlets. Henry had been a familiar face at their camps during the previous years. Woods was confident that an announcement at InterVarsity's summer "Campus in the Woods" meeting on Fairfield Island, Ontario, Canada, would generate interest. Henry also told Norman that he would arrange the courses he was teaching at Wheaton College and Northern Seminary so that *Uneasy Conscience* and *Modern Mind* were the main texts.[12] This was a multiplatform publishing strategy, and it would pay off—handsomely.

THE FIRST ARTICLES

By the beginning of June 1946 Henry had a stack of personal letters with feedback on the article drafts. Some thought he had missed the mark, while others thought his words to be prophetic. Henry wrote to Eerdmans, saying:

> I am getting reactions from fundamentalist leaders, and while we ought not to name them, their comments would make a wonderful advertisement, in enlisting advance interest. I have written the articles sufficiently heavy to be of *Christian Century* caliber, on the theory that we are primarily anxious to do a service to the pastors and teachers who are able to change the plight of the fundamentalist camp.[13]

Henry incorporated some of his readers' suggestions but disregarded others. Henry's professor friend Roland E. Turnbull of Shurtleff College in Alton, Illinois, wrote Henry and suggested that he change the

[12] Letter from Henry to Norman, June 3, 1946.
[13] Carl F. H. Henry to Don Norman, June 10, 1946, Carl F. H. Henry Papers, Rolfing Library, Trinity Evangelical Divinity School.

article's title, then "The Evaporation of Fundamentalist Humanism." Turnbull argued that "Humanism is tied in with the Humanities, i.e. culture from the classics, also of course a liberal view in theology. My impression is that you need the word, 'Humanitarianism' i.e. compassion towards others, & thus to the social questions you raise."[14] Henry soon changed the title to "The Evaporation of Fundamentalist Humanitarianism" and added a footnote in the book to explain his choice: "The word 'humanitarianism' is used in the sense of benevolent regard for the interests of mankind."

Elwyn A. Smith, associate editor for the Board of Christian Education of the Presbyterian Church of the United States (PCUS), also weighed in. His strongly worded comments show that Henry's subject choice had touched a nerve:

> You did oversimplify terribly on the "liberals" and "humanists" and "modernists." You have given little place to what is often called the neo-orthodox; and among persons generally lumped under Niebuhr (whom I suspect you of reading!). . . . Personally I feel the reformation of modern Protestantism will come not from humanist liberals, and only exceptionally from fundamentalists of your own honest type. It will come from the gentiles, Samaritans and outcasts of orthodoxy; the secularists who come to Christ afresh; the intelligentsia who discover the Christian answer; the boys who were the rejectees at Wheaton and Princeton (one of the most conservative places there is, the foofaraw notwithstanding); and those who have looked into the abyss of total unbelief because God gave them the courage to ask, "Do I really believe what I profess?"[15]

Smith's comments underscore the boldness of Henry's venture: he sought nothing less than a "reformation of modern Protestantism," a project noble in aim but complex in prosecution, as the neo-evangelicals would find out.

---

[14] Roland E. Turnbull to Carl Henry, July 4, 1946, Carl F. H. Henry Papers, Rolfing Library, Trinity Evangelical Divinity School.
[15] Elwyn A. Smith to Carl Henry, July 29, 1947, Carl F. H. Henry Papers, Rolfing Library, Trinity Evangelical Divinity School.

In Henry's second article, "The Protest Against Foredoomed Failure," Henry blamed the eschatological views of fundamentalism, with its pessimism about the future, its expectancy of the end of the world, and its postponement theory of the kingdom of God, as the greatest discouragement to evangelicals in being aggressive in the fight against social evil. Henry cautioned, "No voice is speaking today as Paul would, either at the United Nations sessions, or at labor-management disputes, or in strategic university classrooms whether in Japan or Germany or America." Henry was hopeful that there was a rising tide of reaction in fundamentalism that was "a reaction born of an uneasy conscience and determined no longer to becloud the challenge of the Gospel to modern times."[16]

This article also elicited strong comment. In June 1946 Reverend George J. Carlson told Henry that he had failed to emphasize the full effect that modernism had inflicted on fundamentalism:

> Your statement of Fundamentalism's reactions to Religious Liberalism and its world view is no doubt true, but you fail to say that this reaction is the result of Religious Liberalism's paralyzing stroke affecting the trustworthiness of those basic things that Fundamentalism considers divine, authoritative and mandatory for every life situation. I believe critical scholarship has left [its] paralyzing [effect] on traditional Christianity and thereby has affected its reflexes.[17]

Other voices chimed in. Clarence Bouma, editor of the *Calvin Forum* and professor at Calvin Seminary, challenged Henry to dig into the heart of the fundamentalist-evangelical divide:

> I hope that in the remaining articles you may have occasion to dig a bit more deeply into the question why so many fundamentalists are so averse to the application of Christian principles to the social problems of our day. You will then, no doubt, show that the escha-

---

[16] Henry, *Uneasy Conscience*, 34.
[17] Letter from George J. Carlson to Carl Henry, June 15, 1946, Carl F. H. Henry Papers, Trinity Evangelical Divinity School.

tological orientation of many Fundamentalists precludes any real interest in these ethical and social issues. The more the imminence of the Second Coming is taken in the sense of many present-day Dispensationalists and Premillennialists, the less real interest in the ethical task of the Christian Church. It is ultimately a matter of the proper relation between eschatology and ethics.[18]

R. L. Decker, a leading Baptist at the time and future president of the National Evangelical Association, wrote that any deviation from an evangelistic mission would spell doom for a conservative Christian effort:

My impression is that fundamentalists generally are impatient with any formula, plan or program, which is not pre-eminently evangelistic or ecclesiastic in emphasis. Their test question is, "How will this win souls or build up the church?" The postponed kingdom theory, which you mentioned has had and is having a great influence upon the thinking of most premillenarians. This is true because of the large number of books and pamphlets produced by the "Bible School" type of Bible teachers, preachers and evangelists.[19]

Charles W. Koller, president of Northern Baptist Theological Seminary where Henry was teaching, was supportive of Henry's assessment of fundamentalism, saying:

I believe the fundamentalist has fallen into inadequacy for a number of reasons: It is a protest against modernism, which is generally the basis for the social gospel. Part of it is also due to the disillusionment: the first World War, the collapse of the prohibition movement and other things. Also the fundamentalist knows prophecy better than he knows the prophets. Bible Institutes and Seminary (even Northern) have not been gripped by the fundamental message of

[18] Letter from Clarence Bouma to Carl Henry, June 8, 1946, Carl F. H. Henry Papers, Rolfing Library, Trinity Evangelical Divinity School.
[19] Letter from R. L. Decker to Carl Henry, July 16, 1946, Carl F. H. Henry Papers, Rolfing Library, Trinity Evangelical Divinity School.

the prophets, but more by the Messianic and apocalyptic passages. Men who have gone through the Bible Institutes seldom know much about sociology, economics or international affairs: consequently they get their doctrines from the Bible and their social views from the *Chicago Tribune*. This is too often the case.[20]

As Henry continued to make revisions on his articles based on feedback, he confessed to William Eerdmans that "the articles on fundamentalism are being born in pain, but you will have them in good time."[21] As promised, Henry submitted a final draft of the first two articles just before the July 1 deadline. His project was very small in page count but very large in intended effect. As the responses of his peers show, he had a tall order ahead of him if he was to seek unity of mission among fellow believers.

LECTURES AT GORDON COLLEGE

During this time, Henry also carried out doctoral work in philosophy under Edgar S. Brightman at Boston University. While in Boston in the summer of 1946, Henry was invited by T. Leonard Lewis, the new president of Gordon College of Theology and Missions, to teach a summer course in New Testament and to deliver a series of open lectures to students. Henry took this opportunity to present the nascent "uneasy conscience" material, as a trial run, to the student body. These talks helped solidify his framework for the remaining six articles for the *Religious Digest* and later the book.

Throughout July and August Henry continued to send out drafts and receive feedback from peers. The third article was titled "The Most Embarrassing Evangelical Divorce," insinuating that fundamentalism had divorced itself from social engagement. Henry argued boldly, "For the first protracted period in its history, evangelical Christianity stands divorced from the great social reform movements."[22] His respondents wrote with equal boldness. Charles W. Koller believed that asking for

---

[20] Letter from Charles W. Koller to Carl Henry, June 15, 1946, Carl F. H. Henry Papers, Rolfing Library, Trinity Evangelical Divinity School.
[21] Letter from Carl Henry to Don Norman, June 22, 1946, Carl F. H. Henry Papers, Rolfing Library, Trinity Evangelical Divinity School.
[22] Henry, *Uneasy Conscience*, 27.

fundamentalists to participate with secular institutions was naïve, and said as much:

> Fundamentalism is uneasy about its bondage to apostate or corrupt ecclesiastical systems and in that frame of mind is not likely to frame a distinctive constructive ideology. Fundamentalism is too conscious of what it is against. Consequently, it will not join hands with what it considers apostates to secure social reform—as practical as that may be. . . . To ask fundamentalists to join hands with heretics today for the purposes of social reform is to buck the prevailing winds.[23]

Burton Goddard, then dean of Gordon College of Theology and Missions, was also skeptical:

> It occurred to me that you assume that the Church from apostolic days was really organized to achieve social ends, but a cursory reading of the articles did not at all convince me that the apostolic church, for instance, had much of any program along this line. . . . I think it should be brought out more clearly just what the difference, if any, was between the modern Fundamentalist approach and aim, and the preaching and aim of apostolic Christianity.[24]

J. Elwyn Wright, executive secretary of the National Association of Evangelicals, cautioned:

> It is quite evident that our evangelicals have been very delinquent in their interest in social work. On the other hand it has been quite evident that there is a great temptation to let such work become the major to the detriment of the spiritual aspects of the program of the church. This difficulty has been so recurrent that there cannot be too severe censure for those who steer too far to the right of the matter. I think your thesis is timely.[25]

---

[23] Letter from Koller to Henry, June 15, 1946.
[24] Letter from Burk Goddard to Carl Henry, August 6, 1946, Carl F. H. Henry Papers, Rolfing Library, Trinity Evangelical Divinity School.
[25] Letter from J. Elwyn Wright to Carl Henry, September 6, 1946, Carl F. H. Henry Papers, Rolfing Library, Trinity Evangelical Divinity School.

Cornelius Jaarsma, divisional chair of education and professor of philosophy at Wheaton College, warned Henry not to overplay social ethics:

> American fundamentalism, especially the brand found in our fair land, suffers from a lack of a world and life view. The source lies deeper than the absence of ethical responsibility, though this too is a sad omission. . . . A Christian culture, I am sure you agree, is more than the ethical implication of our Christian faith. It is embraced in a total Christian theism, the Christian system of thought. I do not mean this statement by way of criticism of your article. I should say, however, that the article conveys the impression, contrary to your intentions, that the issue is primarily an ethical one. A consistent theism would refute this.[26]

Jaarsma later wrote more in another letter to Henry:

> It is not clear to me from your discussion that we must claim the world of culture, of creative human ingenuity, for Christ, for here too we find the revelation of God, sadly abused by the world, but which can be properly explored by the Christian. The social implications of the gospel do not justify a liberal arts college and a university of a distinctively Christian nature. Ours is more than a social program. The discovery of truth in physics properly oriented in the framework of the Christian postulates of thought is an achievement for the kingdom of God whether any social or personal benefits of a utilitarian or spiritual nature result.[27]

In their article in the *Presbyterian Guardian*, editors Ned B. Stonehouse and Paul Woolley agreed with Henry's assessment of fundamentalism's failure to take leadership outside of the church in education. They wrote:

---

[26] Letter from Cornelius Jaarsma to Carl Henry, June 7, 1946, Carl F. H. Henry Papers, Rolfing Library, Trinity Evangelical Divinity School.
[27] Letter from Cornelius Jaarsma to Carl Henry, August 3, 1946, Carl F. H. Henry Papers, Rolfing Library, Trinity Evangelical Divinity School.

Today the state is doing most of the family's work in education. . . . The church neglects to teach the valid principles of human relationships, and so the state is forced to blunder about trying to learn the principles as well as apply them. . . . Education has in large part been turned over to the state, yet fundamentalists often wash their hands of politics as too sordid for their dainty fingers. . . . The Gospel is a message, which applies to the whole man and to all of life.[28]

Henry's material caused no small amount of comment. But a consensus, however fragile, was emerging among like-minded Christians in this period. While it might have been hard to conceive of *Uneasy Conscience* as a future best seller, it was growing increasingly evident that the book would find an appreciative audience.

Henry's fourth article, titled "The Apprehension Over Kingdom Preaching," called for fundamentalists to restudy the doctrine of the kingdom of God. In a remarkable instance, Henry was cautioned by an unnamed "Fundamentalist spokesman" to stay away from the kingdom because "there is growing reluctance to explicate the kingdom idea in Fundamentalist preaching, because a kingdom-now message is too easily confused with the liberal social gospel, and because a kingdom-then message will identify Christianity further to the modern mind in terms of an escape mechanism."[29] Henry, however, felt strongly that fundamentalists needed to rethink kingdom issues. To his everlasting credit, he wrote, "Nevertheless, the burden of these articles is not to press a personal kingdom viewpoint, but rather to promote an evangelical conviction that nothing is so essential among Fundamentalist essentials as a world-relevance for the Gospel."[30] He argued that no subject was "more frequently on the lips of Jesus Christ than the kingdom."[31] To not speak about the kingdom would be to omit a significant amount of Christ's teaching.

The chapter drew blood as previous selections had. Reverend George J. Carlson, pastor at Tabernacle Baptist Church in Chicago,

---

[28] Ned B. Stonehouse and Paul Woolley, "Fundamentalist Progress," *Presbyterian Guardian* 16 (1947): 231.
[29] Henry, *Uneasy Conscience*, 51–52.
[30] Ibid., 48.
[31] Ibid., 52.

complained that Henry "doesn't seem to have the sympathy he should
for Fundamentalism. . . . As I read it I was trying to think of who these
Fundamentalists are whom you speak of and I failed to make it apply to
the Fundamentalists I know."[32] Like his fellow neo-evangelical leaders,
Henry would face this charge over the years. To some point, his critics
were correct, for despite the monolithic view presented of it in academic
circles, fundamentalism was rarely more than an uneasy coalition of
diverse churches led by vigorous personalities committed to biblical
orthodoxy and separation from perceived sin. As Henry's interactions
demonstrate, these leaders did not hesitate to disagree with one another
in the sometimes strenuous terms endemic to the movement.

THE FOREWORD AND INTRODUCTION
TO *UNEASY CONSCIENCE*

As Henry continued to work on his articles, Eerdmans began plans for
the 1947 launch of the book. Don Norman wrote to Henry, saying:

> Personally, I would like nothing better than to have Dr. Wilbur M.
> Smith write the introduction. As editor of "Peloubets Notes" and
> author of "Therefore, Stand," he is well known throughout the
> country. Furthermore, I understand that he is one of the most highly
> esteemed speakers who ever addressed the meetings of the Inter-
> Varsity Christian Fellowship.[33]

Henry hoped Smith would be willing to serve on the reading committee and interact with the proofs from an early stage. Norman suggested
that Smith could even write the introduction and possibly publish a
review of the book in *Moody Monthly*. Henry told Norman he was
sure Smith would accept the offer: "He may even get a strange delight
out of doing this."[34]

Norman met with Smith and invited him to serve on the reading
committee. Smith declined, so Norman did not invite him to write the

---

[32] Letter from George J. Carlson to Carl Henry, June 15, 1946, Carl F. H. Henry Papers, Rolfing Library, Trinity Evangelical Divinity School.
[33] Letter from Don Norman to Carl Henry, June 17, 1946, Carl F. H. Henry Papers, Rolfing Library, Trinity Evangelical Divinity School.
[34] Letter from Henry to Norman, June 3, 1946.

introduction. A disappointed Henry decided to try his hand at convincing Smith. They met for lunch on Tuesday, June 18, 1946, and Smith once again declined to serve on the reading committee. He did, however, offer to help generally from time to time.

Norman and Henry decided to ask Ockenga to write the introduction. Several weeks later, the preternaturally busy Ockenga sent them a draft and admitted he was not able to give the series as close of a read as he wanted. "However," he said, "I do heartily endorse your series. Get them in print as soon as possible."[35] Henry responded to Ockenga, saying:

> Many thanks for the fine introduction. I have already sent it on to Eerdmans, and a copy of the October issue of "Religious Digest" will be coming your way, as well as the $1 book when it appears at the turn of the year. Somehow I feel that if we could gather 25 men—those who teach Christian ethics in our fundamentalist seminaries and colleges, and some strategic pastors from each big city—we could turn the flank of fundamentalist indifferentism by coming to some common agreement on the outlines of a program.[36]

However, behind the scenes, Henry confessed to Eerdmans that he was disappointed in Ockenga's introduction:

> I'm glad you are ready to proceed with the book on "Uneasy Conscience of Modern Fundamentalism" and that it came along at a timely moment and struck you favorably. Though Harold Ockenga's introduction is brief and perhaps hurried, I think his name nonetheless will mean something to the series, and trust that you will use it; automatically, a few paragraphs by him would commend the whole series to the NAE constituency.[37]

---

[35] Letter from Harold John Ockenga to Carl Henry, August 23, 1946, Carl F. H. Henry Papers, Rolfing Library, Trinity Evangelical Divinity School.
[36] Letter from Carl Henry to Harold John Ockenga, August 28, 1946, Carl F. H. Henry Papers, Rolfing Library, Trinity Evangelical Divinity School.
[37] In quintessentially Henrician fashion, he also pointed out to his publisher, "It occurred to me the other day that I have never signed author's contracts for either of the volumes and, while I have implicit trust, it's just good business for both of us and our heirs to go through the formalities." Letter from Carl Henry to William Eerdmans, September 20, 1946, Carl F. H. Henry Papers, Trinity Evangelical Divinity School.

Henry decided to write his own foreword, which would both fill in
the gaps left by Ockenga and, in his view, better introduce the project as
a whole. By September 1946, he sent the preface to William Eerdmans
and received this response:

> I took your articles with me to New York. Read them on the train,
> and they are superb! . . . But I did not like the introduction by [Ock-
> enga] at all. Seems to me it was hastily written; anyhow did not do
> justice to your thrust. This morning I came down with an idea and
> was busy trying to get that on paper, when Don [Norman] walked
> into my office with your "Forward". And that takes care of it, in a
> very beautiful way. I stopped right after I had read your forward. . . .
> You need no Introduction from anyone. If anyone can, YOU can
> stand on your own legs. And my brother, when we champion a just
> cause, we need no soft-pedaling, or advance trumpet blowing by
> anyone! And so let's go to it. We are ready to make the book. O.K.?[38]

Henry's foreword was powerful and confrontational, setting the
tone for the book. "Some of my evangelical friends have expressed
the opinion that nobody should 'perform surgery' on Fundamentalism just now," he noted, for they considered "it wiser to wait until the
religious scene is characterized by less tension." Henry disagreed with
that assessment:

> I do not share this view that it is wiser to wait, for several rea-
> sons. . . . That it may be somewhat optimistic to speak of a wide-
> spread uneasiness, I also recognize. Many of our Bible institutes,
> evangelical colleges, and even seminaries, seem blissfully unaware
> of the new demands upon us. My hope is that some, who were not
> troubled at the outset of these pages, will become concerned before
> they finish. . . . Unless we experience a rebirth of apostolic passion,
> Fundamentalism in two generations will be reduced either to a toler-
> ated cult status or . . . a despised and oppressed sect.[39]

[38] Letter from William B. Eerdmans to Carl Henry, September 17, 1946, Carl F. H. Henry Papers, Rolfing
Library, Trinity Evangelical Divinity School.
[39] Henry, *Uneasy Conscience*, xv.

This was a courageous move. The young professor had recently been warned that dissecting fundamentalism would bring too much negativity or bad press to the movement. Carlson, pastor at Tabernacle Baptist Church in Chicago, worried, "My first reaction is that this article can be used against Fundamentalists to play upon weak points, and a point of view that many are prejudiced against. . . . We need all the favorable publicity we can get."[40] Other voices found the prescription weaker than the jeremiad. Merrill Tenney, Henry's former professor at Wheaton College, wrote, "The articles impress me as being sane and well written. Possibly they are a bit of an overreaction. . . . You don't prescribe what our definite action should be."[41] Tenney had little sense of how difficult the neo-evangelicals would indeed find formulating "definite action" in the post-1940s period.

PUBLICATION OF THE ARTICLES

In September 1946, the first article in *Religious Digest* was published. To commemorate the series, Henry preached a sermon on Sunday morning, September 1, 1946, to four hundred people at First Baptist Church in Hammond, Indiana, titled "The Uneasy Conscience of Modern Fundamentalism."[42] The second, third, and fourth articles were published in October, November, and December, respectively. In January 1947 the fifth article, titled "The Fundamentalist Thief on the Cross," depicted the two thieves who hung on crosses next to Jesus as "Humanism" and "Fundamentalism." His point was that often the fundamentalist was crucified at the expense of the liberal who has given him an unfair characterization. Henry believed fundamentalists should unite around their shared historical beliefs and not divide over secondary issues. In February, the sixth article, titled "The Struggle for a New World Mind," outlined Henry's philosophical beliefs about modernity and the Christian mind. He argued that fundamentalism needed to regain its intellectual integrity.

The series drew strongly positive comment from Presbyterian

---

[40] Letter from Carlson to Henry, June 15, 1946.

[41] Letter from Merrill Tenney to Carl Henry, July 22, 1946, Carl F. H. Henry Papers, Rolfing Library, Trinity Evangelical Divinity School.

[42] The pastor was Henry's former colleague from Northern Seminary, W. Harry Jellema. Later that night during the evening service, he preached another new sermon, "The Living Apologetic." Henry preached that sermon eight more times before the end of the year, but he never recorded another event where he preached a sermon titled "The Uneasy Conscience of Modern Fundamentalism."

friends. In an article in the *Presbyterian Guardian*, Ned B. Stonehouse and Paul Woolley remarked:

> The heart of the volume comes in the chapter entitled, "The Funda-
> mentalist Thief on the Cross." Here professor Henry points out that
> it is not the discard of doctrinal convictions that is needed. The great
> doctrinal affirmations must continue to be made at the very center.
> But fundamentalists often make "fundamentals" of too much, and
> their beliefs are sometimes out of balance. We cannot define a valid
> fundamentalism "in terms of eschatology only."[43]

One common response to Henry's articles concerned their density, a charge that followed him to the end of his days. He was ever a deep thinker. Earle V. Pierce, editor of the *Watchman Examiner*, said, "My one critique of Dr. Henry's work is that it is expressed in language alto-gether too philosophical. The average fundamentalist who very much needs the book will not read very far in it. . . . There are also very many manufactured words, which are clever, but the book is not read-ily readable."[44]

Clarence Bouma of Calvin Seminary agreed, querying, "Could you simplify your terminology for the average preacher or layman who should read what you have written?"[45] Pastor R. L. Decker suggested that the articles "would be more widely read and quoted if they were written in a more popular style."[46] Clyde Dennis, editor of *Christian Life and Times*, concurred, telling Henry the material was "too heavy for a book condensation."[47]

In March 1947 the seventh article was published under the title "The Evangelical Formula of Protest," where "protest" referred to the refusal of fundamentalists to participate in nonevangelical social efforts. In the 1940s, the best programs battling social and moral evil were non-Christian. Fundamentalists were reluctant to work with them as

---

[43] Stonehouse and Woolley, "Fundamentalist Progress," 231.
[44] Letter from Earle V. Pierce to William B. Eerdmans, May 8, 1947, Carl F. H. Henry Papers, Rolfing Library, Trinity Evangelical Divinity School.
[45] Letter from Bouma to Henry, June 8, 1946.
[46] Letter from Decker to Henry, July 16, 1946.
[47] Letter from Clyde Dennis to Carl Henry, January 13, 1947, Carl F. H. Henry Papers, Rolfing Library, Trinity Evangelical Divinity School.

a result, because their methods were nonredemptive. Elwyn A. Smith, writing from his post on the Board of Christian Education for the Presbyterian Church in the USA, suggested that this meant that one had to essentially write off the fundamentalists:

> First of all, I am grateful to God that at least a voice with both courage and insight has been raised in the desert of Fundamentalism. You know I was raised with the best of them; Moody background, my father's position with the Bible Institute of Penn., Wheaton, etc...; at Harvard, for example, I sat under Ockenga at Park Street. But as far as I am concerned, Fundamentalism is a desert—spiritually, and I am glad.[48]

Henry's reply is instructive for understanding his own conception of fundamentalism. He decried certain aspects of it but refused to write it off altogether: "If Liberalism was to a large extent a footnote on Wellhausen, much of Fundamentalism was a footnote on Darby." The heart of the matter was this: "While you tend to view Fundamentalism as a spiritual, moral and intellectual desert, I see Great Tradition flowing through it, though with enough accretions to make the hour right for a Reformation."[49]

In April 1947, the eighth and final article in the series was published under the title "The Dawn of a New Reformation." Henry wrote, "The evangelical uneasiness is one of the most promising signs of the times, for it may issue in a formula providing a twentieth-century reformation within Protestantism and leading to a global renaissance within modern secularism."[50] This was a lofty ambition and a commendable one. There surely was a revival of sorts that took place in the postwar years, and Henry played a key role in it. The church still awaits a "global renaissance within modern secularism," however.

Henry intended his book to be more descriptive than prescriptive. He knew, however, that some people would not be satisfied with an articulation of the problem. They would want clear solutions. Henry

---

[48] Letter from Elwyn A. Smith to Carl Henry, July 29, 1947, Carl F. H. Henry Papers, Rolfing Library, Trinity Evangelical Divinity School.
[49] Letter from Henry to Smith, August 21, 1947.
[50] Letter from Henry, *Uneasy Conscience*, 61.

wrote to his former Wheaton professor and close friend Gordon Clark, confessing:

> In a few weeks, "The Uneasy Conscience of Modern Fundamentalism" will be off the press and you will get a copy; it is prolegomena, intended to be constructively provocative, for I felt this would be better than to say too much about solutions (and probably I didn't know too much about them anyway). It is only 89 pages, but I have reason to think it may be a lever in evangelical circles.[51]

Some commentators did seize on this possible weakness of the text. Others, however, saw that *Uneasy Conscience* could in finished form help foster a wider conversation oriented toward a positive cultural and social program. Earle Pierce encouraged Henry in this matter, showing that he was stirred by the professor's jeremiad:

> I am not altogether sure just what the climax of the articles might be. At times it seems to me that you were working toward concerted action for the correction of social evils with conservatives and liberals even uniting in some over-all program; at other times it seems as though perhaps the thing in mind was for real conservatives to launch a social program, but in the last chapter your thoughts seemed to be for each man to hammer away in his preaching as best he could, not forgetting the social and economic implications of the Gospel. It would seem to me that in the last article it would be preferable to come to some specific conclusions outlining the main possibilities if that could be done. . . . I am sure that the articles will be very stimulating in any event and congratulate you on the thought behind them. Surely we need to do far more than we have done along these lines.[52]

In one sense, this was all that Henry could have hoped to stimulate: to fan into flame the desire among fellow believers to "do far more" along cultural and social lines than had been done before.

---

[51] Letter from Carl Henry to Gordon Clark, March 9, 1947, Carl F. H. Henry Papers, Rolfing Library, Trinity Evangelical Divinity School.
[52] Letter from Goddard to Henry, August 6, 1946.

THE PUBLICATION OF *THE UNEASY CONSCIENCE* OF *MODERN FUNDAMENTALISM*

By the summer of 1947 all eight chapters had received their final revisions, and Eerdmans published the eighty-nine-page book. The conversation surrounding the text began to quickly heat up. James DeForest Murch, editor and manager of the National Association of Evangelicals' publication *United Evangelical Action*, said:

> You have certainly succeeded in arousing evangelical conscience on social issues. I believe the current discussion is a very healthy sign. Only a dead evangelicalism would fail to react to your splendid treatise in "The Uneasy Conscience of Modern Fundamentalism." Only a dead seminary professor would not be criticized. I believe you rendered our whole cause a great service and the end is not yet. . . . Pray for us.[53]

On June 1, 1947, *United Evangelical Action* announced a contest offering ten dollars for the best essays in both agreement and disagreement with Henry. On July 15, they printed both winning essays in an article titled "Is Doctor Henry Right?" Reverend Paul L. Arnold, pastor of Northwest Presbyterian Church in Detroit, wrote the winning essay in which he agreed with Henry that fundamentalist eschatology provided a great challenge to fundamentalist engagement in society.

Bernard Ramm, who was then serving as professor of apologetics at the Bible Institute of Los Angeles, won the contest on the side of disagreement with Henry. Ramm wrote to Henry privately to express his divergence:

> [The church] is commissioned only to evangelize; we can expect Christian ethics only from the redeemed, and what we as Christians must practice, we cannot expect others to follow. I too am uneasy about the mess we are in. But I find no injunction in Scripture for me to follow but to (1) evangelize, and (2) keep my

---

[53] Letter from James DeForest Murch to Carl Henry, August 20, 1947, Carl F. H. Henry Papers, Rolfing Library, Trinity Evangelical Divinity School.

spiritual life at the right level. Doing this I am salt and light to the world in which I live.[54]

Others sounded further notes of dissension. Some criticized Eerdmans for a sloppy editing job and "cheap" final product. At one point, Henry had written, "Those who read with competence will know that the 'uneasy conscience' of which I write is not one troubled about the great Biblical verities." But the book had misquoted that line, saying, "This is not a revolt against the great Biblical *varieties*." Elwyn A. Smith called it unacceptable and encouraged Henry to find a new publisher. Smith said, "That 'varieties' error was bad. Insist on doing your own proof reading, even jacket blurb, if Eerdmans can't be trusted on it. Our Westminster Press would throw out an expensive printing rather than let a thing like that go through."[55]

Henry himself was no less displeased. He responded, "Eerdmans told me that if I gave [*Remaking the Modern Mind*] to him, he would have it on the market within three months after he had a copy (at a time when other publishers were a year behind with already accepted manuscripts); he gave it priority over 22 books and got it out—so shall I not complain over the unfortunate 50 or 60 typographical errors. But re: *Uneasy Conscience* there was no excuse."[56] Henry was, then and later, a tough taskmaster when it came to less than optimal performance. He was not always as aware of how his own ultra-busy life sometimes contributed to his frustrations, however. This was true of typographical errors, and it would later be true of the broader program of the neo-evangelicals. Wearing the prophet's mantle meant suffering some indignities even as it offered the chance to awaken, and to some extent reinvigorate, the American church.

CONCLUSION

Carl F. H. Henry's conversion occurred when he was twenty years old, working as a journalist in his native New York. Some have wondered

---

[54] "Is Doctor Henry Right?" reply of Rev. Bernard Ramm, professor of apologetics, Bible Institute of Los Angeles, *United Evangelical Action*, July 15, 1947.
[55] Letter from Smith to Henry, July 29, 1947.
[56] Ibid.

how original Henry's ideas were in the *Uneasy Conscience*, surmising, however politely, that he was mostly "reporting" on the ideas of his elder Christian brothers such as Ockenga. For his part, Ockenga recounted his own pleasant amusement: "I am highly complimented that some people think that I might have been the originator of the ideas in 'Remaking the Modern Mind' and 'The Uneasy Conscience.'"[57]

Pastor, professor, journalist, and philosopher—God had provided Henry with a profound diversity of experiences that uniquely qualified him to produce *Uneasy Conscience*, perhaps neo-evangelicalism's single-most important book. On June 22, 1947, Henry wrote a letter to Reverend Elmer Piper, a pastor in Greenville, South Carolina, whom he had known from meetings held at the Broadway Presbyterian Church in New York City. More than any other document save the book itself, this excerpt captures Henry's heart behind the creation of the text. In terms that his later admirers can richly appreciate, Henry suggested that it was not a fight he sought to provoke by the book, or a split, or a position of prestige. No, in the eyes of the young theologian, it was "a second Reformation for which I strive—believing confidently in the second coming of Christ, but feeling that until He comes we are still in the age of grace, showing men that the meaning of life and existence can be found in any and every realm of human experience, in the atoning Christ alone."[58] As for Henry, so may it be for us.

---

[57] Letter from Harold Ockenga to Carl Henry, February 11, 1948, Carl F. H. Henry Papers, Rolfing Library, Trinity Evangelical Divinity School.
[58] Letter from Carl Henry to Elmer D. Piper, June 22, 1947, Carl F. H. Henry Papers, Rolfing Library, Trinity Evangelical Divinity School.

9

The Kingdom of God in the Social Ethics of Carl F. H. Henry

A Twenty-First-Century Evangelical Reappraisal

Russell D. Moore

When I was told of theologian Carl F. H. Henry's death, the first thing I thought of was an unfinished conversation I'd had with him. I was working on a dissertation on the kingdom of God and social ethics and eager to ask him questions about his views on the subject. His health was failing, and I was helping him along, holding his arm as he slowly walked down a corridor. "So are you still a premillennialist?" I asked him. He looked at me with confusion and almost contempt, as though I had asked him, "So are you still opposed to the dictatorship of the proletariat?" He said, "Of course. I've always been a premillennialist, and for three important reasons." I waited to hear them.

First, he said, is the exegesis of Revelation 20. After he spent a few minutes speaking about the reasons he didn't believe the text there could support an amillennial or postmillennial viewpoint, he moved to his second point: the hymnody of the church, which he said had always held the apocalypse to be a cataclysmic event after a time of historical tumult. He then paused and said, "And the third reason—well, I don't remember the third reason. But it is compelling." At the death of Henry, I reflected on the fact that I'll now never know that third compelling reason until he and I both know for certain what the future kingdom looks like.

When many contemporary evangelicals think of Carl Henry, they think of his prophetic call for evangelical social action: *The Uneasy Conscience of Modern Fundamentalism*. What many fail to see, though, is why Henry thought the conscience was so uneasy in the first place: a deficient vision of the kingdom of God. It's easy to remember Henry for his work on issues of epistemology and theology proper but fail to consider how critical was his scholarship on the issues of the kingdom. Whether or not the elderly Carl Henry could remember everything he believed about the kingdom, the young Carl Henry certainly taught the evangelical movement much about the kingdom of God, in both its present and future manifestations.

This chapter will offer a few reappraisals of Henry's understanding of the kingdom of God as it relates to his social ethics.[1] While much could be said on this topic with the benefit of nearly a generation of backward glance, there are three important issues to be considered here: Henry's social ethics as it relates to the reign of God in evangelical eschatology, soteriology, and ecclesiology.

THE KINGDOM, SOCIAL ETHICS, AND *THE UNEASY CONSCIENCE*

Historians rightly identify the first visible rumblings of modern evangelical political engagement with Carl F. H. Henry's 1947 jeremiad, *The Uneasy Conscience of Modern Fundamentalism*.[2] Henry could not have foreseen the way this would go in the generation after it was published.

Henry's *Uneasy Conscience* was not first of all a sociopolitical tract. Instead, it served in many ways to define theologically much of what

---

[1] This essay originally appeared in the *Journal of the Evangelical Theological Society* 55/2, with portions adapted from *The Kingdom of Christ: The New Evangelical Perspective* (Wheaton, IL: Crossway, 2004), and is used here with permission.
[2] Carl F. H. Henry, *The Uneasy Conscience of Modern Fundamentalism* (Grand Rapids, MI: Eerdmans, 1947).

it meant to be a "new evangelical," in contrast to the older fundamentalism.[3] Along with Ramm, Carnell, and others, Henry pressed the theological case for evangelicalism in terms of a vigorous engagement with nonevangelical thought.[4] As articulated by Henry and the early constellations of evangelical theology, such as Fuller Theological Seminary and the National Association of Evangelicals, evangelicalism would not differ with fundamentalism in the "fundamentals" of doctrinal conviction, but in the application of Christian truth claims on to all areas of human endeavor.[5] Henry's *Uneasy Conscience*, which set the stage for evangelical differentiation from isolationist American fundamentalism, sought to be what Harold J. Ockenga called in his introduction to the monograph "a healthy antidote to fundamentalist aloofness in a distraught world."[6]

Thus, the call to sociopolitical engagement was not incidental to evangelical theological identity but was at the forefront of it. Henry's *Uneasy Conscience*, and the movement it defined, sought to distinguish the postwar evangelical effort such that evangelical theologians, as one observer notes, "found themselves straddling the fence between two well-established positions: fundamentalist social detachment and the liberal Social Gospel."[7]

Such "straddling," however, is an inaccurate term if it carries the idea that Henry and his postwar colleagues sought to find a middle way between fundamentalism and the social gospel. The evangelicals charged the fundamentalists with misapplying their theological convictions, but they further charged the social gospel with having no explicit theology at all. "As Protestant liberalism lost a genuinely theological perspective, it substituted mainly a political program," Henry lamented.[8]

---

[3] As the editor of the Billy Graham Evangelistic Association's *Decision* magazine would note, "The book dropped like a bomb into the peaceful summer Bible conference atmosphere of the postwar evangelical community." Sherwood Eliot Wirt, *The Social Conscience of the Evangelical* (New York: Harper & Row, 1968), 47.

[4] This was not only in the social and political arenas. Henry sought to form an evangelical movement that would engage robustly the current streams of philosophy, sociology, scientific thought, and political theory. See, e.g., Carl F. H. Henry, *Remaking the Modern Mind* (Grand Rapids, MI: Eerdmans, 1946).

[5] Evangelicalism was not a repudiation of fundamentalism but a reform movement within it. Henry, even in his most insistent criticisms of fundamentalism, asserted that he wished to "perform surgery" on fundamentalism, not to kill it. Henry, *Uneasy Conscience*, 9.

[6] Harold J. Ockenga, "Introduction," in Henry, *Uneasy Conscience*, 14.

[7] Jon R. Stone, *On the Boundaries of American Evangelicalism: The Postwar Evangelical Coalition* (New York: St. Martin's Press, 1997), 138.

[8] Carl F. H. Henry, *Aspects of Christian Social Ethics* (Grand Rapids, MI: Eerdmans, 1964), 116.

The new evangelical theologians maintained that their agenda was far from a capitulation to the social gospel but was instead the conservative antidote to it.[9] This was because, Henry argued, evangelicalism was a theology calling for engagement, not a program for engagement calling for a theology.

The social-gospel theologians, Henry claimed, "exalt the social issue above the theological, and prize the Christian religion mainly as a tool for justifying an independently determined course of social action."[10] Nonetheless, fundamentalism was also, in many ways, not theological enough for Henry and his cohorts, a fact that lay at the root of fundamentalist isolation, as the evangelicals saw it. Henry commended fundamentalists for their defense of the virgin birth, the deity of Christ, and so forth. This was not enough, however, he warned. "The norm by which liberal theology was gauged for soundness unhappily became the summary of fundamentalist doctrine," he wrote. "Complacency with fragmented doctrines meant increasing failure to comprehend the relationship of underlying theological principles."[11]

This meant, Henry argued, that although conservative Christians could apply the biblical witness to evangelistic endeavors and certain basic doctrinal affirmations, "they have neglected the philosophical, scientific, social, and political problems that agitate our century," such that those seeking to find a theoretical structure for making metaphysical sense of the current situation were forced to find it in Marxism or Roman Catholicism.[12]

Among the primary threats to a cohesive evangelical movement were the skirmishes between Reformed and dispensational theologies, which

---

[9] By segregating political concerns from the gospel, Henry asserted, the fundamentalist evacuation from the public square had conceded it to liberals such as Walter Rauschenbusch, Harry Emerson Fosdick, and their more radical successors. He lamented the fact that the inadequacies of the social gospel were not devastated by conservative orthodoxy but instead by the Christian realism of Reinhold Niebuhr, which was "as destructive of certain essential elements of the biblical view as it was reconstructive of others." Carl F. H. Henry, *A Plea for Evangelical Demonstration* (Grand Rapids, MI: Baker, 1971), 34–35.

[10] Henry, *Aspects of Christian Social Ethics*, 21. The language used by the social gospel pioneers themselves only bolsters Henry's critique. "We have a social gospel," Walter Rauschenbusch proclaimed. "We need a systematic theology large enough to match it and vital enough to back it." Walter Rauschenbusch, *A Theology for the Social Gospel* (New York: Macmillan, 1917; repr. Louisville, KY: Westminster, 1997), 1.

[11] Carl F. H. Henry, "Dare We Renew the Controversy? Part 2: The Fundamentalist Reduction," *Christianity Today*, June 24, 1957, 23.

[12] Henry, *Remaking the Modern Mind*, 12. Henry's argument here would continue as he later argued that "only three formidable movements insist that man can know ultimate reality" in the context of modern Western thought. He identified these as communist materialism, Catholic Thomism, and evangelical Protestantism. Carl F. H. Henry, *Evangelicals at the Brink of Crisis* (Waco, TX: Word, 1967), 7.

Henry viewed as part of a larger trend of evangelical "navel-gazing."[13] This was, however, a real threat to evangelical theological cohesiveness, especially since the debates between the groups predated the postwar evangelical movement itself.[14] This lack of cohesion was even more important given that the bone of contention between evangelical covenantalists and evangelical dispensationalists was the concept Henry identified in *Uneasy Conscience* as most fundamental to an articulation of Christian sociopolitical engagement: the kingdom of God.[15]

The evangelical movement could not dismiss the covenant/dispensational controversies over the kingdom as mere quibbling over secondary matters; nor could these concerns be divorced from the rest of the doctrinal synthesis as though the differences were tantamount to the timing of the rapture. Dispensationalists charged covenant theologians with shackling the biblical witness to a unitary understanding centered on the justification of individuals rather than the larger cosmic purposes of God. Covenant theologians accused dispensationalists of denying the present reality of the kingdom of Christ, divorcing the relevance of the Lord's Prayer and the Sermon on the Mount from this age, and denigrating the centrality of the church by considering it a "parenthesis" in the plan of God. These kingdom-oriented differences were multitudinous, and none of them could be resolved by an umbrella statement on last things appended to the conclusion of the National Association of Evangelicals' statement of faith.

Indeed, Henry set forth his manifesto for sociopolitical engagement, as, above all, a theological statement; more specifically, it was a plea for an evangelical kingdom theology.[16] For Henry, the urgency of such a

---

[13] Carl F. H. Henry, *Evangelicals in Search of Identity* (Waco, TX: Word, 1976), 29.

[14] This is seen in the contentious battles within the Presbyterian communion over the 1941 General Assembly of the Presbyterian Church in the United States controversy over whether dispensationalism was within the bounds of the Westminster Confession of Faith. This move was denounced by Dallas Seminary president Lewis Sperry Chafer in "Dispensational Distinctions Challenged," *Bibliotheca sacra* 100 (1943): 337–43.

[15] As Sydney Ahlstrom observes: "[Dispensationalism] aroused strong resistance among American Protestants by denying what most evangelicals and all liberals firmly believed—that the Kingdom of God would come as part of the historical process. They could not accept the dispensationalist claim that all Christian history was a kind of meaningless 'parenthesis' between the setting aside of the Jews and the restoration of the Davidic Kingdom. This claim aroused violent reactions because it provided a rationale for destructive attitudes and encouraged secession from existing denominations. Especially objectionable was the tendency of dispensationalists to look for the Antichrist among the 'apostate churches' of this 'present age.'" Sydney Ahlstrom, *A Religious History of the American People* (New Haven, CT: Yale University Press, 1972), 811.

[16] So Henry contended that *Uneasy Conscience* was written in order "to urge upon evangelicals the necessity for a deliberate restudy of the whole kingdom question, that the great evangelical agreements may be

kingdom theology was due not only to the theological fragmentation of evangelicals over the kingdom question, but also to the fact that only a kingdom theology could address the specific theological reasons behind fundamentalist disengagement:

> Contemporary evangelicalism needs (1) to reawaken the relevance of its redemptive message to the global predicament; (2) to stress the great evangelical agreements in a common world front; (3) to discard elements of its message which cut the nerve of world compassion as contradictory to the inherent genius of Christianity; (4) to restudy eschatological convictions for a proper perspective which will not unnecessarily dissipate evangelical strength in controversy over secondary positions, in a day when the significance of the primary insistences is international.[17]

The formation of such a kingdom consensus was, however, easier proposed than accomplished, not only because of the internal theological kingdom tensions within evangelicalism, but also because of the role of kingdom theology in nonevangelical American Christianity. After all, a kingdom consensus had indeed been achieved within the ranks of Protestant liberalism by the onset of the early twentieth century.[18]

In the years since *Uneasy Conscience*, however, evangelical theology's "Cold War" over the kingdom has thawed dramatically. Remarkably, the move toward a consensus kingdom theology has come most markedly not from the broad center of the evangelical coalition, as represented by Henry or Ladd, but from the rival streams of dispensationalism and covenant theology themselves. This growing consensus

---

set effectively over against the modern mind, with the least dissipation of energy on secondary issues." Henry, *Uneasy Conscience*, 51.

[17] Ibid., 57.

[18] For a discussion of the varying conceptions of the kingdom in American Protestant theology and biblical scholarship, see Gösta Lundström, *The Kingdom of God in the Teaching of Jesus: A History of Interpretation from the Last Decades of the Nineteenth Century to the Present Day*, trans. J. Bulman (Edinburgh: Oliver & Boyd, 1963); Norman Perrin, *The Kingdom of God in the Teaching of Jesus* (Philadelphia: Westminster, 1963); George Eldon Ladd, *The Presence of the Future: The Eschatology of Biblical Realism* (Grand Rapids, MI: Eerdmans, 1964), 3–42; George Eldon Ladd, *A Theology of the New Testament* (Grand Rapids, MI: Eerdmans, 1974), 54–67; and Mark Saucy, *The Kingdom of God in the Teaching of Jesus in Twentieth-Century Theology* (Dallas: Word, 1997). Reformed theologian Louis Berkhof traced the "new emphasis" on the kingdom of God from Immanuel Kant through Friedrich Schleiermacher to the contemporary scene of theology and biblical scholarship, largely due to its popularization by Albrecht Ritschl.

did not come through joint manifestos, but through sustained theological reflection. Nor has the consensus come through a doctrinal cease-fire in order to skirt the issue of the relationship of the kingdom to the present mission of the people of God. Instead, it has come as both traditions have sought to relate their doctrinal distinctives to the overarching theme of the kingdom of God as an integrative motif for their respective systems.

Thus, the move toward an evangelical kingdom theology is not simply the construction of a broad, comprehensive center for evangelical theological reflection. As the kingdom idea has been explored within evangelical theology, and within the subtraditions of dispensationalism and covenantalism, specific points of contention have been addressed, especially in terms of the way in which the kingdom concept relates to the consummation of all things, the salvation of the world, and the mission of the church. In so doing, this emerging kingdom theology addresses the very same stumbling blocks to an evangelical witness in the public square that were once identified as the roots of conservative Christianity's "uneasy conscience."

THE KINGDOM, SOCIAL ETHICS, AND ESCHATOLOGY

It is not much of an overstatement to say that Carl F. H. Henry's *The Uneasy Conscience of Modern Fundamentalism* is first and foremost a tract on eschatology. In it, Henry tried to triangulate theologically between the kingdom eschatologies of the social-gospel left and the fundamentalist right. It would be a mistake to assume that Henry considered the two eschatological positions to be equal and opposite errors.

Instead, he pointedly asserted that Protestant liberalism had more than a troubled conscience, and had in fact abandoned the gospel itself.[19] For Henry, the challenge for conservative Protestants was somehow to synthesize theologically the relationship between the biblical

---

[19] This is not the only time that Henry would make clear that he did not equate the errors of fundamentalism with the errors of liberalism. Henry corresponded with Billy Graham in June of 1950 with reservations about whether Henry would be the best choice for the editorship of *Christianity Today* because of his firm convictions on this very matter. "I was convinced that liberalism and evangelicalism do not have equal right and dignity in the true church." Carl F. H. Henry, *Confessions of a Theologian* (Waco, TX: Word, 1986), 142. "It is quite popular at the moment to crucify the fundamentalist," he wrote earlier. "That is not the object of this series of articles; there is no sympathy here for the distorted attack on fundamentalism so often pressed by liberals and humanists. . . . The fundamentalist is placed on the cross, while the liberal goes scot-free in a forest of weasel words." Henry, *Uneasy Conscience*, 60–61.

teachings on the "kingdom then" of the future, visible reign of Christ and the "kingdom now" of the present, spiritual reign of Christ. Until this matter could be theologically resolved, Henry believed, evangelical eschatology would remain kindling for the fires of a troubled social conscience.

In the background of fundamentalist eschatological pronouncements stood the ghost of Walter Rauschenbusch. With a full ballast of "kingdom now" rhetoric, for example, Rauschenbusch had called upon socialist organizers in the United States to welcome Christians into their ranks for the good of a common effort to "Christianize the social order."[20] Rauschenbusch employed the language of Christian eschatology, even of millennialism, to the no small controversy within his own Northern Baptist ranks.[21] He redefined, however, the prophetic hope of a "millennium" to mean an imminent possibility of a kingdom of social justice in the present age.[22] It was this view of the present reality of the kingdom, Henry argued, that had led to the fundamentalist eschatological backlash that lay behind the "uneasy conscience." Fundamentalist political isolationism was, at least in one sense, an attempt to defend the future hope of the kingdom from antisupernaturalism of the modernists. Henry may have warned evangelicals that they had overreacted, but he did not tell them their fears had been unfounded.[23] This was true especially in the area of eschatology.

Nonetheless, *Uneasy Conscience* pressed the claim that fundamen-

---

[20] Rauschenbusch wrote: "Why should they erect a barbwire fence between the field of Socialism and Christianity which makes it hard to pass from one to the other? Organized Christianity represents the largest fund of sobriety, moral health, good will, moral aspiration, teaching ability, and capacity to sacrifice for higher ends, which can be found in America. If Socialists will count up the writers, lecturers, and organizers who acquired their power of agitation and moral appeal through the training they got in church life, they will realize what an equipment for propaganda lies stored in the Christian churches." Walter Rauschenbusch, *Christianizing the Social Order* (New York: Macmillan, 1912), 398–99.

[21] See, e.g., the discussion of Rauschenbusch's debate with premillennialist critic James Willmarth, an influential Northern Baptist pastor, in Philadelphia. Paul M. Minus, *Walter Rauschenbusch: American Reformer* (New York: Macmillan, 1988), 90–91.

[22] Rauschenbusch argued therefore: "Our chief interest in any millennium is the desire for a social order in which the worth and freedom of every least human being will be honored and protected; in which the brotherhood of man will be expressed in the common possession of economic resources of society; and in which the spiritual good of humanity will be set high above the private profit interests of all materialistic groups. We hope for such an order for humanity as we hope for heaven for ourselves." Rauschenbusch, *A Theology for the Social Gospel*, 224.

[23] Forty years after the publication of *Uneasy Conscience*, Henry explained: "I had no inclination whatever to commend the modernist agenda, for its soft and sentimental theology could not sustain its 'millennial fanaticism.' Discarding historic doctrinal convictions and moving in the direction of liberalism would not revitalize fundamentalism." Carl F. H. Henry, *Twilight of a Great Civilization: The Drift Toward Neo-Paganism* (Westchester, IL: Crossway, 1988), 165.

talists had overreacted as they tried to avoid the "tendency to identify the kingdom with any present social order, however modified in
a democratic or communistic direction."[24] In so doing, however, the
fundamentalists had strictly relegated the kingdom to the age to come,
thereby cutting off its relevance to contemporary sociopolitical concerns. Moreover, Henry complained, fundamentalism's pessimistic view
of history informed by dispensationalist eschatology fueled an attitude
of "protest against foredoomed failure."[25] Fundamentalism "in revolt-
ing against the Social Gospel seemed also to revolt against the Christian
social imperative," he argued. "It was the failure of fundamentalism to
work out a positive message within its own framework, and its tendency
instead to take further refuge in a despairing view of world history that
cut off the pertinence of evangelicalism to the modern global crisis."[26]

The result, Henry concluded, was that "non-evangelical spokes-
men" were left to pick up the task of sociopolitical reflection "in a
non-redemptive context."[27] Henry did not level all the blame for this
otherworldly flight from the public square on fundamentalist dispensationalism, but he did suggest that dispensationalism carried a dispro-
portionate share of the blame, both in terms of political engagement
and personal ethics.[28]

Henry proposed that fundamentalists did not need to co-opt the
social-gospel vision of the kingdom in order to answer the social and
political dilemmas they faced. Instead, he argued that the postwar evangelical renaissance should capitalize on the theological strengths of both
its premillennial and its amillennial eschatologies. He viewed both
groups as the inheritors of the evangelical eschatological task following

---

[24] Henry, *Uneasy Conscience*, 49.

[25] Ibid., 26.

[26] Ibid., 32.

[27] Ibid.

[28] Thus, Henry explained: "Dispensational theology resisted the dismissal of biblical eschatology and its import for ethics. But in its extreme forms it also evaporates the present-day relevance of much of the ethics of Jesus. Eschatology is invoked to postpone the significance of the Sermon and other segments of New Testament moral teaching to a later Kingdom age. Dispensationalism erects a cleavage in biblical ethics in the interest of debatable eschatological theory. Dispensationalism holds that Christ's Kingdom has been postponed until the end of the Church age, and that Kingdom-ethics will become dramatically relevant again only in the future eschatological era. Liberalism destroyed biblical eschatology and secularized Christian ethics; and the interim ethic school abandoned the literal relevance of Jesus' eschatology and ethics alike; and extreme dispensationalism holds literally to both eschatology and ethics, but moves both into the future. New Testament theology will not sustain this radical repudiation of any present form of the Kingdom of heaven." Carl F. H. Henry, *Christian Personal Ethics* (Grand Rapids, MI: Eerdmans, 1957), 550–51.

the dissipation of postmillennialism, even the more orthodox strands held by relatively evangelical theologians such as James Orr.

Henry argued that evangelical eschatology had the responsibility to provide a biblical and theological alternative to the utopian visions of both evolutionary secularism and Protestant liberalism.[29] Thus, Henry's *Uneasy Conscience* did more than sound the alarm that fundamentalists had neglected "kingdom now" preaching. Henry also indicted fundamentalists for abandoning "kingdom then" preaching. It was not only that fundamentalists were too future oriented to care about sociopolitical engagement, but also that, in the most important ways, they were not future oriented enough. Henry focused the key reason for this "apprehension over *kingdom then* preaching" on what he considered to be the overheated zeal of the earlier generations of dispensationalist popularizers. It was true, Henry asserted, that World War II had demolished the postmillennial predictions of a "Christian century" of world peace and harmony. But the war had demolished just as surely the prophetic predictions of a revived Roman Empire, along with various efforts to identify the Antichrist on the world scene.[30]

Having diagnosed the eschatological impediments to a theology of evangelical engagement, Henry reassured evangelicals that his purpose in *Uneasy Conscience* was not "to project any new kingdom theory; exegetical novelty so late in church history may well be suspect."[31] It would seem, however, that a "new" (at least for American evangelicals) kingdom theology was precisely what he was proposing. In calling on evangelicals to abandon the extremes of the social gospel and fundamentalist withdrawal, Henry simultaneously exhorted evangelical

---

[29] And so he argued: "In the aftermath of the second World War, evangelical postmillennialism almost wholly abandoned the field of kingdom preaching to premillennialism and amillennialism, united in the common conviction that the return of Christ is a prerequisite for the future golden age, but divided over whether it will involve an earthly millennium. Assured of the ultimate triumph of right, contemporary evangelicalism also avoids a minimizing of earthly hostility to the gospel, as well as rejects the naturalistic optimism centering in evolutionary automatic progress. The bright hope of the imminent return of Christ is not minimized, and the kingdom hope is clearly distinguishable from the liberal confidence in a new social order of human making only." Henry, *Uneasy Conscience*, 134.

[30] Ibid., 50.

[31] Henry charged, therefore: "The fact that the West surrendered the radical biblical judgment on history and took Hegel and Darwin rather than Jesus and Paul as its guides, and substituted the optimistic 'social gospel' for the redemptive good news, opened this door for a radical critique of the social order from the Marxist rather than Christian sources. There was plenty to criticize in the sphere of economics a century ago, even as there is today, even if the Marxists overstate and distort the situation. Christianity holds out no hope for the achievement of absolute economic and social righteousness in present history." Henry, *Uneasy Conscience*, 52.

theology to underpin their eschatological convictions with a broader understanding of the kingdom of God. He contrasted the kingdom reticence of American evangelicals with the kingdom exuberance of the apostolic witness of the New Testament. "The apostolic view of the kingdom should likewise be definitive for contemporary evangelicalism," Henry asserted. "There does not seem much apostolic apprehension over kingdom preaching."[32]

For Henry, this would mean that evangelical theology would have to recognize the centrality of the kingdom message to the New Testament and adapt both their elaborate prophecy timetables and their reluctance to proclaim a present role for the kingdom of God to it. This is because, Henry counseled, "no subject was more frequently on the lips of Jesus Christ than the kingdom."[33] And so, Henry maintained, evangelical theology must deal with the biblical data, which seems to indicate a kingdom that has already been inaugurated and yet awaits a future consummation.[34] "No study of the kingdom teaching of Jesus is adequate unless it recognizes His implication both that the kingdom is here and that it is not here."[35]

In other words, it is not simply the kingdom theme that speaks to sociopolitical realities. It is also the way in which the Scripture speaks of the kingdom as both present and future. Thus, Jesus confronts the political authorities in passages such as Matthew 26:63–64 by quoting the "not yet" messianic kingdom references of Daniel 7 while submitting in the "already" to crucifixion, all the while maintaining that the political powers are temporal and derivative in authority. Jesus's words to "render to Caesar" are almost immediately put to the test in the early church as Christ-appointed apostles are indicted for acting "against the decrees of Caesar, saying that there is another king, Jesus" (Acts 17:7). Jesus speaks of the kingdom "in the midst of you" (Luke 17:20–21), that it is given not only to him but to his followers (Luke 22:29), while

---

[32] Ibid., 53.

[33] Henry argued: "He proclaimed kingdom truth with a constant, exuberant joy. It appears as the central theme of His preaching. To delete His kingdom references, parabolic and non-parabolic, would be to excise most of His words. The concept 'kingdom of God' or 'kingdom of heaven' is heard repeatedly from His lips, and it colors all of His works." Ibid., 52.

[34] For evidence of this reality in the New Testament, Henry surveyed the preaching of the apostles in Acts, the references both to a present manifestation of the kingdom and to a future consummation in the epistles of Paul and the writer of Hebrews, and the Apocalypse of John.

[35] Henry, *Uneasy Conscience*, 53.

the apostle Paul mocks the Corinthian followers of Jesus for thinking themselves to be "kings" already (1 Cor. 4:8). The writer of Hebrews contrasts the "not yet" of all things in subjection to Christ with the "already" of his incarnation and atonement (Heb. 2:5–18).

In grappling with these biblical realities, the task of constructing an evangelical theology of sociopolitical engagement has been greatly aided by a growing consensus that evangelical eschatology must focus first not on the sound and fury of millennial meanings but on the invasion of the eschatological, Davidic kingdom into the present age, thus dividing bringing the eschaton into the history of the world in the person of Jesus of Nazareth. By advocating an "already/not yet" model of this fulfillment, evangelical eschatology faces the challenge of integrating these interpretive issues into an understanding of how the present/future reign of Christ impacts contemporary problems of social and political concern.

For Henry, then, a kingdom-oriented, inaugurated eschatology can inform evangelicalism by reminding the movement that all secularist and evolutionary models of utopian progress have "borrowed the biblical doctrine of the coming kingdom of God but cannibalized it."[36] Any theology of evangelical engagement needs such an emphasis so that future generations may recognize, as did Karl Barth and his theologian colleagues in the face of the Third Reich, these "cannibalized" kingdom theologies when they rear their heads.[37]

At the same time, it tempers evangelical theology's temptation to "cannibalize" the kingdom for its own ends. With the adoption of inaugurated eschatology, rooted in an overall commitment to a kingdom-focused theology, evangelicalism has in many ways provided the foundation for the kind of "third way" ethic of sociopolitical engagement that Henry and others were seeking to define against mainline triumphalism and fundamentalist isolationism in the postwar era. In short, the commitment to an "already" of the kingdom protects against

---

[36] Carl F. H. Henry, *Gods of This Age or God of the Ages?* (Nashville: Broadman, 1994), 81.
[37] Barth and his colleagues struggled against the Nazi regime precisely because the "German Christian" movement attempted to recast German identity and historical progress with the kingdom of God. Against this, the confessing church maintained the sole and unrivaled place of Christ as the head of his kingdom. For an analysis, see Rolf Ahlers, *The Barmen Theological Declaration of 1934: The Archaeology of a Confessional Text* (Lewiston, NY: Edwin Mellen, 1986).

an otherworldly flight from political and social responsibility, while the "not yet" chastens the prospects of such activity.

The inaugurated eschatological view of the kingdom that has gained consensus thus addresses the concerns laid out by the postwar evangelical movement, especially in Henry's *Uneasy Conscience*, and provides a starting point for evangelical theological reflection on the relationship between the kingdoms of this temporal age and the eschatological kingdom of God in Christ. Furthermore, this view of inaugurated eschatology has provided the foundation for reexamining some of the implications of two other points of theological and political controversy for the postwar evangelical movement, namely, the doctrines of salvation and the church.

THE KINGDOM, SOCIAL ETHICS, AND SOTERIOLOGY

From the publication of *Uneasy Conscience* and throughout the formative years of postwar evangelicalism, Henry and his allies maintained that an evangelical concern for social and political structures is not, in fact, the first step toward social-gospel modernism. "If evangelicals came to stress evangelism over social concern, it was because of liberalism's skepticism over supernatural redemptive dynamisms and its pursuit of the kingdom of God by sociological techniques only," Henry framed the debate in retrospect. "Hence a sharp and costly disjunction arose, whereby many evangelicals made the mistake of relying on evangelism alone to preserve world order and many liberals made the mistake of relying wholly on sociopolitical action to solve world problems."[38]

The evangelical dilemma over the relationship of redemption to sociopolitical engagement, however, was about more than the priorities given to personal regeneration and public justice. It was more about differing understandings of the present and future realities of the kingdom of God. As such, the question of relating evangelical soteriology to evangelical engagement was interrelated with the prior question of evangelical eschatology.

This was, Henry maintained, a problem of kingdom definition. "The

---

[38] Carl F. H. Henry, "Evangelicals in the Social Struggle," in *Salt and Light: Evangelical Political Thought in Modern America*, ed. Augustus Cerillo Jr. and Murray W. Dempster (Grand Rapids, MI: Baker, 1989), 31.

globe-changing passion of the modern reformers who operate without a biblical context is, from this vantage point, an ignoring of Jesus' insistence that 'all these things shall be added' only after man has sought first 'the kingdom of God and His righteousness,'" Henry charged, citing Matthew 6:33. "Non-evangelicals tend to equate 'kingdom' and 'these things,' reflecting a blindness to the significance of the vicarious atonement of Christ."[39] Thus, Henry contended, the social gospel could not construct a biblical, kingdom-oriented soteriology because of its Hegelian, evolutionary view of the kingdom.[40] It likewise needed an optimistic view of humanity in order to justify the immanence of the kingdom in the historical process.[41] Moreover, Protestant liberalism desperately sought to replace penal substitutionary atonement with social justice primarily because of the social gospel's prior eschatological commitments to a kingdom without a Christ.[42]

Likewise, Henry found the fundamentalist dismissal of the relevance of social and political engagement as a hindrance to the priority of personal evangelism to be a similar issue of kingdom definition. American conservative Protestantism's social and political isolationism reflected its essentially otherworldly view of the kingdom of God, resulting in a view of salvation that concentrated almost solely on the rescue of souls from the imminent cataclysmic world judgment.[43] Henry was in essential agreement with this priority of personal evangelism because this soteriology sought to recognize the Christocentric nature of the biblical kingdom of God.[44] Even so, Henry indicted the otherworldly soteriology of the fundamentalist right for failing to

---

[39] Henry, *Uneasy Conscience*, 27–28.

[40] "Infected with Hegelian speculation Protestant liberalism not only surrendered the Biblical redemptive-regenerative view of man and the world to optimistic evolutionary expectations about the future, but also lost all transcendent and eschatological elements of the Kingdom of God," Henry asserted. "It promulgated, rather, a wholly immanent and essentially politico-economic conception of the Kingdom." Henry, *Plea for Evangelical Demonstration*, 117.

[41] Henry complained that for those who "shared the glow of Dean Shailer Mathews' prospect for a better world," the fundamentalists "who stood with the Hebrew-Christian tradition in a more pessimistic view of contemporary culture were accused of not having any social program." In fact, Henry countered, many of these fundamentalists did indeed have no social program, "though modernism was unjustified in assuming they could have none since they were not optimistic about man." Henry, *Remaking the Modern Mind*, 41.

[42] Henry, *Plea for Evangelical Demonstration*, 92.

[43] Henry, *Evangelicals at the Brink of Crisis*, 68.

[44] "The evangelical vision of the new society, or the Kingdom on earth, is therefore messianic, and is tied to the expectation of the return of Christ in glory," Henry concluded. "It is distrustful of world power, of attempts to derive a just society from unregenerate human nature. And this verdict on human affairs is fully supportive of the biblical verdict on fallen history." Ibid.

take into account the holistic fabric of the biblical portrayal of the messianic accomplishment of salvation. If personal salvation means a transfer into the kingdom (present, future, or already/not yet), then the content of the kingdom must inform the redemptive priorities of Christianity. Indeed, Henry noted, the very idea of the kingdom of God, especially given its centrality in the gospel proclamation of Jesus, means that the kingdom has "a social aspect, as well as an individual aspect" since "redemption is nothing if it is not an ethical redemption, and as such it comprehends more than the restoration of the individual to the image of God."[45]

In the more than fifty years since Henry's jeremiad, evangelical theology has assembled a near consensus on the view that salvation is to be related to the broader picture of the kingdom of God and thus must be conceived from a holistic vantage point, not limited to the individualistic, pietistic, and otherworldly notions of much of earlier fundamentalist revivalism. This consensus soteriology in many cases has grown out of, and has been linked to, the growing evangelical consensus on the inaugurated nature of eschatology. Like the eschatological consensus, it has been articulated both by traditionalist evangelicals on the right and reformist evangelicals on the left of the ideological spectrum of the movement.

Indeed, contemporary evangelical theology must recognize that attention to the doctrinal content of soteriology is the first priority in any effort at a pan-evangelical witness in the social and political arenas. As Henry argued in the 1960s, a reprioritization or redefinition of the evangelistic message of Christian theology skews the very nature of Christian public witness because the evangelical gospel of a forensic justification based on the alien righteousness and substitutionary sacrifice of Christ maintains the centrality of justice in the order of the universe. Henry is largely correct in this emphasis since, as he recognized, a government committed to justice unintentionally aids the church's evangelistic task by inculcating into the culture the importance of justice, righteousness, and certain judgment, thus preparing the way, as it were, for the conviction of sin through the proclamation of the

---

[45] Henry, *Christian Personal Ethics*, 234.

kerygma.[46] Henry's point is bolstered in light of the impact of a social-gospel Protestant liberalism that sought to redefine both the atonement and public philosophy in terms of the centrality of love rather than the centrality of justice.[47]

In examining the philosophically troublesome "love ethic" of American liberalism, Henry rightly tied the sociopolitical difficulties to prior soteriological concessions:

> To misstate the biblical view of the equal status of righteousness and love in God's being brings only continuing problems in dogmatics. Redemption soon loses its voluntary character as divine election and becomes an inevitable if not necessary divine provision. Discussion of Christ's death and atonement in modernism is uncomfortable in the presence of such themes as satisfaction and propitiation. Future punishment of the wicked is revised to conform to benevolent rather than punitive motivations, and hell is emptied of its terrors by man-made theories of universal salvation. The state is no longer dedicated to justice and order, encouraging and enforcing human rights and responsibilities under God, but is benevolently bent toward people's socio-economic wants.[48]

Much of the so-called emerging church is recovering Henry's understanding of the kingdom—a holistic salvation in which social ministry is part of the church's larger task of announcing the reign of Jesus. There are elements of the left wing of the movement, however, that have moved beyond Henry to a recapitulation of the old social gospel. The same could be said of some elements of the right wing of American evangelicalism, whenever it is animated by political concerns rather than by the gospel. A decisive stance on the core issues of the Christian gospel, as Henry warned mid-century, will be the key to keeping evangelical engagement both evangelical and engaged.[49]

---

[46] Henry, *Aspects of Christian Social Ethics*, 94–95.

[47] This thus necessitated the neoorthodox critique of liberal Christian social and political ethics, chiefly in the person of Reinhold Niebuhr.

[48] Henry, *Aspects of Christian Social Ethics*, 169.

[49] Henry brilliantly noted this truth when he asserted in the antiauthoritarian tumult of the 1960s: "Those who know that God deals with men justly and not arbitrarily, and who also have a share in the justification that reinforces His justice in the grace of Golgotha, stand today at the crossroads of a crisis in modern

The key to understanding this kind of kingdom-oriented salvation is a developed christology that takes into account the unity of Christ's person and work along with an eschatology that sees both a present and future element to the reign of Christ. Thus, evangelical theology has grappled with, and come to some consensus on, the relationship between salvation and the kingdom, and the relationship of both to the social and political task of the regenerate community. Because Christ is simultaneously the covenant God who pledged to create a people for himself and the anointed ruler of that people, the Messiah offers a salvation that cannot be truncated into bare spiritual blessings in one dispensation or mere political authority in another. Therefore, although the church does not yet wield political authority over the nations, it must recognize that the redemption it offers has a social and political element that is intrinsically tied to the gospel itself. Matters of sociopolitical engagement cannot therefore be dismissed or reformulated as "unspiritual" or irrelevant to present kingdom activity. If the kingdom is to be understood as having a present reality, and that reality is essentially soteriological, then the kingdom agenda of evangelical theology must focus on the biblical fulcrum of these eschatological, salvific blessings: the church.

SOCIAL ETHICS AND ECCLESIOLOGY

Henry recognized that a sustainable theology of evangelical engagement could not be achieved without some form of consensus on the church. The new evangelical concern over the doctrine of the church was inextricably linked to related soteriological concerns. It was not simply that the denominational church structures had neglected preaching the gospel of individual salvation that galled conservative Protestants. It was also that the liberals had succeeded in turning the denominations into the equivalent of political action committees, addressing a laundry list of social and political issues.[50] The problem with the social-gospel

---

civilization. If they find vision for our day, they can put the world on notice regarding God's claim in creation and redemption, by calling men everywhere to behold anew the demand for justice and the need for justification." Henry, *Evangelicals at the Brink of Crisis*, 72.

[50] Thus, the rationale for the formation of a National Association of Evangelicals as an orthodox alternative to the ecumenical Federal Council of Churches included the particular complaint about the FCC: "It indicated both in pronouncements and practice that it considered man's need and not God's grace as the impelling motive to Christian action and that the amelioration of the social order is of primary concern to

ecclesiology, Henry concluded, was the same anti-supernaturalism that destroyed its soteriology; Protestant liberalism had replaced a regenerate church over which the resurrected Messiah ruled as head with a largely unregenerate visible church.[51] Henry thereby tied the liberal Protestant view of the church and political action directly to a theologically problematic view of salvation, a "neo-Protestant view" that "substitutes the notion of corporate salvation for individual salvation."[52] Thus, even while maintaining the need for individual action in the public square, Henry maintained that the endless political pronouncements of the churches were an affront to the purpose of the church. "The Church as a corporate body has no spiritual mandate to sponsor economic, social, and political programs," he argued in the midst of the omnipolitical 1960s. "Nowhere does the New Testament authorize the Church to endorse specific legislative proposals as part of its ecclesiastical mission in the world."[53] In so doing, Henry pointed out the irony of church officials' proclaiming the certitudes of redemption with less and less certainty while simultaneously making sociopolitical statements that seemed to come with their own self-attesting authority.

At the same time, Henry denied that this position was inconsistent with his call for evangelicals to move beyond the "uneasy conscience" toward a holistic view of redemption and the responsibility toward society. "We do not support the position that the Christian's only concern is the saving of men's souls and that, for the rest, he may abandon the world to the power of evil," he wrote. "Nor do we deny the Church's scriptural right through the pulpit and through its synods,

---

the Church. In this connection it attacked capitalism, condoned communism and lent its influence toward the creation of a new social order." James DeForest Murch, *Cooperation without Compromise: A History of the National Association of Evangelicals* (Grand Rapids, MI: Eerdmans, 1956), 47.

[51] "Insofar as the professing Church is unregenerate and hence a stranger to the power of true love, it should surprise no one that it conceives its mission to be the Christianizing of the world rather than the evangelizing of mankind, and that it relies on other than supernatural dynamic for its mission in the world," Henry noted. "Even ecclesiastical leaders cannot rely on a power they have never experienced." Henry, *The God Who Shows Himself* (Waco, TX: Word, 1966), 15.

[52] Henry, *Evangelicals at the Brink of Crisis*, 74. Henry therefore summed up the defective political ecclesiology of the Protestant left by noting: "The authentic mission of the church is thus asserted to be that of changing the structures of society and not that of winning individual converts to Christ as the means of renewing society. The 'gospel' is said to be addressed not to individuals but to the community. This theory is connected with a further assumption, that individuals as such are not lost in the traditional sense, and that the mission of the Church in the world is therefore no longer to be viewed as the regeneration of a doomed world, but the Church is rather to use the secular structures (political, economic, and cultural) as already on the way to fulfillment of God's will in Christ." Ibid., 74–75.

[53] Carl F. H. Henry, "The Church and Political Pronouncements," *Christianity Today*, August 28, 1964, 29.

assemblies and councils to emphasize the divinely revealed principles of a social order and to speak out publicly against the great moral evils that arise in community life."[54] Still, finding an alternative to the politicized churchmanship of the Protestant left was increasingly difficult for a transdenominational evangelical movement. Evangelicals across the United States did indeed have an identity, Henry editorialized in *Christianity Today*, because their "common ground is belief in biblical authority and in individual spiritual regeneration as being of the very essence of Christianity."[55] Nonetheless, he warned, this common ground was "crisscrossed by many fences" since evangelicals "differ not only on secondary issues but also on ecclesiology, the role of the Church in society, politics, and cultural mores."[56]

From Henry's vantage point, a retarded ecclesiology was an inheritance from fundamentalism, a vestige that evangelicals must address if they were to emerge from "Amish evangelicalism" and provide an alternative to the Protestant mainline. In short, the lack of a coherent evangelical ecclesiology meant the lack of a cohesive evangelical movement.[57] Long after the postwar era, Henry reflected that "the Jesus movement, the Chicago Declaration of young evangelicals, independent fundamentalist churches and even the so-called evangelical establishment, no less than the ecumenical movement which promoted structural church unity, all suffer a basic lack, namely a public identity as a 'people,' a conspicuously unified body of regenerate believers."[58]

With Henry, certain segments of the evangelical conscience were also a bit uneasy about its lack of a coherent understanding of the ecclesiology. Almost from the very beginning of the movement, some evangelicals worried that the parachurch nature of evangelicalism represented

---

[54] Ibid.
[55] Carl F. H. Henry, "Somehow, Let's Get Together!" *Christianity Today*, June 9, 1957, 24.
[56] Ibid.
[57] "Neglect of the doctrine of the Church, except in defining separation as a special area of concern, proved to be another vulnerable feature of the fundamentalist forces. This failure to elaborate the biblical doctrine of the Church comprehensively and convincingly not only contributes to the fragmenting spirit of the movement but actually hands the initiative to the ecumenical enterprise in defining the nature and relations of the churches. Whereas the ecumenical movement has busied itself with the question of the visible and invisible Church, the fundamentalist movement has often been preoccupied with distinguishing churches as vocal or silent against modernism." Carl F. H. Henry, *Evangelical Responsibility in Contemporary Theology* (Grand Rapids, MI: Eerdmans, 1957), 35.
[58] Carl F. H. Henry, *God, Revelation, and Authority*, vol. 1, *God Who Speaks and Shows: Preliminary Considerations* (Waco, TX: Word, 1976), 133.

a problematic individualism that reflected the culture of mid-century America more than the revealed imperatives of the first-century apostolic mandate.[59]

In calling evangelicals to a more theologically workable understanding of the role of the church in social and political engagement, Henry and his postwar evangelical colleagues faced the titanic task of more than simply resolving internecine differences over baptism, church government, and other ecclesiological issues, as daunting as that project alone would have been. Instead, postwar evangelical theology had to confront the question of the relationship between the church and the kingdom of God in order to differentiate their view of evangelical engagement from that of the social gospel and to guard against the isolationism of fundamentalism.

Henry argued that a kingdom theology of evangelical engagement was made necessary by the way in which the relationship between church and kingdom was delineated on both the left and the right of the spectrum of American Protestantism. This was especially true given the low view of the church assigned by the social gospel, in which the primary focus was not the regenerate community, but "the kingdom." Henry complained that this definition of the kingdom could not help but lead to politicized church structures because the "universalistic view that the social order is to be considered as a direct anticipation of the Kingdom of God, whose cosmic rescue and redemption is held to embrace the totality of mankind, regards Christians as the vanguard of a New Society to be achieved through politico-economic dynamisms."[60]

Thus, Henry concluded, conservative Protestantism's lack of an ecclesiological counterproposal had left the theological landscape with two politically problematic alternatives: Roman Catholicism and Protestant liberalism.[61] An evangelical alternative, however, was rendered

---

[59] Ironically, one of the early voices to address this problem was the editor of the Billy Graham Evangelistic Association's *Decision* magazine, Sherwood Wirt. Wirt feared that the evangelical movement's commitment to "the stance of the pristine rugged individualist" would undercut any call to evangelical public engagement. Redemption could not be merely about rescuing individuals, Wirt maintained, but instead meant the creation of a new community, the church. Sherwood Eliot Wirt, *The Social Conscience of the Evangelical* (New York: Harper & Row, 1968), 76, 149.

[60] Henry, *Evangelicals at the Brink of Crisis*, 75.

[61] "Today the wrong understanding of the Christian view of the State is compounded both by the Roman Catholic theory of union of Church and State and the Protestant liberal attempt to spawn the Kingdom of God as an earthly politico-economic development. Neither scheme has escaped the notice of totalitarian

almost impossible by the evangelical debate over the nature of the kingdom. Henry especially fingered the dispensational stream of fundamentalist theology at this point. The construction of an evangelical theology of the role of the church in the world was hindered, Henry concluded, since dispensational ecclesiology virtually severed the New Testament *ekklesia* from the kingdom purposes. This was the result, he explained, of the dispensationalist "postponement theory" in which Jesus's Davidic reign is rejected by the nation of Israel at his first advent. "As a consequence, the divine plan during this church age is concerned, it is said, only with 'calling out' believers," Henry noted. "This theory has gained wide support in the north during the past two generations; many persons automatically identify it not only with all premillennialism, but with all fundamentalism."[62]

Nonetheless, Henry was not therefore resigned to a Reformed position that would see the kingdom simply in terms of the spiritual blessings offered through the church.[63] In the place of these two options, he called for an evangelical ecclesiological appropriation of inaugurated eschatology. In terms of an evangelical doctrine of the church, he argued, the teachings of Jesus must be highlighted, "both that the kingdom is here, and that it is not here."[64]

For Henry, the doctrine of the church is the fulcrum in which eschatology and soteriology meet in the kingdom purposes of God. As such, a kingdom-oriented ecclesiology would be essential to the development of a theology of evangelical engagement. Therefore, the doctrine of the church must be understood biblically in terms of the redemptive progress of the kingdom and the inaugurated reign of Christ over the regenerate community.[65] Only a kingdom-oriented ecclesiology, he argued, could rescue Christianity from the unbiblical and unbalanced futurism he called them to discard.[66]

---

rulers who want to manipulate the Church for their own political objectives." Henry, *Aspects of Christian Social Ethics*, 83.

[62] Henry, *Uneasy Conscience*, 52.

[63] Ibid., 53.

[64] Ibid.

[65] "From his throne in the eternal order the Living Head mediated to the Body an earnest of the powers that belong to the age to come." Henry, *Aspects of Christian Social Ethics*, 28.

[66] So Henry wrote: "Christ founded neither a party of revolutionaries, nor a movement of reformers, nor a remnant of reevaluators. He 'called out a people.' The twice-born fellowship of his redeemed Church, in vital company with its Lord, alone mirrored the realities of the new social order. This new order was

This effort toward a kingdom ecclesiology is seen explicitly in the later, systematic writings of Carl Henry.[67] Henry's later work sketches out an incipient ecclesiology, though such seems to be constructed largely as a series of ad hoc responses to specific issues troubling the evangelical movement and its interaction with rival cognitive systems. Whereas Henry's early statements on the church seem to focus on the political relationships of the church contra the claims of politicized ecumenicalism, the later, more systematic treatment does so contra the claims of liberation theology and other revolutionary movements. As such, Henry self-consciously developed his ecclesiology within the context of his commitments to inaugurated eschatology and holistic soteriology. "When Christianity discusses the new society it speaks not of some intangible future reality whose specific features it cannot as yet identify, but of the regenerate church called to live by the standards of the coming King and which in some respects already approximates the kingdom of God in present history," Henry asserted.[68]

Therefore, he concluded, a distinctively evangelical view of the church emerges from a prior commitment to kingdom theology.[69] With such the case, Henry emphasized that neither personal redemption nor inaugurated eschatology can be understood without a concept of the church as an initial manifestation of the kingdom of God, the focus of the "already" of the kingdom in the present age.[70]

And yet, as many even among Henry's most ardent supporters admit, the plastic nature of the parachurch coalition he envisioned spelled the

---

no mere distant dream, waiting for the proletariat to triumph, or the evolutionary process to reach its pinnacle or truth to win its circuitous way throughout the world. In a promissory way the new order had come *already* in Jesus Christ and in the regenerate fellowship of his Church. The Lord was ascended; he reigned over all. Hence the apostolic church would not yield to other rulers or other social visions." Ibid.

[67] This is ironic given the relatively scant attention given by Henry to the doctrine of the church and the criticism he has received from more confessional evangelicals at this very point. For an analysis of this, specifically in light of Henry's contribution to Baptist ecclesiology, see Russell D. Moore, "God, Revelation, and Community: Ecclesiology and Baptist Identity in the Thought of Carl F. H. Henry," *Southern Baptist Journal of Theology* 8/4 (2004): 26–43.

[68] Carl F. H. Henry, *God, Revelation, and Authority*, vol. 4, *God Who Speaks and Shows, Fifteen Theses, Part 3* (Waco, TX: Word, 1979), 522.

[69] "Marxist exegesis is notably vague in stating what precise form the socialist utopia is to take, and where in history it has been concretely realized. Radical neo-Protestant theologians needlessly accommodate much of this Marxist obscurity over the new man and the new society. For they fail to identify Jesus Christ as the ideal man, fail to emphasize the new covenant that Scripture associates with messianic fulfillment and fail to center the content of the new society in the regenerate church's reflection of the kingdom of God." Ibid.

[70] The role of the church as covenant community, therefore, "is not to forcibly demote alien powers" but "to demonstrate what it means to live in ultimate loyalty not to worldly powers but to the risen Lord in a corporate life of truth, righteousness, and mercy." Ibid., 529.

doom of the evangelical "movement" itself.[71] This is seen in the fact that Henry's theological and apologetic legacy is maintained, not within the broad mainstream of parachurch evangelicalism, but instead within the conservative wing of the Southern Baptist Convention, whose commitment to "denominational distinctives" would no doubt have been labeled "sectarian" by the early evangelical theologians, Henry included. "It would not be going too far to say that Henry has been a mentor for nearly the whole SBC conservative movement," observes one historian, citing Henry's influence on Baptist conservatives such as R. Albert Mohler Jr., Richard Land, and Mark T. Coppenger.[72] When Henry's *God, Revelation, and Authority* volumes were republished near the end of the twentieth century, it was the result of cooperative efforts between an evangelical publisher and a think tank led by confessional Southern Baptists.[73]

A confessional evangelicalism, informed at crucial points by Henry's theological contributions, therefore, must confront an evangelical left that is now even more "parachurch" than Henry and his postwar colleagues. With this "uneasy conscience" of evangelical ecclesiology, the renewed attention to the doctrine of the church offered by the various expressions of kingdom theology should be welcomed. It is this problem that prompts theologians such as Richard Lints to suggest that the movement needs fewer "evangelical theologians" and more "Baptist theologians, Presbyterian theologians, and so on."[74]

The only structure that can cultivate the revelational atmosphere in which biblically ordered families can thrive is the church. It is this aspect

---

[71] R. Albert Mohler Jr., perhaps Henry's closest theological successor, cites Henry's goal to create "an international multi-denominational corps of scholars articulating conservative theology," and concludes that Henry emphasized the movement more than the church, thereby destabilizing the movement itself. R. Albert Mohler Jr., "Reformist Evangelicalism: A Center Without a Circumference," in *A Confessing Theology for Postmodern Times*, ed. Michael S. Horton (Wheaton, IL: Crossway, 2000), 133. John Muether, for instance, rightly notes that Henry's "indifference to ecclesiology and confessionalism may explain the failures of the evangelical movement, failures he so candidly describes." John Muether, "Contemporary Evangelicalism and the Triumph of the New School," *Westminster Theological Journal* 50 (1988): 342.
[72] Barry Hankins, "The Evangelical Accommodationism of Southern Baptist Convention Conservatives," *Baptist History and Heritage* 33 (1998): 59.
[73] This describes the 1999 collaboration between Crossway and the Carl F. H. Henry Institute for Evangelical Engagement of the Southern Baptist Theological Seminary. This is especially significant given Fuller Seminary's almost complete repudiation of the epistemological and apologetic contributions of Henry. See, e.g., the counterproposal on issues of theological prolegomena offered by Fuller Seminary philosopher Nancey Murphey, *Beyond Liberalism and Fundamentalism: How Modern and Postmodern Philosophy Set the Theological Agenda* (Valley Forge, PA: Trinity Press International, 1996).
[74] Richard Lints, *The Fabric of Theology: A Prolegomenon to Evangelical Theology* (Grand Rapids, MI: Eerdmans, 1993), 321.

of a claim to authority that likewise protects evangelical ecclesiology from the self-conscious sectarianism of communitarians such as Stanley Hauerwas. Carl Henry was correct in maintaining that the difference between an engaged evangelical ecclesiology and the post-liberal communitarian vision of the church is the nature of the truth.[75] The church's internal counterculture is not enough, Henry rightly asserted, if "truth—universally valid truth" is "a concern as vital to the Church's public involvement as are forgiveness, hope and peace."[76] Such resonates with a Protestant commitment to a New Testament teaching basing the community of the church on a prior commitment to prophetic/apostolic authority.[77]

This means, therefore, that evangelicals ought not abandon the public square for the sake of the church. This is precisely the isolationist stance described and denounced in Henry's *Uneasy Conscience*. Contrary to this position, the orientation of the church as a manifestation of the kingdom means that evangelicals cannot be concerned only about the "counterculture" of the churches, because the scope of the kingdom informs the scope of evangelical concern. As such, the concerns of the community itself at times require attention to matters of political concern, including electoral politics.[78] Some civil society theorists, and a traditionalist conservative political theorist, are right that culture informs politics and is therefore the more important of the two. Nonetheless, history bears out that treacherous cultural movements are given teeth through political processes.[79]

---

[75] It is this lack of an ability to articulate an objective moral standard that unravels the communitarian project. See, e.g., the devastating critique of theorists such as Amitai Etzioni in J. Budziszewski, "The Problem with Communitarianism," *First Things*, March 1995, 22–26.

[76] Carl F. H. Henry, "The Church in the World or the World in the Church? A Review Article," *Journal of the Evangelical Theological Society* 34 (1991): 382. Henry similarly devastates Hauerwas's claim to a distinction between the church and the world, when Hauerwas is unwilling to draw the distinction "between the faithful Church and the pseudo-church or apostate church." Ibid., 383. It would appear that Henry's critique of Hauerwas keeps in mind the similar problems with Rauschenbusch and the social gospel.

[77] Such that, for instance, the apostle Paul claims that "it is in the sight of God that we have been speaking in Christ, and all for your upbuilding, beloved" (2 Cor. 12:19). The issue of apostolic biblical authority is directly correlated to the structuring of the life of the community. This is consistent with the canonical witness. It is the authority of revelation that shapes and defines the Old Testament community (Ex. 19:5–6; Deut. 27:9; 29:13). Likewise, the New Testament *ekklesia* is built on the authoritative revelation of the identity of Jesus as the Messiah (Matt. 16:13–19).

[78] This means that a commitment to civil society generically, or to ecclesiology particularly, does not reduce the need for direct political engagement, a mistaken emphasis sometimes implied by civil society theorists. For a more balanced view, see Christopher Been, *The Necessity of Politics: Reclaiming American Public Life* (Chicago: University of Chicago Press, 1999).

[79] Thus William F. Buckley Jr. rightly warns: "Our principal afflictions are the result of ideology backed by the power of government. It takes government to translate individual vices into universal afflictions. It was government that translated *Mein Kampf* into concentration camps." William F. Buckley Jr., *Let Us Talk of Many Things: The Collected Speeches* (New York: Random House, 2000), 107.

At the same time, the developments toward a kingdom ecclesiology remind evangelicals of the limits of political activity. Political solutions are first implemented within the community of the local church. When political solutions are offered to the outside world, they must always be couched in language that recognizes the futility of cultural reform without personal regeneration and baptism into the body of Christ. The church, as a multinational Spirit-body, has been forbidden the power of the sword by the Son of David himself (John 18:11). The church, understanding its place in the kingdom program, cannot then proclaim itself or any national government to be a "new Israel" with the authority to enforce belief in Christ or any conformity to revealed religion.[80] It recognizes the inherent distinction between the church and the state. Realizing that the church is not the full consummation of the kingdom prevents the church from seizing the Constantinian sword, as did the application of Augustinian kingdom theology early in the history of the church.[81]

As evangelicals move toward a coherent kingdom ecclesiology, it becomes clearer that the church is inherently eschatological and soteriological. In an inaugurationist kingdom theology, the church is reminded that, as Henry argues, the people of God live "with renewable visas" on earth, even as they live out their heavenly citizenship in the counterculture of the church.[82] At the same time, every church building represents by its very existence a latent political challenge to the powers that be. Because the evangelical consensus at this point recognizes the church as an initial form of a coming global monarchy, they proclaim by their very presence on the landscape that the status quo will one day be shaken apart in one decisive act of sovereign authority. As such, the evangelical conscience remains always a bit "uneasy" even as it engages vigorously the social and political structures. This is because the

---

[80] As did some efforts at Puritan church/state alliances. For an analysis of this phenomenon, see Conrad Cherry, ed., *God's New Israel: Religious Interpretations of American Destiny*, rev. and exp. (Chapel Hill, NC: University of North Carolina Press, 1998). For a theological interpretation of the conflict between the political theories of Puritan New England with that of dissenter Roger Williams, see A. J. Beitzinger, *A History of American Political Thought* (New York: Dodd, Mead, 1972), 51–60.

[81] Michael J. Scanlon convincingly argues that it is Augustine's recapitulation of Cyprian's understanding of the church as the kingdom of Christ on earth that led to Charlemagne's appropriation of *The City of God* in the construction of the "Holy Roman Empire" and "the identification by medieval Christendom of the church with the kingdom of God." Michael J. Scanlon, "Eschatology," in *Augustine through the Ages: An Encyclopedia* (Grand Rapids, MI: Eerdmans, 1999), 317.

[82] Henry, "The Church in the World or the Word in the Church?," 383.

doctrine of the church is, after all, the concrete display of the already/ not yet of the kingdom. As such, it reminds evangelicals that although they are to submit to the governing authorities, they are claimed by no transient political entity but by a coming messianic kingdom, which they see even now breaking in around them through Spirit-propelled reconciliation, peace, and unity.

CONCLUSION

In the generation after Carl Henry, dispensationalist apocalyptic is still around. Prophecy teacher Tim LaHaye signed a contract for yet another series of end-times novels. And the evangelical market will buy them. The social gospel is also still with us—on the left and on the right— and so is the sectarian isolationist model—again on the left and on the right. Nonetheless, Carl Henry's integration of the kingdom of God with evangelical social ethics is more fruitful than ever.

The relevance of the kingdom of God for social ethics is assumed, even among evangelicals who disagree about the theological or practical particulars. Conservative evangelicals are not simply speaking to issues of personal morality or religious liberty but are addressing issues of the global AIDS crisis, orphan care, environmental protection, and human trafficking, as well as the questions of what expanding technologies mean for human nature and human flourishing. On the whole, such activism is not placed in opposition to gospel preaching but put in a context of the very kind of holistic redemption matrix Henry called for a half century ago. Evangelical Christianity is, in many places of the world—perhaps especially through the Pentecostal movements in Latin America and Africa—addressing the "uneasy conscience" of evangelicalism, and the "uneasy consciences" of unbelievers.

As evangelicals engage such issues, very few recall the role of Henry in building a framework for such activism in a kingdom understanding of eschatology, soteriology, and ecclesiology. In the long run, that doesn't matter. What matters is that evangelical Christianity embrace a kingdom vision that leads to the mystery of Christ and the love of his church. Along the way, we might do well to remember Dr. Henry's place in reminding us of Jesus's announcement of the kingdom, and that it was compelling.

Selected Bibliography

Henry, Carl F. H. *Pacific Garden Mission: A Doorway to Heaven*. Grand Rapids, MI: Zondervan, 1942.

———. *Successful Church Publicity: A Guidebook for Christian Publicists*. Grand Rapids, MI: Zondervan, 1943.

———. *Remaking the Modern Mind*. Grand Rapids, MI: Eerdmans, 1946.

———. *Such as I Have: The Stewardship of Talent*. New York: Abingdon-Cokesbury, 1946.

———. *The Uneasy Conscience of Modern Fundamentalism*. Grand Rapids, MI: Eerdmans, 1947.

Henry, Carl F. H., and R. L. Decker, eds. *Evangelical Pulpit*, vol. 1. Grand Rapids, MI: Eerdmans, 1948.

Henry, Carl F. H. *Notes on the Doctrine of God*. Boston: W. A. Wilde, 1948.

———. *The Protestant Dilemma: An Analysis of the Current Impasse in Theology*. Grand Rapids, MI: Eerdmans, 1948.

———. *Giving a Reason for Our Hope*. Boston: W. A. Wilde, 1949.

———. *Fifty Years of Protestant Theology*. Boston: W. A. Wilde, 1950.

———. *The Drift of Western Thought*. Grand Rapids, MI: Eerdmans, 1951.

———. *Personal Idealism and Strong's Theology*. Wheaton, IL: Van Kampen, 1951.

———. *Glimpses of a Sacred Land*. Boston: W. A. Wilde, 1953.

———. *Christian Personal Ethics*. Grand Rapids. MI: Eerdmans, 1957.

———, ed. *Contemporary Evangelical Thought: A Survey*. Great Neck, NY: Channel Press, 1957.

———. *Evangelical Responsibility in Contemporary Theology*. Pathway. Grand Rapids, MI: Eerdmans, 1957.

———, ed. *Revelation and the Bible*. Contemporary Evangelical Thought. Grand Rapids, MI: Baker, 1958.

———, ed. *The Bible Expositor: The Living Theme of the Great Book*. 3 vols. Philadelphia: Holman, 1960.

———, ed. *Basic Christian Doctrines*. Contemporary Evangelical Thought. New York: Holt, Rinehart, & Winston, 1962.

———. *Aspects of Christian Social Ethics*. Grand Rapids, MI: Eerdmans, 1964.

———, ed. *Christian Faith and Modern Theology*. Contemporary Evangelical Thought. New York: Channel Press, 1964.

———. *Frontiers in Modern Theology*. Chicago: Moody, 1966.

———. *The God Who Shows Himself*. Waco, TX: Word, 1966.

———, ed. *Jesus of Nazareth: Saviour and Lord*. Grand Rapids, MI: Eerdmans, 1966.

———. *Evangelicals at the Brink of Crisis: Significance of the World Congress on Evangelism*. Waco, TX: Word, 1967.

———. *Faith at the Frontiers*. Chicago: Moody, 1969.

———, ed. *Fundamentals of the Faith*. Grand Rapids, MI: Zondervan, 1969.

———. *A Plea for Evangelical Demonstration*. Grand Rapids, MI: Baker, 1971.

———, ed. *Prophecy in the Making: Messages Prepared for the Jerusalem Conference on Biblical Prophecy*. Carol Stream, IL: Creation House, 1971.

———. *New Strides of Faith*. Moody Evangelical Focus. Chicago: Moody, 1972.

———, ed. *Baker's Dictionary of Christian Ethics*. Grand Rapids, MI: Baker, 1973.

———. *Evangelicals in Search of Identity*. Waco, TX: Word, 1976.

———. *God, Revelation, and Authority*. Vol. 1, *God Who Speaks and Shows, Preliminary Considerations*. Waco, TX: Word, 1976. Reprint, Wheaton, IL: Crossway, 1999.

———. *God, Revelation, and Authority*. Vol. 2, *God Who Speaks and Shows, Fifteen Theses, Part 1*. Waco, TX: Word, 1976. Reprint, Wheaton, IL: Crossway, 1999.

———, ed. *Horizons of Science: Christian Scholars Speak Out*, Contemporary Evangelical Thought. San Francisco: Harper & Row, 1978.

———. *God, Revelation, and Authority*. Vol. 3, *God Who Speaks and Shows, Fifteen Theses, Part 2*. Waco, TX: Word, 1979. Reprint, Wheaton, IL: Crossway, 1999.

———. *God, Revelation, and Authority*. Vol. 4, *God Who Speaks and Shows, Fifteen Theses, Part 3*. Waco, TX: Word, 1979. Reprint, Wheaton, IL: Crossway, 1999.

———. *God, Revelation, and Authority*. Vol. 5, *God Who Stands and Stays, Part 1*. Waco, TX: Word, 1982. Reprint, Wheaton, IL: Crossway, 1999.

———. *God, Revelation, and Authority*. Vol. 6, *God Who Stands and Stays, Part 2*. Waco, TX: Word, 1983. Reprint, Wheaton, IL: Crossway, 1999.

———. *The Christian Mindset in a Secular Society: Promoting Evangelical Renewal and National Righteousness*. Critical Concern. Portland, OR: Multnomah, 1984.

———. *Christian Countermoves in a Decadent Culture*. Critical Concern. Portland, OR: Multnomah, 1986.

———. *Confessions of a Theologian*. Waco, TX: Word, 1986.

———. *Twilight of a Great Civilization: The Drift Toward Neo-Paganism*. Wheaton, IL: Crossway, 1988.

Henry, Carl F. H., and Kenneth S. Kantzer, eds. *Evangelical Affirmations*. Grand Rapids, MI: Zondervan, 1990.

Henry, Carl F. H. *Toward a Recovery of Christian Belief*. Rutherford Lectures. Wheaton, IL: Crossway, 1990.

———. *The Identity of Jesus of Nazareth*. Nashville: Broadman, 1992.

———. *Gods of This Age or the God of the Ages?* Edited by R. Albert Mohler Jr. Nashville, TN: Broadman, 1994.

———. *Has Democracy Had Its Day?* Nashville: Ethics and Religious Liberty Commission, 1996.

Contributors

D. A. Carson is research professor of New Testament at Trinity Evangelical Divinity School and president of The Gospel Coalition.

Timothy George is founding dean of Beeson Divinity School of Samford University and general editor of the Reformation Commentary on Scripture.

Matthew J. Hall is vice president of academic services at the Southern Baptist Theological Seminary, where he also teaches courses in church history.

Paul House is professor of divinity at Beeson Divinity School, where he teaches courses in Old Testament.

R. Albert Mohler Jr. is president of the Southern Baptist Theological Seminary, the flagship seminary of the Southern Baptist Convention, where he also serves as the Joseph Emerson Brown Professor of Christian Theology.

Russell D. Moore is president of the Ethics and Religious Liberty Commission.

Richard J. Mouw is professor of faith and public life at Fuller Theological Seminary, where previously he served as president for twenty years.

Ben Peays is executive director of The Gospel Coalition.

Owen Strachan is assistant professor of Christian theology and church history at the Southern Baptist Theological Seminary and Boyce College. He also serves as president of the Council on Biblical Manhood and Womanhood and director of the Carl F. H. Henry Institute for Evangelical Engagement at Southern Seminary.

Gregory Alan Thornbury is president of The King's College in New York City. He previously served as the founding dean of the School of Theology and Missions at Union University.

John Woodbridge is research professor of church history and the history of Christian thought at Trinity Evangelical Divinity School.

General Index

Scripture Index

"A must for every Christian leader."
REVEREND BILLY GRAHAM

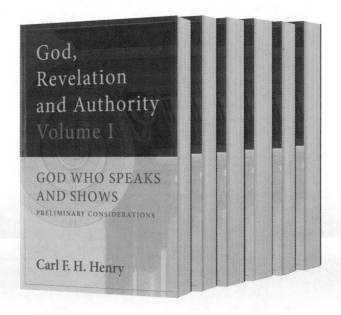

GOD, REVELATION AND AUTHORITY
CARL F. H. HENRY
6-Volume Set

"God, Revelation and Authority *is a biblically faithful rock in the twentieth-century sea of theological experimentation.*"

JOHN PIPER, Founder, desiringGod.org; Chancellor, Bethlehem College and Seminary

"*A sure-footed guide to a great many aspects of evangelical theology.*"

D. A. CARSON, Research Professor of New Testament, Trinity Evangelical Divinity School

"*These volumes are a landmark work, fully biblical, intellectually coherent, powerfully persuasive, and genuinely spiritual.*"

DAVID F. WELLS, Distinguished Senior Research Professor, Gordon-Conwell Theological Seminary

For more information, visit crossway.org.